ON MISSION WITH GOD

LIVING GOD'S PURPOSE FOR HIS GLORY

AVERY T. WILLIS, JR.

HENRY T. BLACKABY

LifeWay Press
Nashville, Tennessee

ISBN: 0-6330-1855-4

This book is a resource in the Ministry category
of the Christian Growth Study Plan.
Course CG-0705

Dewey Decimal Classification Number: 248.84
Subject Heading: GOD\CHRISTIAN LIFE

Printed in the United States of America

Adult Ministry Publishing
LifeWay Church Resources
One LifeWay Plaza
Nashville, Tennessee 37234-0175

Unless otherwise noted, Scripture quotations are from
the Holy Bible, *New International Version*, copyright
1973, 1978, 1984 by International Bible Society.

Scripture quotations marked AMP are from
The Amplified Bible copyright, The Lockman
Foundation 1954, 1958, 1987. Used by permission.

Scripture quotations marked *Phillips* are from
The New Testament in Modern English, Revised
Edition, copyright J. B. Phillips 1958, 1960, 1972.

Scripture quotations marked NKJV are from the
New King James Version. Copyright © 1979, 1980, 1982,
Thomas Nelson, Inc., Publishers.

Cover Photograph: PhotoDisc®

GROUP COVENANT

To encourage a high level of trust, love, and openness in my *On Mission with God* group and in order to dedicate myself to God and to my *On Mission with God* group, I make the following commitments.

I commit to—

- acknowledge Jesus Christ as Lord of my life each day;

- attend all group sessions unless providentially hindered;

- complete each week's assignments prior to the group session;

- keep in confidence anything personal that others share in the group sessions;

- share of myself and my challenges and victories s a participant rather than a spectator in the process of experiencing God as I join Him on His mission;

- be a good steward of the time that I spend in a group session. I will share of myself as God leads while I remember to condense and edit my remarks so as to be fair to myself and others;

- pray for myself, my group leaders, and other group members.

_____

Signed

_____

Date

CONTENTS

THE AUTHORS

AVERY T. WILLIS, JR., the author and developer of *MasterLife*, is the senior vice-president of overseas operations at the International Mission Board of the Southern Baptist Convention. The original *MasterLife*, published in 1980, has been used by more than 250,000 people in the United States and has been translated into more than 50 languages for use by untold thousands. Willis is also the author of *Indonesian Revival: Missions, MasterBuilder: Multiplying Leaders, BibleGuide to Discipleship and Doctrine*, and several books in Indonesian.

Willis served for 10 years as a pastor in Oklahoma and Texas and for 14 years as a missionary to Indonesia, during which he served for 6 years as the president of the Indonesian Baptist Theological Seminary. Before assuming his present position, he served as the director of the Adult Department of the Discipleship and Family Development Division, the Sunday School Board of the Southern Baptist Convention, where he introduced the Lay Institute for Equipping (LIFE), a series of in-depth discipleship courses.

HENRY T. BLACKABY, the author of *Experiencing God: Knowing and Doing the Will of God*, is the president of Henry Blackaby Ministries and the former special assistant to the presidents of the following agencies of the Southern Baptist Convention: LifeWay Christian Resources, the International Mission Board, and the North American Mission Board. Blackaby was a pastor in the Los Angeles area before accepting a call to Faith Baptist Church in Saskatoon, Saskatchewan. He wrote *What the Spirit Is Saying to the Churches*, the story of God's activity among His people at Faith Baptist Church. In addition to *Experiencing God*, a study that encourages believers to discover where God is working and join Him, he has also written *The Man God Uses* and *Abraham: Born to Be God's Friend*. Blackaby has led conferences in the United States, in Canada, and around the world.

INTRODUCTION

The heart of this book is to help you examine God's mission and your experience through the lives of the seven most significant characters in the Bible—Abraham, Moses, David, Jesus, Peter, Paul, and John. You will study these eternal truths from five perspectives.

- **The individual (close-up) perspective.** You will study a specific experience of the character using the seven realities of *Experiencing God*.

- **The lifetime (wide-angle) perspective.** You will study what God did through the character's life as he experienced the seven spiritual markers of being on mission with God.

- **The corporate (180-degree, extra wide-angle) perspective.** You will study the way God used these same seven spiritual markers in each character's life to influence the people of God in his generation to be on mission with God.

- **The eternal (360-degree) perspective.** You will study the way God revealed a central, eternal aspect of His mission through His relationship with each of the characters and His people.

- **The personal perspective.** At every point along the way God will apply these teachings to your life and to the lives of the people of God to help you and your church join Him on mission and accomplish His purpose.

Two diagrams (figures 1 and 2 on page 10) in this book illustrate the concept of experiencing God on mission. The first day of each week's study you will examine the way each biblical character initially experienced God from an individual encounter with Him (illustrated in figure 1).

The second diagram (figure 2) depicts the same mission of God and the goal of the glory of God with seven spiritual markers that every believer personally and the people of God corporately experience when they join Him on mission. Days 2 and 3 will view all your experiences on mission with God from your lifetime perspective and from the corporate perspective.

In addition to the seven primary biblical figures you will study, two weeks provide supplemental articles on women who experienced God on mission. Sarah is featured on pages 52–53, and Mary is featured on pages 120–22.

OVERALL GOAL

What can you expect God to do in your life as you work through this book and meet weekly with a small group for eight weeks, studying a different Bible character each week? By the conclusion of this study you will be able to relate your daily life to God and His mission and will be able to bring glory to God as you actively pursue God's will for your life.

PERSONAL GOALS

Additionally, you will achieve these personal goals.

1. You will experience God developing a love relationship with you and inviting you to be on mission with Him and His people so that He will be glorified and worshiped by all peoples of the earth.
2. You will worship God more fully as you get to know Him better.
3. You will be able to respond obediently to God's leading as He connects you to His purpose.
4. You will be able to find your place in God's mission and find fulfillment as you experience His heart for all peoples.
5. You will be able to formulate God's personal plan for your involvement in His mission that is biblical, practical, and appropriate.
6. You will express your God-given concern for the unreached peoples of the world.
7. You will be able to mobilize others to be involved in God's mission to all peoples.

This book is written for those who want to go further in experiencing God and to find practical, mind-expanding ways to join God on mission.

Each week you will be reminded that God's desire is to encounter each of us in personal ways. Since the beginning of creation God has been involved in the world He created. He didn't create the world, then go off and play celestial golf and let His world merrily spin along on its way without Him.

God loves His creation. The Bible says He knows every sparrow and every other living thing on the earth. He not only knows but He also cares deeply about every aspect of His creation, especially for us humans, whom the Bible says He created in His own image.

All through the Bible God reveals Himself to you so that you can know Him personally. God initiates a personal, loving relationship with you and invites you to join Him in His work. As God speaks to you, you experience a crisis of belief that calls for major adjustments in your life so that you can be related to Him and His mission.

As you make the necessary adjustments and obey God, He moves you into the middle of His activity—God's mission. The purpose of this study is to spell out God's mission and how He involves you in it.

HOW TO STUDY THIS BOOK

Each day for five days a week, I encourage you to study a segment of the material in this workbook and to complete the related activities. You may need from 20 to 30 minutes of study time each day. Even if you find that you can study the material in less time, spreading the study over five days will give you time to apply the truths to your life.

Set a definite time and select a quiet place to study with little or no inter-ruption. Keep a Bible handy to find Scriptures as the material directs. Memorizing Scripture is an important part of your work. Set aside a portion of your study for memory work. You will find each week's memory verse in the margin of the first page of the week's study under the heading "Heart Focus." Unless I have deliberately chosen another version for a specific emphasis, all Scriptures in

On Mission with God are quoted from the *New International Version* of the Bible. However, feel free to memorize Scripture from any version of the Bible you prefer.

In writing this book, we have chosen to use the personal pronoun *I* for Avery. This prevents the awkwardness of switching back and forth between two authors.

Frequently in the text you will find the word *peoples*, a term you may be unfamiliar with. Whereas the word *people* is a general term that applies to persons collectively, the word *peoples*, with an *s*, refers to groups that have their own identities. When you see the word *peoples*, understand that I am not talking about humanity in general but about distinctive groups, each with its own group characteristics.

This book has been written as a tutorial text. Study it as if I were sitting at your side, helping you learn. When I ask you a question or give you an assignment, respond immediately. Each assignment appears in boldface type. As your personal tutor, I will often give you feedback about your response— for example, a suggestion about what you might have written. This process is designed to help you learn the material more effectively. Do not deny yourself valuable learning by omitting the learning activities.

At the end of each week's study, members gather for a group session. The group sessions help you reflect on the concepts and experiences that *On Mission with God* presents and apply them to your life. You will share insights gained, look for answers to problems encountered, and gain strength from the fact that others encounter similar struggles and victories.

Plan to study *On Mission with God* as part of a group. Although you may benefit from completing the studies totally on your own, without a group experience you will have missed the critical element Jesus' disciples experienced: relationships with one another in Christ's presence. You will find that growth occurs more quickly when you participate in a group.

If you have started to study *On Mission with God* and you are not involved in a group study, try to enlist some friends or associates who will work through this course with you. A husband and wife are encouraged to work through the material together. The *On Mission with God* leader guide, which begins on page 193, provides guidance and learning activities for the group sessions. Do not attempt to conduct a group without using these leader helps.

A KEY DECISION

Key to this study is the decision to trust Jesus as your Savior. If you have not done this already, I encourage you to make this decision as the study begins. On page 219 you will find biblical guidance for making that decision. You will benefit more from this course if you go through the material already having committed your life to Christ and allowing Him to guide you to join Him on mission.

FIGURE 1

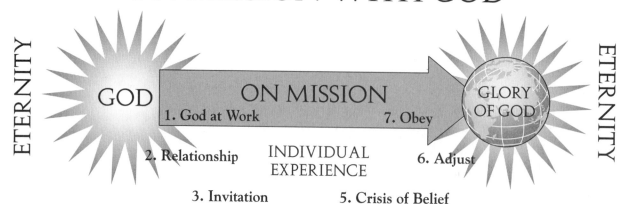

ON MISSION WITH GOD

ETERNITY

GOD

ON MISSION

1. God at Work   7. Obey

GLORY OF GOD

ETERNITY

2. Relationship   INDIVIDUAL EXPERIENCE   6. Adjust

3. Invitation   5. Crisis of Belief

4. God speaks

FIGURE 2

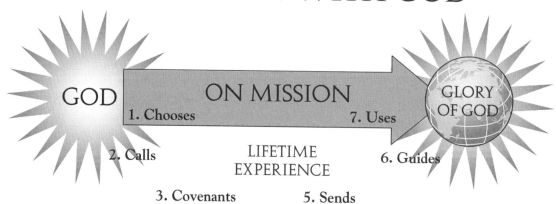

ON MISSION WITH GOD

GOD

ON MISSION

1. Chooses   7. Uses

GLORY OF GOD

2. Calls   LIFETIME EXPERIENCE   6. Guides

3. Covenants   5. Sends

4. Prepares

INTRODUCING YOUR SEVEN MENTORS FOR THE JOURNEY

This Week's Lessons

Day 1: God Reveals His Mission
Day 2: Experiencing God Personally
Day 3: Seven Spiritual Markers
Day 4: Influencing Your Generation
Day 5: Filled with the Glory of the Lord

This Week's Learning Focus

You will be able to explain God's pattern of doing extraordinary things through ordinary people to glorify His name among all peoples.

Heart Focus
"The Spirit helps us in our weakness. We do not know what we ought to pray for, but the Spirit himself intercedes for us with groans that words cannot express" (Rom. 8:26).

 DAY 1

GOD REVEALS HIS MISSION

The tropical sun beat down on my van as I wound through the dusty East Java roads. I was looking for a village on the unmarked road. When I finally stopped a man and asked where the village was, he replied, "Kesana," which, loosely translated, means "thataway." He pointed down the road with his thumb. I asked how far it was and how I would know when I got to my destination. After reiterating, "Kesana," several times, he said, "I'll show you," and hopped in the car. I had asked for a road map, but instead I got a personal guide!

You usually ask God for a road map of your life, and He replies, "I am the Way. I will personally lead you. Follow Me and My commands, and you will get to the destination." On the way you discover that you may not get to the destination you first had in mind, but you will get to *His* destination for your life—a far better arrival point than you had planned. That's what it means to be on mission with God. You let Him be your Guide and direct you, because you believe He has a purpose for you. His purpose is not just your own personal gain. As His disciple, you commit yourself to His purpose and His mission.

Figure 1 on page 10 shows that you experience God as you obey Him and join Him on mission. His mission is that the "earth will be filled with the knowledge of the glory of the Lord, as the waters cover the sea" (Hab. 2:14). The personal application of that is "living God's purpose for His glory."

You may not get to the destination you first had in mind, but you will get to *His* destination for your life.

"The earth will be filled with the knowledge of the glory of the Lord, as the waters cover the sea" (Hab. 2:14).

"At the name of Jesus every knee should bow, in heaven and on earth and under the earth, and every tongue confess that Jesus Christ is Lord, to the glory of God the Father" (Phil. 2:10-11).

"He made known to us the mystery of his will according to his good pleasure, which he purposed in Christ, to be put into effect when the times will have reached their fulfillment—to bring all things in heaven and on earth together under one head, even Christ. In him we were also chosen, having been predestined according to the plan of him who works out everything in conformity with the purpose of his will, in order that we, who were the first to hope in Christ, might be for the praise of his glory" (Eph. 1:9-12).

Read Habakkuk 2:14, Philippians 2:10-11, and Ephesians 1:9-12 in the margin. In your own words describe the connection between God's mission and His glory.

_____

_____

Think of God's glory as who He is—His presence. Think of His mission as what He does—His purpose. God is always at His work everywhere to fulfill His purpose. Jesus said, " 'My Father is always at his work to this very day, and I, too, am working' " (John 5:17). God is moving to accomplish His mission. As you join Him on mission, you experience God and the glory of His presence.

A distinction exists between *mission* and *missions*. By *mission* I mean the total redemptive purpose of God to establish His kingdom. *Missions*, however, is the activity of God's people—the church—to proclaim and to demonstrate the kingdom of God cross-culturally to the world. We are focusing on God's mission, not on our missions. God isn't interested in merely giving you a missions experience but in your being on mission with Him.

This study does not attempt to call you to be a missionary. It helps you understand the heart of God and His mission. God reveals Himself to you so you can adjust your life to Him and join Him on His mission. He wants to reveal His glory to a waiting world through you. He can do that anywhere He chooses when you allow Him to manifest Himself through you. As you experience God on mission, you do not choose your assignment or your location. He does. Your ultimate goal is to allow God to reveal Himself to you and then through you as He did through the people in the Bible.

When I was seeking the East Java village, I was on mission with God. I thought I would be on mission there for years, but God had other plans. Being on mission is not a profession, a vocation, or a location. In fact, since I, at age 19, committed myself to be on mission with God, I have been a laborer in a milling company, salesperson, volunteer director of a rescue mission, pastor, missionary, professor, author, director of adult discipleship for my denomination, and now vice-president of my denomination's mission board. When was I most on mission with God? In every case! No doubt, I followed more closely and obeyed God more at some times than others, but still I was on mission with God all the time.

Henry Blackaby had a similar experience. Henry and Marilynn committed themselves to be missionaries, only to be turned down because of their son's health. They ended up back in Canada, Henry's birthplace. Henry was the pastor of a small church there. During that time Marilynn experienced difficulty in understanding what being on mission with God meant. Marilynn recalls, "Henry traveled a lot; I was at home with our four boys. I remember asking myself after a long day of washing dishes, cooking meals, and running after kids. *Is this being a missionary?* Later, as I was vacuuming, God answered my question: 'Yes, Marilynn, it is. This is your mission field.' And with that realization my daily work took on a different meaning because I knew without a doubt that it was what God had given me to do."[1]

In the margin write the roles you have filled when you have been on mission with God.

God's glory is His demonstrated presence. For the people of Israel the manifest glory of God was His presence among them (see Ex. 33:15-18 in the margin). The people of Israel did not bring God glory; they reflected His glory. God wants to manifest His presence—His glory—through you. He wants to show His glory to a watching world as His people experience Him. Your worship, obedience, attitudes, and relationships are to reflect His glory like shining lights on a mountaintop (see Matt. 5:16 in the margin).

THE STANDARD FOR EXPERIENCES WITH GOD

God gave you the Bible so that you could know Him and join Him on mission. Since the Bible is a book about God, why are 60 percent of its stories about people? God has chosen to reveal Himself as He interacts with people. The Bible's accounts show ways people interacted with God and His mission. God reveals Himself, His purpose, and His ways through the lives of the people He has included in the Holy Book.

You can depend on God's revelation to you through the Bible. Because in this course you can't study every character in the Bible, how can you know God's mission? I believe that if you understand what God revealed through the most significant characters of the Bible, you will have a standard of experiencing God's glory as you accompany Him on His mission. You can base your experiences on ways God has worked with people in the Bible. Later you will be able to use the pattern that we will teach you to study the rest of the biblical characters on your own.

My wife and I traveled to Nepal to visit missionaries who were experiencing a tremendous response to the gospel. I had always wanted to see the Himalayan mountain range. More than 30 peaks rise to heights greater than 24,000 feet. We took a small plane and saw a panorama of 8 of the world's 10 highest peaks, including Mount Everest—the world's highest peak at 29,023 feet!

Mount Everest is awesome! When I compare this mountain range to the main characters of the Bible, I see Jesus as the highest peak. But ascending toward Him from either side are other peaks that point to His grandeur—men and women of the Bible through whom God revealed Himself and His mission. We will study three of these characters from the Old Testament and three from the New Testament. Each point to Christ. We will also study Jesus Himself.

When God is about to do something, He takes the initiative and comes to one or more of His servants. He invites them to adjust their lives to Him so that He can accomplish His mission through them.

We will look at the lives of the seven most significant people in the Bible— Abraham, Moses, David, Jesus, Peter, Paul, and John. Each moved and reflected God's kingdom purpose in his day. Each joined God on mission, and through them the Holy Spirit helps us understand what God is doing today. I have many favorite biblical characters, but when limited to seven, I am compelled to stay with the ones you will study. Just think how many lives these persons have influenced! After this, we will refer to them as the Seven. If you know what

"Then Moses said to him, 'If your Presence does not go with us, do not send us up from here. How will anyone know that you are pleased with me and with your people unless you go with us? What else will distinguish me and your people from all the other people on the face of the earth?' " (Ex. 33:15-18).

" 'In the same way, let your light shine before men, that they may see your good deeds and praise your Father in heaven' " (Matt. 5:16).

God has revealed through these seven biblical characters, you will understand God's heart and mission. Look what God revealed through these Seven.

- Through Abraham God revealed Himself as the Lord, the Almighty Provider, who wants to bless all the peoples of the world through His people.
- Through Moses God revealed Himself as the great I AM, whose plan is to show His glory to the world through His people, as a kingdom of priests to all peoples.
- Through David God revealed that His Seed would rule all nations and His kingdom would be for all peoples.
- Through Jesus God revealed His love and His purpose to reconcile the world to Himself and to send His disciples as ministers of reconciliation to all peoples.
- Through Peter God demonstrated how the Holy Spirit would empower His people to be His witnesses to all peoples.
- Through Paul God revealed the mystery of the ages that He includes all peoples in His redemption and sends missionaries to all nations, tribes, tongues, and peoples.
- Through John God revealed that all nations, tribes, tongues, and peoples will worship and glorify Him forever in heaven.

Take a few minutes to review these seven revelations about God's mission. In a minute I will ask you some questions about these men.

I hope you will see each character as God sees him. Starting with week 2, we will study each of the Seven from five perspectives. In each case, you will see your own life from each of these same perspectives.

- **Close up.** The first perspective will view the personal experiences with God as the top of one peak in a mountain range.
- **Wide-angle.** I will ask you to back up so you can view the whole mountain, representing the character's lifetime of experiences with God.
- **180 degrees (extra wide-angle).** The third perspective will back up to an extra wide-angle view of the peaks (that is, other persons) immediately surrounding the character, who represent his generation's experiences with God.
- **360 degrees.** The fourth perspective will be a 360-degree view from eternity. You will learn how God accomplished His mission through the character and through his generation.
- **The personal perspective.** At every point along the way God will apply these teachings to your life and to the lives of the people of God to help you and your church join Him on mission and accomplish His purpose.

All through the Bible God reveals Himself to you so that you can know Him personally. If you've studied *Experiencing God: Knowing and Doing the Will of God*, you already know the seven realities in the diagram at the top of page 15.

ON MISSION WITH GOD

God is at work all the time, and He initiates a personal, loving relationship with you and invites you to join Him in His work. As God speaks to you, you experience a crisis of belief that calls for major adjustments in your life so that you can relate to Him and His mission. As you make the adjustments and obey Him, He moves you into the middle of His activity—as a part of God's mission.

As you look at God's mission through the eyes of His chosen servants, be assured that it is God who is on mission. The mission is His, not yours. But He has determined to accomplish His mission through His people. He is actively working to involve His people with all the peoples of the world so that they may know Him and worship Him.

God's mission will be accomplished when Christ delivers the kingdom to the Father. Meanwhile, He gives you every opportunity to be on mission with Him so that He can exalt the Son and draw all peoples to worship Him.

See if you can remember what God revealed through each of the Seven. (Hint: I have scrambled the order.)

- Through _____ God demonstrated how the Holy Spirit would empower His people to be His witnesses to all peoples.
- Through _____ God revealed Himself as the Lord, the Almighty Provider who wants to bless all the peoples of the world through His people.
- Through _____ God revealed His love and His purpose to reconcile the world to Himself and to send his disciples as ministers of reconciliation to all peoples.
- Through _____ God revealed Himself as the great I AM whose plan is to show His glory to the world through His people who are to be a kingdom of priests to all peoples.
- Through _____ God revealed that his Seed would rule all nations and His kingdom would be for all peoples.
- Through _____ (in Revelation) God revealed that all nations, tribes, tongues, and peoples will worship and glorify Him forever in Heaven.
- Through _____ God revealed the mystery of the ages that He includes all peoples in His redemption.

Check your answers with the previous list on page 14.

DAY 2

EXPERIENCING GOD PERSONALLY

Have you wondered whether the seven realities in *Experiencing God* apply to all people or just to Moses? Let's review the realities to see how God uses them to reveal His glory in the lives of the Seven.

1. God is always at work around you.

God is always at work all the time, wherever you are! In John 5:17 Jesus said, "My Father is always at his work to this very day, and I, too, am working." As you wait on Him this week, watch to see where He is at work around you. Note opportunities that the Lord places in your path as the great God of eternity moves by His mighty Holy Spirit in the lives of those around you!

2. God pursues a continuing love relationship with you that is real and personal.

Read John 3:16 (in the margin) and meditate on God's love for you.

" 'God so loved the world that he gave his one and only Son, that whoever believes in him shall not perish but have eternal life' " (John 3:16).

When Adam and Eve sinned, God did not pack up and leave the earth behind. He didn't decide to start over with His creation. Instead, He lovingly, patiently, painstakingly, and continually works to bring the fallen world back to Himself.

God is intricately involved in details of worldwide significance; yet He is also concerned about individuals like you and me. God cared enough for you and me and every other person on the earth to send His Son to give His life on the cross for our salvation. He gives you the choice to repent of your sin, believe in Jesus, and commit yourself to following Him, and you will be saved.

Stop right now and recall your salvation experience. Can you recall a time in your life when you prayed to ask Christ to come into your life and to be your Savior and your Lord? Yes ☐ No ☐

If you checked *no*, turn to page 119, where you can read how Christ can save you. Then pray and ask God to forgive you of your sins, come into your heart, and live there forever. Plan to share your experience with your group.

God numbered the hairs of your head. You are much more valuable than the birds and the flowers for whom He cares. Your experience with Jesus was not a one-time event. God's Holy Spirit is present to make Christ real to you on an ongoing basis.

As a Christian, how would you assess your personal relationship with God right now? Check your response.
☐ I am far too busy to even think about my relationship with God.
☐ I wonder where in the world I'm going and where God is.
☐ I am pondering the fact that God loves me and wants me to obey Him.

☐ After studying *Experiencing God*, I know that God loves me, but I am not yet fully involved in His mission.

☐ I am experiencing God daily as He reveals Himself to me, and I am joining Him in His work and world.

Take time now to pray that you will encounter God through this study in such a way that you will be caught up in His activity and irresistibly involved with Him on His mission!

3. God invites you to become involved with Him and His work.

When God reveals Himself or His activity to you, that is His invitation for you to join Him. When He speaks through your Bible reading or brings a thought to mind while you pray, He is giving you a personal invitation.

God took the initiative with the Seven you are studying in this book. They did not come to God saying, "What great thing can I do for You?" God came to them and told them what He was about to do and invited them to be a part of it.

Match the person in the margin with what God was about to do.
_____ 1. Deliver His people from slavery, giving them the Promised Land
_____ 2. Save His people from their sins
_____ 3. Equip/empower His people to witness to all peoples
_____ 4. Begin a race of people who would bless all peoples
_____ 5. Break out of Judaism, taking the gospel to all peoples
_____ 6. Reveal that representatives of all peoples will worship Him
_____ 7. Introduce a Kingdom that would have no end

a. Abraham
b. Moses
c. David
d. Jesus
e. Peter
f. Paul
g. John

In each case, God's activity was not the person's agenda. God revealed what He was doing and invited the person to join Him. The correct order of what God was doing through each character is *b, d, e, a, f, g,* and *c.*

You may think you were saved to go to heaven when you die, but God says, "I saved you to be on mission with Me to redeem a broken world." For a follower of Christ He sets the direction and tells you where He is and where He is going.

Read John 4:35 and Matthew 9:37-38 in the margin. Underline the three commands Jesus gives about the fields that belong to "the Lord of the harvest." Then write *yes, no,* or *not yet* beside each question below.
_____ Are your spiritual eyes open?
_____ Are you looking at the ripe spiritual harvest fields in God's world?
_____ Are you asking Him to send out workers into His harvest?
_____ Are you willing to be one of those workers?

4. God speaks by the Holy Spirit through the Bible, prayer, circumstances, and the church to reveal Himself, His purposes, and His ways.

We want to be right in the middle of God's redemptive activity. But how do we know which way God is moving at the moment? God used many ways to reveal His glory and speak to the Seven.

" 'Do you not say, "Four months more and then the harvest"? I tell you, open your eyes and look at the fields! They are ripe for harvest' " (John 4:35).

"He said to his disciples, 'The harvest is plentiful but the workers are few. Ask the Lord of the harvest, therefore, to send out workers into his harvest field' " (Matt. 9:37-38).

a. Abraham
b. Moses
c. David
d. Jesus
e. Peter
f. Paul
g. John

"In the past God spoke to our forefathers through the prophets at many times and in various ways, but in these last days he has spoken to us by his Son, whom he appointed heir of all things, and through whom he made the universe" (Hebrews 1:1-2).

" 'I have much more to say to you, more than you can now bear. But when he, the Spirit of truth, comes, he will guide you into all truth. He will not speak on his own; he will speak only what he hears, and he will tell you what is yet to come. He will bring glory to me by taking from what is mine and making it known to you. All that belongs to the Father is mine. That is why I said the Spirit will take from what is mine and make it known to you.' " (John 16:12-15).

"Without faith it is impossible to please God, because anyone who comes to him must believe that he exists and that he rewards those who earnestly seek him" (Heb. 11:6).

Fill in the blank with the letter from the margin matching the biblical character with one of the ways God used to speak to him.
____ 1. God spoke through a prophet to show what he would be and do.
____ 2. God spoke through a burning bush.
____ 3. God spoke from heaven so that others could hear at His baptism.
____ 4. The resurrected Christ appeared to him, showing future visions.
____ 5. God blinded him with a bright light and told him what to do next.
____ 6. We don't know how, but God spoke, and he knew it was He.
____ 7. He had to interpret a trancelike vision to understand God's will.

This exercise may challenge you, depending on how well you know the lives of these men. By the end of this study, you will know ways each of the Seven heard God speak and ways they responded. The answers were *c, b, d, g, f, a,* and *e.*

Underline the phrases from Hebrews 1:1-2 and John 16:12-15 in the margin that describe how God most often speaks today.

God speaks to you through the Son and the Spirit. For you to hear God and participate in what He is doing, attune your ear to the voice of the living God to know what He is about to do next.

5. God's invitation for you to work with Him always leads you to a crisis of belief that requires faith and action.

Everything God says to you requires faith and action on your part. Without faith you cannot please Him (see Heb. 11:6 in the margin). You may try to dismiss His speaking or rationalize it away, but when God speaks, you must respond. The Seven discovered that when they had faith to respond to God's invitation, He not only met them but also spoke again and continued to stretch their faith. That's how you join Him on mission. God's invitation leads to a crisis of belief, followed by an adjustment and obedience. The key is your responding to God with faith and action.

What do you sense God is asking you to do by faith now? (*example: I sense He is asking me to teach a Sunday School class when I have no previous experience.*)

_____

_____

6. You must make major adjustments in your life to join God in what He is doing.

Heeding God's invitation and responding positively require major adjustments on your part. Can you imagine what the Seven would say if you could eavesdrop on them talking in heaven about the major adjustments they were asked to make? It might go something like this.

Abraham: My family and I were happy living in Ur. I didn't ask God to send me to another country. He encountered me and told me what I was to do to reveal His glory to all the peoples of the earth. Can you imagine how I had to explain that to Sarah? When I did, she obediently followed, too.

Moses: I was content living in the desert far away from my troubles in Egypt. I didn't go looking for that burning bush and the glory of God's presence. I certainly did not want to go back to Egypt for any sort of showdown with Pharaoh. God had to do a job on me to get me to join Him.

David: I was the baby in my family. I would have loved to spend my days tending sheep, playing my harp, and writing poetry.

Jesus: I left My throne in heaven to give Myself to redeem all peoples. I could have stayed in heaven, but I knew that the cross was ordained for Me before the foundation of the world.

Peter: I was proud and arrogant, but I learned that only with God's strength could I really do anything. When I finally caught on, God did far more through me than I could have imagined.

Paul: I tried to stamp out Christianity. When Jesus encountered me and showed me His glory (see Acts 9:1-22), He turned my life upside down.

John: I thought I should get to sit next to Christ in glory (see Mark 10:35-37). I wanted things my way, but I realize now God really did know best.

Are you seeking God, or have you allowed God to encounter you?

Look back over the seven biblical figures in this study. Below check the one with whom you most identify right now (in any of the seven realities).

❑ Abraham   ❑ Moses   ❑ David   ❑ Jesus
❑ Peter   ❑ Paul   ❑ John

Describe why you chose the one you did.

_____

_____

When God encounters you, He wants you to join Him on His mission and experience His glory. He doesn't enter your life to pamper you or indulge you. He comes to involve you in the greatest adventure of life—experiencing His glory as you accompany Him on His mission.

7. *You come to know God by experience as you obey Him and He accomplishes His work through you.*

God has a greater purpose for you to obey Him than you ever dreamed. He wants you to experience His glory. God's purpose for including you in His mission is to make your character like Christ's. Through your character God will bless a whole world. By joining His mission, you will experience God and be forever changed. You are not just a channel through which God does something. You are a transformed part of His eternal purpose to make all peoples like His Son for His glory. God affirms the glory of His presence as you experience the seven realities.

⚛️— DAY 3 —⚛️

SEVEN SPIRITUAL MARKERS

Being on mission with God means experiencing Him all your life! When you someday look back at your life, you will be fascinated to see what God was doing the entire time. From His eternal perspective God knows your life from beginning to end. David understood this when he said, "All the days ordained for me were written in your book before one of them came to be" (Ps. 139:16).

Step back from individual experiences with God and see life as God does—from a lifetime perspective. In terms of the Himalayan mountain-range analogy earlier, with this 180-degree, wide-angle view, look at the whole mountain. Most of the time we are so involved in the moment that we have only fleeting thoughts about our whole life's impact.

Have you noticed that as people talk about those who have impacted their lives, they seldom mention the things the person would mention? They may give specific instances of what the person did but only to illustrate the life message of that individual. Your life message relates to the kind of person you are more than to your accomplishments.

Looking at spiritual markers in your life can help you see the direction God is leading you. A spiritual marker is a time when you knew that you experienced God and did His will.

Let's consider seven spiritual markers that all people will experience if they follow through on God's initiatives. The diagram below pictures them. The seven realities you studied yesterday may be repeated over and over at each of these spiritual markers as you have a continuing relationship with God.

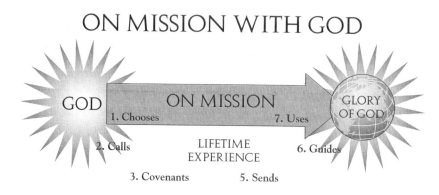

ON MISSION WITH GOD

GOD — ON MISSION — GLORY OF GOD

1. Chooses   7. Uses

2. Calls   LIFETIME EXPERIENCE   6. Guides

3. Covenants   5. Sends

4. Prepares

1. God chooses you to involve you in His mission to reconcile the world to Himself.

We have already established that God takes the initiative with each person to become a part of His kingdom and His mission. He desires for each person to experience the glory of His presence. When He saved you, He knew how He would use you in His kingdom.

> **Read the Scripture in the margin about God's choice. Check the statement that you believe is correct.**
> ☐ God's choice of people is accidental.
> ☐ God's choice of people is coincidental.
> ☐ God's choice of people is providential.

"He chose us in him before the creation of the world to be holy and blameless in his sight. In love he predestined us to be adopted as his sons through Jesus Christ, in accordance with his pleasure and will" (Eph. 1:4-5).

Every time you see God's choice in the Bible, you see that the choice relates to something He wants to do through that person. A photograph of a group of people best illustrates the meaning of the words in Ephesians 1:4-5 (in the margin). God marks or circles the persons He chooses for His purposes. He then begins to shape them and mold them to be like Christ. God's choice of people is neither accidental nor coincidental but providential.

In each week's study we will examine God's choice of individuals one day and of peoples the next day. Your interest in experiencing God on mission is evidence that God has chosen you. But you were not chosen so that you could take pride in being God's choice. He chose you by His grace and in spite of your sin. Before you were born, God chose you for His purposes.

> **Read Jeremiah's experience in Jeremiah 1:4-7, in the margin. Write the reason you think God might have chosen you.**

_____

2. God calls you to Himself so that you can be on mission with Him.

Look at three principles related to God's call.

A. God calls you first to be in relationship with Him.
The first call of God is a call to relationship—not to an activity or a place. The place and activity will follow.

"The word of the Lord came to me, saying,
  'Before I formed you
    in the womb I
    knew you,
  before you were born
    I set you apart;
  I appointed you as
    a prophet to
    the nations.'
'Ah, Sovereign Lord,' I said, 'I do not know how to speak; I am only a child.' But the Lord said to me, 'Do not say, "I am only a child." You must go to everyone I send you to and say whatever I command you' " (Jer. 1:4-7).

> **Check the best answer from the statements listed below.**
> ☐ God saved me so that when I die, I'll escape hell and go to heaven.
> ☐ God called me to a relationship more than to an activity for Him.
> ☐ I am more interested in a missions call than in intimacy with God.
> ☐ The place and activity of God's call are most important to me.
> ☐ I must figure out what my mission for God in life will be.

Have you understood the first principle of God's call—God calls you to a relationship with Him? The best answer is the second in the list.

B. God's call to salvation is a call to service.

Look back at the second principle of God's call. Then write in your own words what you think it means.

_____

_____

_____

God had a purpose in calling you to Himself. He wants you to follow Him and fellowship with Him on the journey. However, in Jesus' call He usually relates the call to service.

Complete these verses.
"If anyone would come after me, he must deny himself _____

_____ and follow me" (Luke 9:23).

"Come follow me," Jesus said, "and I will make you _____

_____" (Matt. 4:19).

"Now that I, your Lord and Teacher, have washed your feet, you also should

_____" (John 13:14).

Since God is at work to accomplish His mission, that means you will join Him by carrying His cross, catching fish, or washing feet.

C. Your relationship with God will determine your activities.

God retains the right to determine what you do, when you do it, and how you do it. He is the Master Guide; you are the servant follower. You have been called. The question is, how will you respond?

Your response to each encounter with God determines the nature of the next. If you respond obediently, He blesses; if you respond in disobedience, He disciplines. Because He encounters you every day, the longer you stay in an unwilling response, the more you are standing against the flow of His purpose.

Picture this: if you stand against a river, many things will hit you! Instead of going with the flow, the whole river will pass you by. Eventually, you find yourself in a whirlpool going round and round. Have you been there? God has better things in mind for you than that. He wants to lead you step-by-step to experience Him on mission. God doesn't just choose you and call you; He promises to be with you and bless you.

Your response to each encounter with God determines the nature of the next encounter.

3. God initiates a covenant of promise and obedience with you in order to accomplish His mission and to glorify Him.

God makes covenants with those He calls. He expects commitments from them as a part of fulfilling His promises. God initiates a mission covenant of promise, obedience, and blessing with you. You'll discover that God made covenants with all of the Seven—promises to them based on their obedience. In the equation in the margin, what happens if you leave out one of the components?

Covenant
=
Promise
+
Obedience
+
Blessing!

All parts of the equation must be in balance for the covenant to work. God writes all covenants. They are not negotiating sessions. You can't bargain with Him and fulfill His mission. God's covenants are permanent: for His glory and your good and the good of all peoples.

A covenant lifts the level of your involvement and gives it permanence and significance. If you break covenant with God, repent and return to it as quickly as you can under His conditions. After Moses and David failed God, they didn't dictate the conditions on which they were restored to Him. God did. When they returned, God restored them. Have you understood what was entailed in keeping God's covenants, or do you feel that you have failed Him through disobedience? If so, stop now and bow before Him in repentance. Allow Him to restore you to His covenant to bless you and make you a blessing.

DAY 4

INFLUENCING YOUR GENERATION

4. God prepares and equips you to be on mission with Him.

God prepares you to experience Him on mission. Part of your preparation is a fundamental orientation to reject the ways of the world and adopt God's ways. He has to shape your character to match your assignment. God took many years to shape the character of the Seven. The bigger the assignment, the longer or more challenging circumstances He used to prepare them.

- God spent 40 years readying Abraham to be the father of faith who believed God enough to offer his son.
- God took 80 years to prepare Moses to lead the Israelites out of slavery.
- David spent 10 of the worst years of his life after he was anointed to be king because God needed to prepare him to establish His kingdom instead of the people's kingdom.
- Peter spent every day for three years with Jesus in preparation, but God had to keep preparing him for another 10 years before he was willing and able to lead the church to be on mission to the Gentiles.
- God sent Paul to Arabia for 3 years of personal training, 10 years in his hometown of Tarsus, and another year in Antioch with Barnabas before He sent him on his first missionary trip.
- God waited until John was age 90 before He used him to write the Gospel of John and the Revelation.

"Not only so, but we also rejoice in our sufferings, because we know that suffering produces perseverance; perseverance, character; and character, hope. And hope does not disappoint us, because God has poured out his love into our hearts by the Holy Spirit, whom he has given us" (Rom. 5:3-5).

"Consider it pure joy, my brothers, whenever you face trials of many kinds, because you know that the testing of your faith develops perseverance. Perseverance must finish its work so that you may be mature and complete, not lacking anything" (Jas. 1:2-4).

"Our fathers disciplined us for a little while as they thought best; but God disciplines us for our good, that we may share in his holiness. No discipline seems pleasant at the time, but painful. Later on, however, it produces a harvest of righteousness and peace for those who have been trained by it" (Heb. 12:10-11).

Note what God is doing in your life right now, because He is preparing you for your assignment. Your next assignment may occur tomorrow, or your ultimate assignment may be 20 years from now, but God is preparing you according to His foreknowledge and wisdom. When He puts you in a situation that calls for preparation, He has already equipped you to handle it by His grace. The adversity you face today prepares you for your assignment tomorrow.

Read the three passages in the margin. Describe why God prepares you.

_____

_____

_____

God wants you to rejoice in your hardships and suffering because they will mature you, equip you, and help you share in His glory. Ultimately they will produce a harvest of holiness, righteousness, and peace in your life. God is shaping your life to match your message.

5. God sends you where He can best work through you to accomplish His mission.

Each of the Seven reflected God's kingdom purpose by moving to the place God had planned to bless and use them. Their experiences will help you to know and understand where God is working in your life.

Where did God send each of the Seven? Match the following.

____ Abraham   1. Sent back to his own people
____ Moses   2. Stayed with his own people
____ David   3. Sent from heaven to earth
____ Jesus   4. Sent to a far country
____ Peter   5. Sent to a faraway island
____ Paul   6. Sent to all peoples but served in his country
____ John   7. Sent to the Gentiles

Each of the Seven had a different destination as he joined God on mission. One of them could not do the work of any of the others. God knows where to send you to best accomplish His mission through you. The correct order of the above exercise is 4, 1, 2, 3, 6, 7, and 5.

John 15:16 (in the margin on page 25) assures us that when God chose you, He knew your assignment. He asks you to adjust your life to join Him. God covenants with you and promises He will complete what He began in you (Phil. 1:6, also in the margin on page 25). He prepares you and sends you where He can best accomplish His mission through you.

Jesus prepared His disciples by sending them on many small assignments before He issued the Great Commission. God does not lock you in a greenhouse and then send you out fully grown. He equips you on the way. He sends you according to His plan and timing—whether next door or to an unreached people group. Everyone rightly related to Him is on mission with God. He drops you into the time line of His local, global, and eternal kingdom activity.

Let's review that again.
Whenever you adjust your life to join God where He is working, you are

dropped into the time line of His _____, _____, and

_____ kingdom activity.

God is at work all over the world, and He cares for all peoples. He is establishing His kingdom locally, globally, and eternally. Only God can determine where you go—unless you think you are smarter than God or you have your best interests at heart more than He does. Jonah thought he knew his assignment better than God; look what happened to him! Pray that God will send you where He has planned for you to go.

6. God guides you step-by-step on His mission to glorify Him among all peoples.

God's guidance is critical to your joining Him on mission. The place is not the only important thing. How He gets you there is also important. The Holy Spirit guides willing and obedient harvesters to the right place. He can use any means along the way to be sure you get there.

God told Paul at his conversion that he would testify of the Lord before kings. He would never have chosen prison, but during two years in jail, Paul witnessed to King Agrippa and Felix. Then he appeared before Caesar. While in prison Paul had time to write letters to the churches; those letters now make up almost half of the New Testament. When you are in difficult circumstances, remember Paul. God will reveal what He wants you to do when you get to the place where He can best use you in His mission.

7. God uses you to fulfill His mission for His glory.

Many of the heroes in the Hall of Faith in Hebrews 11 would not make *Time* magazine's "Heroes of the Millennium," but they are recorded in heaven. Until you reach heaven you will not be able to see your influence on your generation. Only eternity will reveal your significance.

Prayerfully write your own personal mission statement that states how you would like your contribution to be recorded in heaven.

_____

_____

_____

" 'You did not choose me, but I chose you and appointed you to go and bear fruit—fruit that will last. Then the Father will give you whatever you ask in my name' " (John 15:16).

"Being confident of this, that he who began a good work in you will carry it on to completion until the day of Christ Jesus" (Phil. 1:6).

God will reveal what He wants you to do when you get to the place where He can best use you in His mission.

" 'You yourselves have seen what I did to Egypt, and how I carried you on eagles' wings and brought you to myself. Now if you obey me fully and keep my covenant, then out of all nations you will be my treasured possession. Although the whole earth is mine, you will be for me a kingdom of priests and a holy nation.' These are the words you are to speak to the Israelites" (Ex. 19:4-6).

"You are a chosen people, a royal priesthood, a holy nation, a people belonging to God, that you may declare the praises of him who called you out of darkness into his wonderful light" (1 Pet. 2:9).

"My prayer is not for them alone. I pray also for those who will believe in me through their message, that all of them may be one, Father, just as you are in me and I am in you. May they also be in us so that the world may believe that you have sent me. I have given them the glory that you gave me, that they may be one as we are one: I in them and you in me. May they be brought to complete unity to let the world know that you sent me and have loved them even as you have loved me" (John 17:20-23).

God wants to use you to apply the seven spiritual markers to all members of His body so they can also be on mission with Him. When God invites you to join Him on mission, He invites you to function as a member of that body. As God reconciles us to Himself, He reconciles us to each other—churches, races, and a broken world. The stronger and more complete the interdependence in the body, the sooner His mission will be done.

Read Exodus 19:4-6 and 1 Peter 2:9 in the margin. Underline why God called His people and circle what he called them to be.

God designed us to function together. Your life is linked with others by God's design. You cannot love Him and refuse to love those He put around you.

Read John 17:20-23 in the margin. Write below how and why God wants His people to join Him on mission.

How? _____

Why? _____

Jesus wants all His disciples to be one so that the world may believe in Him and experience His glory. If the people of our generation understood Christ's purpose for the corporate life of the church (and churches) working together, we would see one of the greatest movements of God in history.

God plans for the body of Christ to function together as a unit to reach the world for Him in this generation. If God makes you an eye, your primary function is not for you to see but to help the whole body to see. If He makes you a hand, it is not for you just to feed yourself but to help the body reach the lost. If you are a foot, you are not designed to take a walk by yourself, but to help the body walk to where God wants it to be.

If you get frustrated and pull yourself out of the body, you deny the body the use of your gifts, and you end up without a body! If you go to the mission field as a Lone Ranger and the whole body doesn't get involved, the world remains lost. If the whole body is to be marshaled for God's glory, you must personally adjust to God and patiently help your church adjust to God from top to bottom! Then you go on mission with God, and they "go with you."

The early church experienced tangible unity and harmony in the Holy Spirit. Paul believed that all the churches were responsible for functioning together the moment they heard of need. He assumed that he had the right to appeal to the churches for an offering for the saints in Jerusalem or to help him go to Spain. God used His people in previous generations to go on great expeditions with Him to spread His glory. Similarly, in the past 10 years people in many denominations and mission organizations have had a wake-up call from God to go with Him on mission.

Each week as you study the life of one of the Seven, you will use the seven spiritual markers studied in yesterday's lesson to guide you. However, in this introductory unit I want you to see the ultimate reason God wants His people to join Him on mission.

In your Bible look up the verses listed in the margin that support God's reason for the seven spiritual markers for His people. On the lines following, write why God gave each of the spiritual markers.

1. Chooses _____

2. Calls _____

3. Covenants _____

4. Prepares _____

5. Sends _____

6. Guides _____

7. Uses _____

Chooses:
Ephesians 1:3-6
Calls:
2 Peter 1:3-4
Covenants:
Romans 4:20-21
Prepares:
Romans 8:17
Sends:
Isaiah 43:6-7
Guides:
Isaiah 58:8
Uses:
1 Peter 4:11

Did you get the point? God is involving His people in His mission so that everyone will glorify Him in everything. He wants His name celebrated in all generations. Psalm 45:17 says, "I will perpetuate your memory through all generations; therefore the nations will praise you for ever and ever."

Describe ways you will influence others to be on mission with God.
(example: I will enlist a prayer partner to help me pray for missionaries.)

_____

_____

≈≈≈ DAY 5 ≈≈≈

FILLED WITH THE GLORY OF THE LORD

God lives in eternity but created time. Time is a capsule for our sake—not His. Time takes its significance from eternity. God reveals Himself to us in time, and He works in time to carry out His eternal mission. We may tend to think the whole meaning of life is about us, our time, and how little time we have, but God works for His eternal purpose.

You can't understand what God did in history apart from His eternal purpose. Reconciliation only makes sense in the light of eternity. If eternity—heaven and hell—was not real, the cross would be unnecessary.

Often we are so self-centered and so human-focused that we focus on ourselves and not on God. When I preached in our church on the subject "What Is the Bible All About?" I began by asking the questions "What is God's real purpose? What is the message of the Bible?"

**The people at my church gave these answers to my questions.
Check the one answer you would choose.**

☐ The road map for life   ☐ Faith that comes by hearing
☐ Redemption   the Word of God
☐ Love   ☐ Reconciliation
☐ To bring people to Himself   ☐ Giving praise to God

When I heard the last answer, I congratulated the person who got it right. All the others missed it. The Bible includes the story of salvation, the story of what's happened in the past, and predictions of what will happen in the future. But even these do not represent the primary message of the Bible!

The Bible is the story of God's glory. The mission of God is that all peoples glorify Him. Glorifying God is God-centered, not people-centered. All the wonderful things listed above contribute to our understanding of His Word, our redemption, our salvation, and our understanding of His love, but they all exist to glorify Him. Salvation certainly involves us, but we usually stop with our end—our deliverance—and don't get to God's end—His glory."

Read Psalm 96 in your Bible. Underline how you are to worship God. Circle who is to praise God.

Wow! Are you amazed at God's wanting everyone to glorify Him? The psalmist urges all creation to join in praising God. Let me ask you some questions and then give you my sometimes shocking answers.

Each question below is followed by a Scripture passage that answers the question. In your Bible read the Scripture passages. Below check whether you agree with the answer you find in Scripture.

☐ Who is the most God-centered being in the universe? (Isa. 45:22-24)
☐ Of what is God most jealous? (Josh. 24:19-20)
☐ Why did God save the Israelites? (Isa. 48:9-12)
☐ Why does God save humankind? (Jude 25)
☐ What is the reason for all to confess Jesus as Lord? (Phil. 2:10-11)

The answers are sometimes shocking. Most church members give one of the answers our congregation gave when I asked what the Bible is about.

Complete the following sentence: The Bible is about ...

_____

The glory of God is "the visible splendor or moral beauty of God's manifold perfections." "When the Scripture speaks of doing something 'for God's name's sake' it means virtually the same as doing it 'for his glory.' "[2]

If you have difficulty with the concept of God's wanting everyone and everything to glorify Him, that's your problem, not God's. Look at it this way. God doesn't have an equal. Who else could He, in all good conscience, recommend for you to worship, other than Himself? God knows you will find your greatest joy and fulfillment in worshiping Him. God is complete in Himself. Complete unselfishness, worship, and counsel exist among the Father, Son, and Holy Spirit (John 14:10).

God made Adam in His image to be a mirror of God and His glory (Isa. 43:7). But Adam failed to glorify God when Satan tempted him to try to be as God, knowing good and evil. Since then all humans have displayed the glory of God through a warped, broken mirror that focused back on themselves instead of God. At the Tower of Babel (see Gen. 11:1-4) the people said, "Let's make a name for ourselves, lest we be scattered." They wanted to establish a name for themselves and to be self-sufficient instead of glorifying God.

I stated that the message of the Bible is the theme of God's glory. If that statement is correct, then a study of seven of the most significant persons in the Bible should substantiate it. Right? Let's see.

Read the verses in the margin about each of the Seven. In your Bible underline phrases indicating that God worked in them to show His glory.

It's unanimous! All of the Seven glorified God and His name. Abraham "grew strong in his faith, giving glory to God." Moses showed how God got the glory over Pharaoh "for his namesake, that he might make known his mighty power." David urged all nations to glorify God, His name, and His praise. Jesus said that He had glorified the Father as intended and then said He endured the cross to glorify His name. Peter said that in everything God is to be glorified through Jesus Christ. Paul said when Christ returns, He will be glorified by all the saints and marveled at by all who have believed. John pictures all peoples praising, glorifying, and worshiping God. The Bible is the message of God's glory.

But you may ask, "How will I know that I have experienced God's glory?" You will experience God's glory as the Seven did.

Choose the correct character from the margin. Write the name on the most appropriate blank. (The verses you just read will help you answer.)

1. When God gives you a *promise* that you claim by faith as _____ did, you will experience God's glory.
2. When you, like _____, see God do things that you know only God can do, you will know that you have seen the glory of God's *presence*.
3. When you, like _____, experience God in worship that overwhelms you with God's holiness, love, righteousness, splendor, majesty, or wonder, you experience God's glory in *praise*.
4. When you receive _____ as Lord and sense His abiding in you and you in Him, you know you are experiencing the glory of God in *person*.
5. When you are filled with the Spirit like _____ and God works through you to speak His Word, lead people to Christ, give sacrificially to help others, or accomplish other spiritual purposes, you experience God's glory in His *people*.
6. When you are caught up in Christ and sense that His presence is more important than anything you suffer for His sake, like _____, you experience God's glory in His *purpose*.
7. When you are in the Spirit like _____ and worship the Lamb and the One who sits on the throne, you *personally* experience God's glory.

Abraham
(Rom. 4:20-21)

Moses
(Ex. 14:4,18; Ps. 106:6-8)

David
(1 Chron. 16:10,24, 28-29,35-36)

Jesus
(John 17:4; 12:27-28)

Peter
(1 Pet. 4:10-11)

Paul
(1 Cor. 10:31)

John
(Rev. 5:8-14)

"Moses said to him, 'If your Presence does not go with us, do not send us up from here. How will anyone know that you are pleased with me and with your people unless you go with us? What else will distinguish me and your people from all the other people on the face of the earth?' " (Ex. 33:15-16).

One day you will personally experience the reality of God's glory when you see Him with your eyes, hear His voice like the thunder of many waters, and fall down before Him in adoration. For now you experience God's glory when you sense His presence in you and around you while you pray, worship, read the Word, serve Him, undergo persecution, and go through daily activities.

Like Jacob when he woke from his dream, you may say of a very ordinary place: " 'Surely the Lord is in this place, and I was not aware of it' " (Gen. 28:16). Or, like David you may say: "You have made known to me the path of life; you will fill me with joy in your presence" (Ps. 16:11).

Stop now and pray the prayer in the margin (Ex. 33:15-16).

God is on mission to do three things so that all peoples will glorify Him.

1. God is reconciling the world to Himself through Jesus Christ.

" 'This gospel of the kingdom will be preached in the whole world as a testimony to all nations, and then the end will come' " (Matt. 24:14).

God is gearing all things toward gathering in the harvest. His Spirit is stirring the church to respond to His great purpose, so that all peoples will glorify Him throughout eternity. More people and more churches are praying and adopting unreached people groups. They are no longer content to merely give money. They want to be involved in preaching "this gospel of the kingdom … as a testimony to all nations" (Matt. 24:14).

2. God is bringing all things together under one head, Jesus Christ.

"He made known to us the mystery of his will according to his good pleasure, which he purposed in Christ, to be put into effect when the times will have reached their fulfillment—to bring all things in heaven and on earth together under one head, even Christ" (Eph. 1:9-10).

Read Ephesians 1:9-10 in the margin. In your own words write what you think it says.

_____

_____

In Greek the words "bring together" are used to mean to "sum up," like adding a column of figures, except the Greeks put the sum at the top of the list instead of the bottom as most cultures do. God made Christ the head; everything in heaven and earth will be put under Him.

Read 1 Corinthians 15:24-28 in your Bible. Write *T* (true) or *F* (false) beside each statement below.
____ 1. Time will never end.
____ 2. Christ will destroy all dominions, authorities, and powers.
____ 3. The last enemy Christ will destroy is death.
____ 4. God is included in everything under Christ's feet.
____ 5. Christ is included in everything that is subject to God.

What a glorious hope we will have when Christ is crowned Lord over everything and then presents it all to God for His glory. As His witness, don't be shy, afraid, or defeated. God will win! God continues to work through His Son to reconcile all things to Himself. As people of God, we can drop into the middle of God's mission and watch the mighty presence and power of God reconcile all things to Himself. Joining God on mission is simply being involved with God as He reconciles all things to Himself through Christ (see Eph. 1:21-22 in the margin). God put everything under Christ's feet in order to reconcile everything to Himself. Statements 1 and 4 in the exercise are false.

3. God is bringing all peoples to worship Him.

The great Alpha and Omega will eternally rule and reign over the new heaven and new earth. We will join the angelic hosts and the unnumbered peoples around the throne giving God praise for all eternity. What a motivation— to experience people from every nation on the face of the earth praising God around His throne.

> **Read Isaiah 66:18-19 in the margin. Underline God's purpose for bringing all peoples to Himself.**

God's mission on earth is to accomplish what needs to be done for eternity. In the whole Bible you see how God chose a people and prepared them to be His ambassadors in the world. He wants you to be involved in bringing all peoples to glorify Him! When God shows you where He is at work, He invites you to be a part of His eternal purpose!

At no time in history have so many diverse peoples and nations intersected in so many ways. With a push of a remote control or click of a mouse, you can know anything about any place on the globe. Travel and mobility have put more ethnic diversity in your backyard than your grandparents ever dreamed. God constantly provides you opportunities to join Him in seeing His glory fill the earth.

> **From God's point of view, why do you think that He, at this time in history, is connecting you so easily to the other nations?**

_____

_____

God has placed you in this unique era of His kingdom's advance. He wants you to join Him on mission to bring all peoples of the world to glorify His name.

"Far above all rule and authority, power and dominion, and every title that can be given, not only in the present age but also in the one to come. And God placed all things under his feet and appointed him to be head over everything for the church" (Eph. 1:21-22).

"I, because of their actions and their imaginations, am about to come and gather all nations and tongues, and they will come and see my glory. I will set a sign among them, and I will send some of those who survive to the nations— to Tarshish, to the Libyans and Lydians (famous as archers), to Tubal and Greece, and to the distant islands that have not heard of my fame or seen my glory. They will proclaim my glory among the nations" (Isa. 66:18-19).

---

[1] Ivey Harrington Beckman, comp., "Family Album," *HomeLife*, February 2001, 15.
[2] John Piper, *Desiring God* (Sisters, OR: Multnomah Books, 1996), 255.

ABRAHAM
ON MISSION WITH GOD:
A BLESSING FOR ALL PEOPLES

Heart Focus

"I will make you a great nation; and I will bless you; I will make your name great, and you will be a blessing. I will bless those who bless you, and whoever curses you I will curse; and all peoples on earth will be blessed through you"
(Gen. 12:2-3).

This Week's Lessons

Day 1: A Personal Encounter
Day 2: A Willing Heart
Day 3: Experiencing God on Mission
Day 4: God Encounters Your Generation
Day 5: God Will Use You for His Glory

This Week's Learning Focus

You will be able to understand and explain how God is connecting your life, like Abraham's, to His mission to bless all peoples for His glory.

DAY 1

A PERSONAL ENCOUNTER

Can you recall a time when you knew you were making a decision that would affect your entire life? I experienced such a time while on stateside assignment after 14 years as a missionary in Indonesia. Three denominational agencies asked if I could remain in the U.S. and work with them. These requests confused me; I had planned to be a missionary for the rest of my life.

Month after month I wrote in my journal, "Lord, I don't know what You are saying, but I sense You telling me You want to do something else in my life." I couldn't imagine God would call a missionary back from Indonesia to serve in the U.S. when only 325 evangelical missionaries in Indonesia were seeking to reach 150 million people.

God also showed me promises of what He would do if I obeyed Him. My wife, Shirley, and I set aside a day for fasting and prayer. He clearly showed us these verses in Isaiah 43:18-19:

"Forget the former things;
do not dwell on the past.
See, I am doing a new thing!
Now it springs up; do you not perceive it?"

Those verses were like arrows through my heart. I knew God was telling me I wouldn't return to Indonesia. Through my tears, I read the verses that followed in Isaiah 43:20-21:

"I provide water in the desert …
to give drink to my people, my chosen,
the people I formed for myself
that they may proclaim my praise."

I saw that God wanted to form (disciple) His people to proclaim His praise. Then He showed me Isaiah 44:3:

"I will pour water on the thirsty land,
and streams on the dry ground;
I will pour out my Spirit on your offspring,
and my blessing on your descendants."

Through these words, God assured me He would bring revival among His people and bless the world's peoples. For us to return to America was more difficult than going as missionaries had been. But like Abraham, I knew God had spoken. Now it was my turn to obey even though I could not understand. I couldn't teach others to obey if I was disobedient. I could not see, as commentator Paul Harvey says, "the rest of the story."

I could not envision how God would change lives through *MasterLife* and the hundreds of other resources we would produce. I could not see how God would later lead us back into missionary work as a vice president with the International Mission Board. On the day God encounters us, most of us, like Abraham, cannot envision the part that God wants us to play in His mission.

God is at work everywhere all the time! When you adjust your life to join Him where He works, He drops you into the timeline of His global and eternal kingdom activity. In this diagram you will observe how God includes you in His mission through a personal encounter. You may recognize the diagram from *Experiencing God: Knowing and Doing the Will of God.*

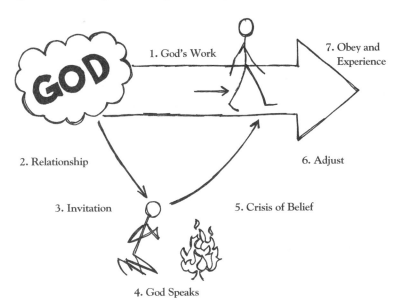

The arrow in the diagram represents time. God has been at work before you joined Him. He will be at work after you complete the assignments He gives you. God is moving from eternity to encounter you in time to lead you into eternity.

I saw that God wanted to form His people to proclaim His praise.

"The Lord had said to Abram, 'Leave your country, your people and your father's household and go to the land I will show you. I will make you into a great nation and I will bless you; I will make your name great, and you will be a blessing. I will bless those who bless you, and whoever curses you I will curse; and all peoples on earth will be blessed through you.' So Abram left, as the Lord had told him; and Lot went with him. Abram was seventy-five years old when he set out from Haran. He took his wife Sarai, his nephew Lot, all the possessions they had accumulated and the people they had acquired in Haran, and they set out for the land of Canaan, and they arrived there. Abram traveled through the land as far as the site of the great tree of Moreh at Shechem. At that time the Canaanites were in the land. The Lord appeared to Abram and said, 'To your offspring I will give this land.' So he built an altar there to the Lord, who had appeared to him. From there he went on toward the hills east of Bethel and pitched his tent, with Bethel on the west and Ai on the east. There he built an altar to the Lord and called on the name of the Lord" (Gen. 12:1-8).

The seven realities in the *Experiencing God* diagram, which will form the outline for your work today and tomorrow, show how God leads you to obedience. Once God has your ongoing obedience, you are ready to participate in advancing His kingdom purpose. This study will help you make the necessary adjustments to join God's mission in this generation.

1. God is always at work around you.

You experience God's glory when He manifests His presence to you. We do not know how God appeared personally to Abraham, but from the beginning we see that God was going to reveal His glory through His promises.

Read Genesis 12:1-8 in the margin. Underline phrases that indicate God would bless Abraham so that Abraham could be a blessing.

As you observe this wandering bedouin, you may believe you could never be like Abraham, "the man of faith" and "God's friend" (Jas. 2:23). Yet Abraham started out as a person plagued by persistent fear—the opposite of faith!

Abraham was afraid of many things. God had a lot of work to do to transform Abram into a model of faith, for all time. God encountered Abraham in Ur (which today is in modern Iraq). Later in Haran God met Abraham and told him to leave everything and go to a distant land.

Go back to the Genesis 12:1-8 passage that you just read. What three things did God ask Abraham to leave behind?

1. _____

2. _____

3. _____

A man riddled with fear would find leaving his country, his people, and his father's household a difficult adjustment, but at age 75 Abraham left them all and followed God, not knowing his destination. All he knew was that God promised to make a name for him, bless him, and make him a blessing to all peoples.

Recently, I talked with a group of people who had followed God's call to leave their homes and homelands to join God on mission. Most of them thought they were heading for a particular country only to find that in the process God redirected them to another! They felt a bit like Abraham did.

How might you feel if God called you today to something different from what you are doing now? Check the answers that apply.
☐ I dislike change, so I couldn't possibly make a shift.
☐ I feel very insecure outside my comfort zone, so I'd probably fail.
☐ I'd like to think I could be available to God, but I'd have to rely totally on His strength and not on my own.
☐ I want to be obedient. I'm ready if He calls me.
☐ Other _____

Stop and pray. If your answer in the above exercise reflected any hesitation, ask God to make your heart open to follow wherever He leads, even if that requires some adjustment.

2. God pursues a continuing love relationship with you that is real and personal.

When God encountered Abraham, amazingly, Abraham responded in faith. God initiated a love connection that changed Abraham's heart forever. God chose him from a pagan culture and called Abraham to a one-on-one relationship with Himself. When God gives you a promise like He gave Abraham, claim it by faith.

> **Read again the Genesis 12:1-8 passage on page 34. Draw parentheses around the phrases showing that Abraham worshiped God.**

You probably put parentheses around the phrases indicating that Abraham built altars to the Lord as examples of his worship. Similarly, God encounters you every day on His way to redeem the world, and He invites you to join Him. In a life-changing encounter called salvation, God pursued and won your heart. Now that you are a part of His people, He intends to involve you in His mission to the world. He particularly speaks to you when you deeply worship Him, as Abraham did. His encounters are always directed to move you into the flow of His eternal and global kingdom activity. God encounters you every day on His way to redeem the world, and He invites you to join Him.

3. God invites you to become involved with Him in His work.

God's invitation to Abraham involved his descendants, who would be the means of blessing the nations. However, after he arrived in the promised land, Abraham left without consulting God. Although Abraham at first believed God's promise about his becoming a great nation, his chronic weakness—fear—almost took away his wife and the mother of the promised son!

> **Read Genesis 12:10-20 in your Bible. Star the verses that reveal Abraham's fear and lack of faith in God.**

Famine sent Abraham scuttling for Egypt, and his fear placed Sarah in jeopardy with the Pharaoh. Note that Abraham asked her to say she was his sister (a half-truth), to save his own skin. God intervened to salvage the situation, but can you imagine what the Egyptian ruler thought about this faithless behavior on Abraham's part?

> **How do you feel when you realize, by reading the story of Abraham's flaws, that God does not expect perfection from you—only obedience and willingness on your part? Check any statements at the top of page 36 that describe your reaction to this.**

☐ I'm a perfectionist by nature. I'm sure I can never change.
☐ My flaws are too great. I don't believe that God can overlook them.
☐ Abraham's life inspires me. If God can overlook his lack of faith, then
   I have hope that He can use me in spite of my weaknesses, as well.
☐ I'm willing and want to be obedient.
☐ Other _____

DAY 2

A WILLING HEART

An encounter with God is an opportunity to respond to Him. Prepare to respond by carefully listening. Attune yourself to the ways He speaks.

4. God speaks to you by the Holy Spirit through the Bible, prayer, circumstances, and the church to reveal Himself, His purposes, and His ways.

Without the Scriptures how did Abraham hear from God? The passages we've read show God spoke to Abraham clearly and specifically. By his faithful worship, Abraham put himself in the position to hear from God. As God's child, you have more than Abraham had. You have the Holy Spirit residing in you to illuminate the written Word. As you wait on God, He speaks through His Word, circumstances, the church, and prayer to make sure you know His mission for you.

> **Check the ways God continues to encounter you.**
> ☐ As I sense His presence and love when I pray
> ☐ In His Word as I read the Bible or hear it explained
> ☐ During times of praise and worship
> ☐ When I experience the beauty of His creation
> ☐ Through other people and their testimonies
> ☐ Through the witness of His Holy Spirit within me
> ☐ Through everyday life experiences in which He speaks to me
> ☐ Through times of discipline
> ☐ Other _____

You can be sure that each time He encounters you, He has a loving purpose to involve you in His work.

You may have marked several or all of the previous statements as ways God encounters you. You can be sure that each time He encounters you, He has a loving purpose to involve you in His work.

5. God's invitation for you to work with Him always leads you to a crisis of belief that requires faith and action.

Even with his fear and other human weaknesses Abraham was a person of faith and action. You saw how he left his homeland and replaced stable living with nomadic wanderings. Crises often occurred which tested his faith until it was refined to God's standard. Many crises were within his own family, as God worked through him to bless his family and, through them, all peoples.

Read Genesis 13:5-18 in your Bible. Mark the following questions T (true) or F (false), based on the Bible account of Abraham and Lot.
_____ Abraham and Lot had a personal quarrel.
_____ The Lord invited Abraham to take the lush Jordan Valley.
_____ Lot allowed Abraham to choose the area he preferred.
_____ God invited Abraham to walk the length and breadth of the land He was giving to him and his offspring.

As Lot's and Abraham's herdsmen quarreled, the patriarch permitted his nephew to take the most fertile plain of the Promised Land. God invited Abraham to walk the whole land, reassuring him that he and his descendants would inherit it. All statements above except the last one are false.

In the margin jot down any crises of faith that face you in your immediate or extended family as you join God in His work.

6. You must make major adjustments in your life to join God in what He is doing.

As Abraham joined God on His mission, he struggled with many major adjustments. At one point this peace-loving patriarch was called on to battle four kings to rescue his nephew Lot and family (see Gen. 14:11-24). Abraham could have let Lot reap the consequences of his selfish choice to live in Sodom. Instead, he acted immediately, routed the enemy, and recovered the people and plunder.

In Genesis 14:11-24 in your Bible underline verses that show how Abraham glorified God by his actions.

Because he recognized that the glory belonged to God, Abraham made sure human actions would not be cited as the reason for his blessings. You may have found that human nature rebels against wanting to respond immediately to God's directive. Fear, anxiety, comfort, and untold excuses may try to deter you. You are probably discovering, however, that when you obey, God blesses beyond measure any adjustments you make to follow Him.

God blesses beyond measure any adjustments you make to follow Him.

Can you recall a time when God blessed an adjustment you made to follow Him? If so, describe it here.

_____

_____

_____

7. You experience God's purpose as you obey Him and He accomplishes His work through you for His glory.

Abraham gradually learned who God is. His faith grew when he obeyed God and saw Him intervene. I am most aware of the glory of God's presence when He works through me to accomplish His will. I am amazed when He leads someone to believe in Him through my witness. God demonstrates His purpose and His glory when He works through you.

> **Review the seven realities of *Experiencing God* that you have studied. Answer these questions.**
>
> 1. Which step are you on now in your experience with God? Reality #____
>
> 2. What holds you back from taking the step to the next reality?
>
> _____
>
> **Read Psalm 139:23-24 in the margin. Write anything you think God sees in your heart that could hold you back from obeying Him.**
>
> _____
>
> **Stop and pray. Ask the Lord to reveal any areas of rebellion or hardness of heart. Ask Him to make you willing to be obedient.**
>
> **Study the following diagram.**

"Search me, O God, and know my heart; test me and know my anxious thoughts. See if there is any offensive way in me, and lead me in the way everlasting" (Ps. 139:23-24).

ON MISSION WITH GOD

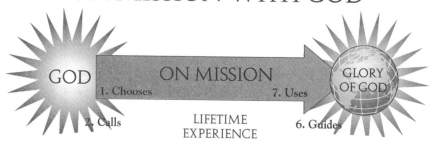

GOD   ON MISSION   GLORY OF GOD

1. Chooses   7. Uses

2. Calls   LIFETIME EXPERIENCE   6. Guides

3. Covenants   5. Sends

4. Prepares

You have explored the *Experiencing God* picture—how God works in an individual experience. For the rest of today you will encounter the bigger picture of what God is doing with your entire life as He brings you into His mission.

You will study the seven spiritual markers God uses with His people. You will see how the Lord chooses you, calls you, covenants with you, prepares you, sends you, guides you, and uses you to accomplish His mission so that the glory of God will cover the earth.

1. God chooses you to be on mission with Him to reconcile a lost world to Himself.

God's purpose in choosing Abraham wasn't merely to bless him but to bring glory to God by making him a blessing to all nations. God has a bigger picture than your personal salvation in mind. He has chosen you to be involved in His worldwide kingdom. Could God possibly see you as a channel through whom He can share His gospel and display His glory and grace to all the nations?

If you know Him, you realize that God chose you to be His child. He cared enough about you to find you. He encountered you to show you His love and brought you to a crisis of belief in which you trusted Him, made the adjustment to follow Him, and obeyed Him. Why did God do that? Because He sees you as a part of what He will do in the world during your generation!

2. God calls you to Himself to be on mission with Him.

God calls you just as He called Abraham. You may say, "But I'm not called to be a preacher." Abraham wasn't a preacher, either. When God tells you to follow Him, He is not obligated to reveal your destination immediately. I did not know where God wanted me to serve until 11 years after I answered God's call to be on mission with Him. Just before we were to be appointed as missionaries, the Lord revealed it was Indonesia.

If you follow Him in faith, He will lead you to the place where He can best use you. See what Hebrews 11:6 in the margin says about pleasing God when you obey Him. You obey by faith!

3. God calls you to Himself to initiate a covenant of promise and obedience with you.

God's nature is to love, bless, and redeem. He not only chooses and calls you, He also makes a covenant with you, just as He did with Abraham. The covenant God made with Abraham about blessing the nations, appears at right.

Read Genesis 12:1-3 in the margin. Underline the principal blessing God promised to Abraham. Draw a double line under the corresponding responsibility Abraham had.

God's principal blessing includes all His promises of blessings for you, but your responsibility is that all peoples of the world will be blessed through you. If you experience only the blessing, you're only halfway there! For every top-line blessing exists a bottom-line responsibility.

In Genesis 15 Abraham complained that he didn't have a son and that his servant would receive his inheritance. God promised that Abraham would have a son and gave him an object lesson. Read Genesis 15:4-6 in the margin. When

"Without faith it is impossible to please God, because anyone who comes to him must believe that he exists and that he rewards those who earnestly seek him" (Heb. 11:6).

"The Lord had said to Abram 'Leave your country, your people and your father's household and go to the land I will show you. I will make you into a great nation and I will bless you; I will make your name great, and you will be a blessing. I will bless those who bless you, and whoever curses you I will curse; and all peoples on earth will be blessed through you.'" (Gen. 12:1-3).

"The word of the Lord came to him: 'This man will not be your heir, but a son coming from your own body will be your heir.' He took him outside and said, 'Look up at the heavens and count the stars—if indeed you can count them.' Then he said to him, 'So shall your offspring be.' Abram believed the Lord, and he credited it to him as righteousness" (Gen. 15:4-6).

God makes a promise, He gives His word that it will come to pass. As Abraham surveyed the eastern sky, he experienced God's glory. God's promise went far beyond anything Abraham could imagine—Abraham's descendants would be as uncountable as the stars. This promise challenged Abraham's faith. God let Abraham experience the glory of His mission as He enlarged His promise.

Abraham experienced God's love in a vivid way. This occurred when God told Abraham to do something, and Abraham responded. In your Bible read Genesis 15:9-18. Below place into sequential order the steps involved in how this happened.
___ As the sun set, Abraham fell into a deep, almost coma-like sleep.
___ Abraham cut the animals in half and arranged the halves across from each other.
___ Abraham was told to bring a heifer, a goat, and a ram to sacrifice.
___ A firepot and blazing torch appeared, passing through the animals.

> Remember: God is the one who initiates a covenant, not you.

In Abraham's culture and time, persons entered a binding agreement as they cut a covenant. This made the agreement binding on both parties. To do this, they walked between the two halves of sacrificed animals. In this vision Abraham saw himself and God walk between the sacrificed animals. The order of steps above is 3, 2, 1, 4. Remember: God is the one who initiates a covenant, not you. Making a covenant with God is much more serious than you may realize. Your covenant with Him is your response to His initiative. God promises you many things, but each depends on how you obey Him. When God makes a covenant, He keeps His word, and He expects you to, also!

Below write any promise you believe God has made to you. If it is a Bible promise, write the reference and what you believe God has promised you through it.

_____

_____

DAY 3

EXPERIENCING GOD ON MISSION

In day 2 you studied the first three spiritual markers in God's lifetime plan for you. Today you will study the other four.

4. God prepares you for His mission.

God took 25 years to shape Abraham's character so he could be the father Isaac needed. During that time God dealt with Abraham's greatest weakness. Even though he believed God's promise about an heir, Abraham's fear fed on Sarah's continuing childlessness. God had a lot of work to do with Sarah, as well, before she could become the mother God wanted her to be.

Read Genesis 16:1-5 in the margin. Underscore the false and self-centered statements with which Sarah filled Abraham's ears.

Sarah blamed God for her barrenness and turned to her maidservant to provide an heir. Then she blamed Hagar for her sufferings. Before God was finished with Abraham and Sarah, He would transform their faithlessness and fearfulness into faithfulness and fearlessness. Meanwhile, God tested them and allowed them to have problems that He would use to transform their character.

When you have woes, realize that God is shaping and molding you for His purpose. A diamond was once a piece of black coal. With pressure, time, and cutting, it became a beautiful jewel. The grand design for diamonds in God's kingdom is that all the peoples of the world will be blessed through His people!

If God sees you as a diamond in the rough, what do you think are some of the rough edges in your character that God needs to work on to use you to the maximum on mission with Him? *(example: He needs to silence my tongue so that I will say only helpful and not hurtful things to others.)*

_____

_____

5. God sends you to the place where He can best work through you to accomplish His mission.

The day finally arrived when Isaac, the child of promise, was born. Abraham and Sarah must have thought they were home free in their faith-walk with God. In Genesis 17 Abraham immediately obeyed God when He introduced the covenant of circumcision. In Genesis 21:11-14 the distressed patriarch submitted to God in sending away his other son, Ishmael. Abraham must have hoped that his trials were over. But the biggest test was yet to occur. God was getting ready to send Abraham on a journey that would cut him to his very core.

In your Bible read Genesis 22:1-18. Underscore the phrases that show Abraham's seasoned trust in God.

What must have run through Abraham's mind when God sent him on this harrowing expedition! I can just imagine him saying something like, "But God, I'm over one hundred years old. My heart won't take these shocks. You gave me this child. The heathen do abominable things like human sacrifice. How can this possibly glorify you?" But Abraham had heard the voice of God enough to know when God was speaking. Early the next day he set out on his sad journey. Knowing that Isaac was his only hope for name, inheritance, and blessing to all peoples, Abraham trusted that God would raise Isaac from the dead if necessary (see Heb. 11:19). He believed God and hoped in Him.

> "Now Sarai, Abram's wife, had borne him no children. But she had an Egyptian maidservant named Hagar; so she said to Abram, 'The Lord has kept me from having children. Go, sleep with my maidservant; perhaps I can build a family through her.' Abram agreed to what Sarai said. So after Abram had been living in Canaan ten years, Sarai his wife took her Egyptian maidservant Hagar and gave her to her husband to be his wife. He slept with Hagar, and she conceived. When she knew she was pregnant, she began to despise her mistress. Then Sarai said to Abram, 'You are responsible for the wrong I am suffering. I put my servant in your arms, and now that she knows she is pregnant, she despises me. May the Lord judge between you and me'" (Gen. 16:1-5).

> Abraham must have hoped that his trials were over. But the biggest test was yet to occur.

> Abraham had heard the voice of God enough to know when God was speaking.

Has God brought you through a physical or emotional experience in which He was your only hope? If so, describe it below. Remember that a loving Father's grace is sufficient in your weakness (see 2 Cor. 12:9).

_____

_____

6. God guides you on mission with Him.

As he prepared to sacrifice his son, Abraham could not have understood the mission and the glory God would receive from it . From the very outset, however, God knew that He would have to guide Abraham unerringly to foreshadow the sacrifice of His only begotten Son years later. The showdown came on the very mountain, Moriah, where Christ would be crucified!

In your Bible read Genesis 22:1-12. Write the number of the verse that corresponds to each event in Abraham's experience.
1. The place _____
2. The answer _____
3. God's intervention _____
4. God's provision _____

> The happy ending occurred when God provided the ram and made Isaac the answer to Abraham's hope.

God not only guided Abraham to the right mountain (see Genesis 22:2) but also provided prophetic words to answer his son's question (see v. 8). God intervened at the crucial moment (see vv. 10-12). Finally, the One Abraham called "The Lord Will Provide" showed him the ram (see v. 13) caught in the thicket—the sacrifice that would take Isaac's place. The happy ending occurred when God provided the ram and made Isaac the answer to Abraham's hope. The patriarch had finally moved from fear to faith that God would fulfill His promises!

Have you had a faith encounter with God? Compare the way God met you with the way you see Him answer Abraham. Write below how God met you in each of the same ways.

1. The place _____

2. The answer _____

3. God's intervention _____

4. God's provision _____

If God has not led you through such an experience yet, ask Him to guide you to one. When missionaries sacrifice to go with God, they rarely mention the deprivation they encounter. More often they say, "This is great. I'm doing what God wants me to do. I enjoy living here. Compared with what Jesus did, this is no sacrifice!" God calls you to present your body "a living sacrifice, holy, acceptable to God, which is your reasonable service" (Rom. 12:1). Such sacrifices bring a "soothing aroma" to Him (Lev. 1:13,17). Sacrificing yourself daily will guarantee that you will experience His glory through His daily guidance in your life!

7. God uses you to bring glory to His name as He accomplishes His mission through you.

From studying Abraham, you realize that everything begins with God and not with you. Sometimes you may think you have a better idea and want to bargain with God: "If You'll make this happen, I'll serve You. If You'll bless me, I'll give You a tithe or an offering." This is the opposite of what God does. He covenants with you and tells you what He will do through you, as He did with Abraham.

When God first began to convict me about missions, I responded, "I don't want to live in a grass hut in Africa!" I tried to bargain with God. I told Him, "If I marry a girl who wants to be a missionary, then I'll be one, too." Now that was a bold decision, wasn't it? Actually, God got it settled before I started dating her.

When I finally surrendered to be a missionary, I sensed God leading me to be an evangelist instead. I responded, "But God, now I want to go." He said, "Be an evangelist." I replied, "But I really want to go be a missionary." God said, "You'll go someday, but now I want you to be an evangelist." For the next 11 years I did evangelism and was the pastor of three churches before He let me go to another land.

If you struggle with God's call and you still feel Him calling, obey. God can still use you to accomplish His mission. Whether His call is to another people or to your own, God is working to lead you to join His mission.

If you don't respond to God to be on mission with Him, you will miss experiencing His glory through your life. You may not realize why you, like Abraham, have undergone trials and testing. Hopefully, this study has helped you see how God is working in your life. Times of testing could be God's indications that He has a significant assignment for you. God is using these to shape you into His image and prepare you to be on mission with Him.

Read Philippians 2:13 and 4:4-6 in the margin. Then stop and thank God that He cares enough to work in you and through you to accomplish His mission in the world.

DAY 4

GOD ENCOUNTERS YOUR GENERATION

1. God chooses His people to be on mission with Him to reconcile a lost world to Himself.

When God chose Abraham, He had in mind a much greater purpose than saving one individual. God's mission was to make Abraham into a great nation to bless all peoples on the face of the earth. His covenant with Abraham was confirmed with his son, Isaac.

Sometimes you may think you have a better idea and want to bargain with God. This is the opposite of what God does.

"It is God who works in you to will and to act according to his good purpose" (Phil. 2:13).

"Rejoice in the Lord always. I will say it again: Rejoice! Let your gentleness be evident to all. The Lord is near. Do not be anxious about anything, but in everything, by prayer and petition, with thanksgiving, present your requests to God" (Phil 4:4-6).

Read Genesis 26:1-5 and 28:10-15 in your Bible. In your own words write in the spaces provided how God confirmed to Isaac and Jacob the promises He made to Abraham.

1. Land/place _____

2. Descendants _____

3. Blessings _____

*"The Lord will guide
   you always;
he will satisfy your needs
   in a sun-scorched land
and will strengthen
   your frame.
You will be like a well-
   watered garden,
like a spring whose waters
   never fail"*
(Isa. 58:11-12).

God continued to bless Abraham's descendants. God's plan in choosing Abraham included not only the nation of Israel but the coming of Christ, the promise of the Holy Spirit, and salvation for Gentiles as well as Jews.

When Shirley and I faced the decision I mentioned in day 1 she said, "Isaiah 44:3 says, 'I will pour out my Spirit on your offspring and my blessing on your descendants.' We need to ask for some Bible promises for our kids." God led us to other promises that we claimed for our five children (see one of those promises, Isa. 58:11-12, in the margin).

We have the promise of God that He will bless our descendants for all time! I wish I had time to tell you how God has blessed our descendants already. Our five children are all walking with Jesus and serving Him—two of them in church-related vocations. They are training our 13 grandchildren to follow Christ. Henry and Marilynn Blackaby have claimed promises for their five children, too. All five of them are in ministry or missions, and the Blackabys are praying for their 13 grandchildren.

Have you been praying for your descendants? We have the promise of God that He will bless our descendants for all time!

If God has given you promises for your descendants, write these below and describe what you believe God has promised you through them. If you do not yet have any promises, begin now to ask God to give you Scriptures that you can claim for your physical or spiritual children as you study *On Mission with God*. When He does, write them below.

_____

_____

2. God calls your generation to Himself to be on mission with Him.

God knew when He called us that leaving us on our own to do His mission would not be a good idea. Instead, He put His Holy Spirit within us and made us members of Christ's body (see Eph. 5:30). The Lord designed the church to be a multifaceted group with varying gifts (see Rom. 12:4-6a; 1 Cor. 12:12,14,18,27). Just as God chose Israel to be His special people in the Old Testament, He has called out the church to be its New Testament counterpart.

As part of the body of Christ, we have an interdependent relationship with others in the church. Through worship and the Word, God works in and through His church so that, together we accomplish His mission in the world.

In this generation the Lord is bringing a new unity and harmony in His body so that the world will believe on Him. Christ prayed for you before He left this world and intercedes for you in heaven even as you read this (see Heb. 7:25).

Read John 17:16-23 in the margin. Mark each statement T (true) or F (false).

_____ 1. You are to be "of the world."

_____ 2. You are sent into the world by Christ as He was by the Father.

_____ 3. Christ's prayer was only for His twelve disciples.

_____ 4. People will believe in Christ through the preached message.

_____ 5. Jesus will be satisfied with partial unity in His church.

_____ 6. Unity demonstrates to the world that the Father sent Jesus.

God has called you to pursue unity in His church and to work with your brothers and sisters in Christ. Only then will His glory rest on you as you, in partnership with others in the body of Christ, seek to join Him on mission. I hope you answered in the above exercise that statements 1, 3, and 5 are false.

3. God initiates a covenant of promise and obedience with your generation.

In *The Experiencing God Bible* Henry Blackaby defines the church as "the body of people God has chosen to enter into love relationship with him through faith in Jesus Christ as Lord and Savior, having committed themselves to obey Him and join in the work He is doing. God's chosen people, Israel, were the precursor or forerunner of the church, only a faithful remnant serving as God's people."[1]

Read 1 Peter 2:9 in the margin. Circle all the uses of "people" (plural).

God chose a single individual to begin a nation, but His purpose is to bring together a covenant people from every nation, tribe, tongue, and people. In our individualistic society, you may find fitting in with a group of believers difficult. Realize that God's purpose is so great that you can't experience it alone. Jesus said, " 'I have given them the glory that you gave me, that they may be one as we are one' " (John 17:22). You experience God's glory in the presence of His people.

4. God prepares His people in your generation for His mission.

Paul said to Timothy, a young person of his generation, "Endure hardship with us like a good soldier of Christ Jesus" (2 Tim. 2:3). God is giving this generation a great deal of on-the-job training and character-building opportunities as He prepares His people for His heavenly purpose.

I see many heartbreaking situations as I relate to missionaries all over the world. A young missionary battles cancer. Another lost his son to disease. Christian believers have their homes ransacked or are arrested and interrogated. Some are imprisoned. Some have been martyred. Does this sound like a modern catalog of heroes, like those in Hebrews 11? Times have not changed much when you look at the whole world.

" 'They are not of the world, even as I am not of it. Sanctify them by the truth; your word is truth. As you sent me into the world, I have sent them into the world. For them I sanctify myself, that they too may be truly sanctified. My prayer is not for them alone. I pray also for those who will believe in me through their message, that all of them may be one, Father, just as you are in me and I am in you. May they also be in us so that the world may believe that you have sent me. I have given them the glory that you gave me, that they may be one as we are one: I in them and you in me. May they be brought to complete unity to let the world know that you sent me and have loved them even as you have loved me' " (John 17:16-23).

"You are a chosen people; a royal priesthood, a holy nation, a people belonging to God, that you may declare the praises of him who called you out of darkness into his wonderful light" (1 Pet. 2:9).

In your Bible read Hebrews 11. Below write the difference in the people verses 1-34 mention and those verses 35-38 mention.

_____

That great cloud of witnesses is looking over the banisters of heaven, urging you and Christ's church on to final victory.

People in the latter group suffered persecution and death for their faith. That great cloud of witnesses (see Heb. 12:1) is looking over the banisters of heaven, urging you and Christ's church on to final victory as we work with God to win the world to Jesus Christ in our day. Time is running out. I have been impressed with many in today's younger generation who are ready to go wherever He is on mission. In your day that is literally to the ends of the earth!

5. God sends this generation of His people to the place where He can best work through them to accomplish His mission.

Throughout history God has been moving people from one place to another for His purposes. You've seen how Abraham had to travel long distances to be in the place of God's choosing. Similarly, 70 members of the family of Jacob went down into Egypt, where God would make of them a great nation (see Ex. 1:1). More than 400 years later, He brought them out of Egypt into the land of Canaan. Later, they were taken captive to Babylon and returned to Palestine after 70 years of captivity (see Jer. 25:8-14). In the New Testament the disciples were scattered after the stoning of Stephen (see Acts 8:1-4). The destruction of Jerusalem in A.D. 70 dispersed God's people throughout the Roman world. When you look at all of history, it seems that God has always had His people on the move.

**How many persons in your church would you estimate have traveled out of your country in the past three years for any reason? _____
How many from your church have gone on mission trips in the past three years? _____ How many missionaries have been called from your church?_____**

Stop and ask God to make your church a world missions-strategy center to commission people to be on mission with Him.

In the whole Bible you see the account of the way God has chosen a people and prepared them to be His representatives, His ambassadors, His reconcilers in the world. He wants your church to be involved in His redemptive purpose!

6. God guides His people in this generation to be on mission.

Because the mission belongs to God, He takes responsibility for guiding a willing group of people to the proper destination. God guided Abraham. God can guide His people today. He cares as much about this generation as any other.

More than two hundred years ago Adoniram Judson and Luther Rice heard God's call and left America to go to India. On the trip overseas they studied their Bibles and became Baptists. On arrival they were baptized by William Carey. They were not allowed to serve in India, so Judson and his wife, Ann, went to Burma. Because their support would no longer come from the Congregationalists who sent them out as missionaries, Rice returned to America to raise money. From his efforts came the Triennial Baptist Convention, the precursor to the American Baptist Convention and the Southern Baptist Convention.

Judson served for six years before he saw his first convert. I visited Myanmar (Burma) in 1999. The Baptist convention there had 700,000 members divided into 15 people-group conventions. Judson could not have imagined that his work would bless so many people. Rice could never have imagined that one of the conventions (the Southern Baptist Convention) he helped start would become the largest missionary-sending body in the world. Like Abraham, Judson and Rice acted on faith.

7. God is using this generation to fulfill His mission.

God has designed us to function as a people united with one heart and mind. Your life is linked with others by God's design. Previously, you may not have seen the church as a people God put together on purpose to be on mission with Him.

In your generation one of the great moves of God in revival is to have people understand the value of corporate life among churches, associations, and denominations, and Christian organizations as part of His kingdom.

Below write ways God might use you to bring unity and harmony among fellow Christians.

_____

_____

Describe what you desire for your church to do as a part of God's people to bring glory to Him among all peoples.

_____

_____

_____

⇒⇒ DAY 5 ⇐⇐

GOD WILL USE YOU FOR HIS GLORY

1. God's blessings come to us to move through us.

One expression of God's nature and character is that He loves to bless. One of the first times in Scripture God blessed occurred when He made people in His image and likeness. Genesis 1:28 says that immediately, "God blessed them and said to them, 'Be fruitful and increase in number; fill the earth and subdue it.

God's blessings came to Adam and Eve to move through them to bless the entire creation.

Rule over the fish of the sea and the birds of the air and over every living creature that moves on the ground.' " God's blessings came to Adam and Eve to move through them to bless the entire creation. Today God desires to do the same through you!

Tom Elliff says, "In the biblical sense a 'blessing' is an act of God by which He causes someone or something to supernaturally produce more than would be naturally possible. When you ask the Lord, for instance, to bless a certain missionary, you are asking God to give him the ability to accomplish more than is humanly possible. Praying that God bless an offering indicates a desire for God to superintend the use of that money so that it accomplishes more than it would if dispensed on the basis of human cleverness."[2]

Write your own definition of the word *blessing*.

_____

He desires that through you, the knowledge of His glory will increase and fill the whole earth.

God desires to bless you by making you fruitful in every good work (see Col. 1:10) and watching you increase in faith (see 2 Cor. 10:15) so that the gospel can be furthered. He desires that through you, the knowledge of His glory will increase and fill the whole earth (see Hab. 2:14). He wants you to walk in His authority as you go and disciple all nations (see Matt. 28:18-19), subduing the kingdom of darkness (see Rom. 16:20), so that you may rule and reign in His kingdom (see Rev. 5:10).

Although God began His creation by blessing Adam and Eve in the garden of Eden, the primary revelation of God's desire to bless all nations occurred through Abraham. As part of God's covenant of blessing with Abraham, God prospered him *physically* and *spiritually* in everything he did. God blessed him with great wealth and flocks and herds (see Gen. 13:2). Abraham had so many physical blessings that he and his nephew Lot parted company because the land could not support all their possessions (see Gen. 13:6).

State one way God has blessed you to make you physically and spiritually fruitful. *(example: He gave me godly parents who taught me about Him from an early age; now I need to pass this on to others.)*

Physically:_____

Spiritually:_____

" 'I have chosen him, so that he will direct his children and his household after him to keep the way of the Lord by doing what is right and just, so that the Lord will bring about for Abraham what he has promised him' " (Gen. 18:19).

Scripture indicates that the patriarchs blessed their children. This blessing was based on the fact that God had blessed them. It affirmed God's blessings to their offspring. Certainly, the fathers bequeathed physical blessings to their offspring, especially the firstborn. The inheritance included the idea that spiritual blessings from God overshadowed them and would continue through the generations. Today the idea of a blessing by one's parents is important, although it is seldom formal. Sometimes parental approval while the person lives is more important psychologically than is actual physical inheritance.

God promised that His blessing would extend to all the world's peoples through Abraham and his descendants. God continues to bless anyone connected with Abraham, right down to you if you are a believer (see Gal. 3:7). The blessings to your forefather Abraham are designed to flow to you and to bless the nations of the world through you.

2. God's blessings are based on obedience.

As you've already seen, God chose Abraham, knowing he would obey Him. God says as much in Genesis 18:19 (in the margin on page 48). Note that God's blessing hinged on Abraham's obedience. Disobedience could bring a curse—the opposite of blessing—as it did to Adam and Eve (see Gen. 3:14-23), to Noah's generation (see Gen. 6), and to Babel (see Gen. 11). God's promise to Abraham included his descendants, the land, and the blessing. God blessed Abraham abundantly for leaving his family and friends. Know that God's call to Christians to reach the nations will result in rich rewards of relationships enduring into eternity!

Read Jesus' words in Mark 10:29-30, in the margin. Mentally count the blessings God has given you as you have followed Him.

The promised land was another part of the blessing God gave to Abraham. His willingness to leave culturally rich Ur to wander throughout foreign countries was a genuine step of faith for him. Several times during Abraham's lifetime God confirmed the call to Canaan.

Read Genesis 12:7 and 13:14-15 in the margin. Circle the word *land* each time it is used.

Interestingly, the only part of the promised land that Abraham possessed during his lifetime was the cave of Machpelah, which he bought to bury Sarah. It was a token of the promise which would later be fulfilled to the nation Abraham fathered. Read Hebrews 11:9-10 in your Bible. It sums up Abraham's experience of faith in God's promise.

You may or may not own a home in the place where you currently live. God may ask you, like Abraham, to leave your homeland and live in a temporary dwelling anywhere in the world. If He does, you will join the ranks of those whose hope rested in God—the founder of an eternal city. There, throughout eternity, you will no longer be a stranger or a foreigner but a child of the King and a citizen of the heavenly kingdom!

The third part of the promise was the blessing itself.

In Genesis 12:2-3 (in the margin), circle or highlight the word "bless" in God's promise to Abraham.

Did you underline *bless* five times in the verses? When God first called Abraham, God informed him that he was about to be blessed—in ways Abraham would see in his lifetime and in ways Abraham was unable to foresee or even remotely understand. Not only was Abraham blessed, he would become the means of blessing all peoples on earth. Blessing is never just for yourself; it is always to be passed on to others!

" 'I tell you the truth,' Jesus replied, 'no one who has left home or brothers or sisters or mother or father or children or fields for me and the gospel will fail to receive a hundred times as much in this present age (homes, brothers, sisters, mothers, children and fields—and with them, persecutions) and in the age to come, eternal life. But many who are first will be last, and the last first' " (Mark 10:29-30).

"The Lord appeared to Abram and said, 'To your offspring I will give this land.' So he built an altar there to the Lord, who had appeared to him" (Gen. 12:7).

"The Lord said to Abram after Lot had parted from him, 'Lift up your eyes from where you are and look north and south, east and west. All the land that you see I will give to you and your offspring forever'" (Gen. 13:14-15).

"I will make you into a great nation and I will bless you; I will make your name great, and you will be a blessing. I will bless those who bless you, and whoever curses you I will curse; and all peoples on earth will be blessed through you" (Gen. 12:2-3).

3. God's promised blessings to those who believe are as sure as the promises He has already fulfilled.

The mission to bless all the peoples of the world is to bring all peoples into the family of God. God is not interested in blessing your life just so that you will prosper. The final scene of history is not a throng of individuals standing before the throne recounting their blessings. Rather, it is a scene of all the people of God (see Rev. 7:9-10)—a people drawn from every tribe, language, and people—giving honor and glory to the rightful Lord of all!

Remember the diagram that summarizes this study (see p. 10)? God's promise of blessing on your life is not the target. Look at the target the arrow points to—the glory of God. In order to join God on mission, keep His target in view. He is on His way to the world. He initiates encounters with you so that you can join Him, not so that He can join you.

You can see that God has been lifting you into the flow of His kingdom work. Often, when problems around you overwhelm you, God has strategically placed you there to advance His kingdom. You may be the only person in a situation who can pray or give godly wisdom or laugh with hope that comes from deep inside. God has connected His life to yours because He wants His "family life" extended to places where only you can take it.

Some four thousand years ago God gave Abraham the promise that all peoples would be blessed through him. Yet today approximately 2,100 distinct peoples, numbering some 1.7 billion individuals have little or no access to the gospel and have never heard God's promise of salvation.

> You may be the only person in a situation who can pray or give godly wisdom or laugh with hope that comes from deep inside.

Check all the statements that seem to answer the following question. Why are the 1.7 billion individuals represented by these groups still not reached with the message of the gospel?
- ☐ 1. Satan does not want redemption to come to them.
- ☐ 2. God has not made it obvious to the church what He wants done.
- ☐ 3. Satan blinds believers to the big picture, so he is free to reign over vast areas of the earth.
- ☐ 4. Believers get too busy passing the blessing back and forth to one another to consider why God has blessed them in the first place.
- ☐ 5. God is more concerned that you live in a godly, comfortable, economically secure nation than He is that His kingdom be advanced.
- ☐ 6. Other _____

You cannot underestimate the spiritual battle that underlies God's mission. Every people without a church is a people Satan has locked in captivity. He will not easily give up these people. He will blind believers to God's mission. He will convince you that God is more concerned about you than He is about them. I hope you checked 1, 3, and 4 above.

> Every people without a church is a people Satan has locked in captivity.

In your words state why God has encountered, called, and blessed you.

_____

_____

Ultimately, God is shaping your life so that you can join Him on mission. When you align your life with His purpose, you can live with hope and significance.

Check the areas where you have already been involved in helping to extend the kingdom of God to the ends of the earth.

☐ Intercessory prayer

☐ Participating with my Sunday School class in adopting a missionary

☐ As a business person, working toward racial reconciliation

☐ Giving to missions/missionaries

☐ Joining a volunteer mission trip

☐ Praying for persecuted Christians

☐ Becoming involved in student missions

☐ Reading the newspaper or listening to televised newscasts and learning about world events so that I can pray for missionaries who work in troubled areas around the globe

☐ Doing a short-term missions assignment

☐ Teaching missions education programs in my church

☐ Befriending internationals, such as students, in my community

☐ Working in a foreign country and bearing witness to Christ

☐ Other _____

You may have noted ways you have already been involved in global purposes or ways you would like to be involved. Ask God to help you see the ways you can join Him in blessing the nations!

Pray and reflect about the things God is impressing on your heart. Then check one of the following.

☐ Lord, I am willing to look among the nations. I want to know and understand what You are doing. I want to be a part of it. Help me see the ways You connect my life to Your mission to glorify Your name among all the world's peoples.

☐ Lord, I am willing, but I confess I am still not convinced that this whole world mission has anything to do with me. Help me understand how Your mission to bless all peoples of the world connects to my life.

---

1 *The Experiencing God Bible* (Nashville: Broadman & Holman, 1994), 179.

2 Thomas D. Elliff, *Praying for Others* (Nashville: Broadman Press, 1979), 79.

Women on Mission

SARAH
ON MISSION WITH GOD

We tend to look at Abraham as the father of faith. But Sarah, his wife, also played a major role in God's plan. Because of her obedience Sarah was the mother of multitudes. Her spouse was experiencing God, but she was on mission, as well. Sarah is a model for anyone—male or female—who wants to be used as God's vessel, especially for an individual whose mate has a life-changing encounter with God and who finds himself or herself wondering how he or she fits into this experience.

1. Realize that God is at work around your life at the same time He is at work around your spouse's life.
God's promise to Abraham was also a promise to Sarah because she was an integral part of God's plan. Anything God says to your spouse involves you. So when you see Him working in your spouse's life, pay attention to anything God wants to say to you (see Gen. 12:1-3).

2. God loves you just as much as He does your spouse and seeks a relationship with you that is real and personal.
Later, in Genesis 12:14-20 Abraham told Sarah to say she was his sister so that Pharaoh would not kill him to get his wife. Abraham was so wrapped up in himself that he did not realize that God loved Sarah as much as He did him. Abraham failed to believe God, and it almost cost Him his wife's purity and their marriage. His lack of consideration could have cost him the promise of God. Abraham had to learn this lesson again because he failed to learn it the first time (see Gen. 20:1-17). In each case Sarah was submissive, but her faith had to be in God, not in Abraham, who had just had a great experience with God. The Bible doesn't tell us how Sarah felt, but in His love God spared her.

3. God's invitation to your spouse is addressed to both of you.
Without Sarah, Isaac could not be the heir of God's promises. When God calls one member of the couple, He calls both. God doesn't will that one fulfill His purpose without the other. Sarah was disappointed that year after year she could not bear a child. Finally, she gave her servant to Abraham and told him to have children by her. She failed to believe that the invitation to her spouse included her. Abraham's lack of faith caused him to yield to the line of least resistance. That spawned the Arab-Israel conflict that continues to this day!

4. God speaks to you as well as to your spouse.

Don't just accept God's speaking to your spouse as the only thing God says to you. God repeatedly spoke to Abraham. In Genesis 18:9-15 God sent the message to Sarah that she would bear a son even though she was, in her words, "worn out" and her husband "old." She couldn't believe it at first, but when the angel challenged her, she accepted God's word to her. When God speaks to your spouse, ask Him to speak to you also.

5. God's invitation to work with you and/or your spouse always leads you to a crisis of belief that requires faith and action from both of you.

God spoke to Abraham in Genesis 17:15-22, but Abraham laughed when God told him that Sarah would bear Isaac. He was 100 years old, and his wife was past 90—obviously past the time of childbearing. Sarah also laughed when told she would bear Isaac. They both laughed, but when challenged, they believed. About a year later, Isaac was born!

6. You must make a major adjustment in your life to join God in what He is doing in your life and in the life of your spouse.

After they made the adjustment to God's plan for His people to come from Isaac, Sarah sent Hagar and Ishmael away because she now accepted God's plan. She determined to remain faithful to the promise that God had answered and not to trust any longer in her plan. God also acted, responded to Hagar's prayer of faith, and rescued her and Ishmael. God does more than you expect when you adjust your life to God and His plan for your spouse.

7. You come to know God by experience as you obey Him and He accomplishes His work through you.

God not only accomplished His mission through Abraham and Sarah to create a people for Himself, but He also used both of them as models for us.

Abraham

"He is also the father of the circumcised who not only are circumcised but who also walk in the footsteps of the faith that our father Abraham had before he was circumcised" (Rom. 4:12).

Sarah

"This is the way the holy women of the past who put their hope in God used to make themselves beautiful. They were submissive to their own husbands, like Sarah, who obeyed Abraham and called him her master" (1 Pet. 3:5-6).

When God is working in your spouse's life, He is also at work in your life. The two of you are one, and God has a wonderful plan for you together! Are you listening to God when He speaks to your spouse? Believe Him, obey Him, and experience Him as He accomplishes His work through you.

MOSES

ON MISSION WITH GOD: A PEOPLE RESPONSIBLE FOR ALL PEOPLES

Heart Focus
"But I have raised you up for this very purpose, that I might show you my power and that my name might be proclaimed in all the earth" (Exodus 9:16).

This Week's Lessons
Day 1: A Purposeful Encounter
Day 2: God Speaks to You Individually
Day 3: Have Faith and Trust in God
Day 4: God Prepares His People
Day 5: On Eagles' Wings

This Week's Learning Focus
You will be able to understand and explain how, when God encounters you personally, He wants to use you to make His name known to the nations for His glory.

DAY 1

A PURPOSEFUL ENCOUNTER

Have you ever been in a seemingly forsaken place and wondered whether God had forgotten you? Henry Blackaby felt that way as the pastor of faithless, 12-member Faith Baptist Church, of Saskatoon, Saskatchewan, Canada. This seemingly unpromising pastorate capped a varied career. Henry had also been an oiler on a one-ton loraine clam bucket, a deck hand on a coast steamer, a salesman for a gas company, and a worker for Coca-Cola. His father was a lay preacher-banker who started churches in fishing villages in British Columbia.

After God called Henry to preach, he moved to San Francisco to attend seminary while serving as a music director and then the pastor of a small church. After graduation he pastored in east Los Angeles. Six years later, Faith Baptist Church called him to be its pastor. The handful of members left in this declining church threatened to disband if he did not accept their invitation to become their pastor. The only thing attractive about this opportunity was God. Faith Church became a laboratory for experiencing God as Henry served for 12 years in this out-of-the-way place.

As a result of his obedience, Henry experienced God working in special ways in the Saskatoon Revival. It may have been an obscure place, but God knew where Henry was and shaped him there.

The only thing attractive about this opportunity was God.

As He did with Henry, God knows your address, too. He is at work in your life and has you in the place He wants you for you to follow Him. He may have you in a "whale of a belly" as He had Jonah, or he may have you imprisoned as He did Paul, but He wants to speak to you about His mission for your life.

In week 2 we learned that obedience moves us into the flow of God's glory as He fulfills His promises. God promised a blessing through Abraham for all the peoples of the world. He responded in obedience and experienced God's glory. Next, we'll see that God plans for His blessings to flow through His people to all people. We'll see how God moved Moses into His mission.

God plans for His blessings to flow through His people to all people.

Read Exodus 3:1-10 in your Bible. Below check the statements that show how God revealed His glory to Moses.
☐ God showed His glory in the flames of a bush that did not burn up.
☐ God called Moses by name and then revealed His name.
☐ God revealed His character to Moses.
☐ God manifested His presence to Moses.
☐ God revealed His purpose for His people.

If you checked all of the above statements, you are correct. In this week's study you will see how God revealed Himself more fully to Moses than even in the burning bush. No doubt the presence of God and the purpose of God for his life affected Moses dramatically.

God called Moses at the burning bush, but He had been shaping Moses for 80 years. God not only saved Moses' life as a baby, but He also provided for Moses to learn Hebrew history and culture. He allowed him to participate in the best schooling available in the world while he watched the ins and outs of the great nation of Egypt. Moses had to flee Pharaoh's court and spend 40 years on the back side of the desert after he tried to begin an Israelite revolution. But God had not forgotten him, and God still cared for Moses. Moses was gaining personal knowledge of every trail, well, and mountain in the desert of Midian and Sinai. He would rely on these experiences later as he led the Israelites to freedom in the promised land.

God prepares you for your part in His mission by encountering you in various ways, too. When you join God on mission, He reveals His presence to you in your daily life. Your life is linked to His eternal certainty. God interacts with you daily because He is personally concerned for you.

God interacts with you daily because He is personally concerned for you.

You may be involved in an incredibly painful personal experience or family trouble. You may wonder what your life has to do with God's mission. The Israelites in Egypt must have thought the same thing before Moses arrived!

God had been working long before Moses, just as He had been in Abraham's time. In fact, when the children of Israel were just beginning their 430-year sojourn in Egypt, Joseph had prophesied: " 'God will surely come to your aid and take you up out of this land to the land he promised on oath to Abraham, Isaac and Jacob' " (Gen. 50:24). Centuries later, God would tap Moses to be the leader in this momentous event that would fulfill His promise.

ON MISSION WITH GOD

ETERNITY

GOD

ON MISSION
1. God at Work   7. Obey

GLORY OF GOD

INDIVIDUAL EXPERIENCE

2. Relationship   6. Adjust

3. Invitation   5. Crisis of Belief

4. God speaks

ETERNITY

1. God is always at work around you.

God was working at the time of Moses' birth to prepare him for His mission. Moses had the best of both worlds—Egyptian culture and education plus Hebrew devotion to God.

God had a purpose for and revealed Himself to Moses. God has a purpose for and reveals Himself to you when you accompany Him as He completes His mission to be glorified by all peoples.

> **Why and how has God been working all around you and in your life since before you were born? Check the best response.**
> ☐ God is at work in my life because He wants to give me a purpose.
> ☐ God is at work in my life because He has an eternal mission and wants to uniquely involve me in His purpose.

God shapes you, just as He was shaping Moses, to be a part of His mission!

The second choice best describes the core idea of *On Mission with God*. God reveals His glory to you when you accompany Him as He completes His mission to be glorified by all peoples. God shapes you, just as He was shaping Moses, to be a part of His mission!

2. God pursues a continuing love relationship with you that is real and personal.

As Moses grew up in Pharaoh's palace, perhaps he questioned, as you might have at some point, "Why am I here? Does God even know about me? Why is it so difficult for me to find my place in His plan?" Moses, who had been told the deeds of his forefathers, must have wondered if the God who had a personal relationship with Abraham had any interest in him.

Perhaps the Israelites were hoping the Hebrew prince in the palace would resolve their plight. Moses probably saw himself as their deliverer. When he was grown, he took a walk among his people. God includes in the Exodus record the result of Moses' intervention for the sake of the Hebrews.

Read Exodus 2:11 in the margin. Below check the comments you think reflect what Moses might have experienced during that walk.
- ☐ He felt a connection to his own people—he experienced an ethnic identity with the Hebrews.
- ☐ He saw the Hebrews working at hard labor—prisoner-slaves forced to do the impossible with meager supplies.
- ☐ He saw a cruel Egyptian taskmaster beat one of these Hebrew slaves.
- ☐ He saw God's covenant being mocked by the captivity of God's people.

"One day, after Moses had grown up, he went out to where his own people were and watched them at their hard labor. He saw an Egyptian beating a Hebrew, one of his own people" (Ex. 2:11).

The cruelty and injustice of the Egyptian oppression probably overwhelmed Moses. He may have made the connection that he had come to the kingdom for such a time as this. Hebrews 11:25 (in the margin) tells us he made a conscious decision to throw in his lot with the despised slaves rather than enjoy the pleasures of sin for a season. Moses took matters into his own hands. Encountering an Egyptian abusing an Israeli slave, he intervened and killed the Egyptian. He may have thought Israel would respond to his revolutionary act, follow him, and win freedom from Egyptian bondage. But when he tried to make peace between two quarreling Israelites, their response showed that others knew he had murdered the Egyptian. He fled to the desert in Midian for the next 40 years!

He chose to be mistreated along with the people of God rather than to enjoy the pleasures of sin for a short time (Heb. 11:25).

Moses attempted to do God's work by himself. When he failed, he ran from the responsibility God wanted to give him. Later, this weakness exerted itself again when Moses complained that the people weren't following him. You will see that this weakness, near his life's end, caused Moses to disobey God and kept him from entering the promised land.

Have you ever believed, like Moses, that a situation was intolerable and that something had to be done? Did you sense you should do something or that God was up to something? God indeed may have been grabbing your attention. The most important thing in Moses' life was indeed the plight of the Israelite people and his role in their cause. God will use events and people around you to open your eyes to what He is determined to accomplish.

Jot down an instance in the past 24 hours when you saw, read, or thought about some other part of the world or about the world's lost, distraught, suffering peoples that you think God may be using to get your attention.

---

3. *God invites you to become involved with Him in His work.*

God showed His glory to people in Scripture because He is on His mission to fulfill His purpose. God encounters you because He is on His way to a well-defined end. He wants to involve you in what He is about to do.

God encounters you because He is on His way to a well-defined end.

Again read Exodus 3:1-10 in your Bible. Underscore what God said and did. Put parentheses around Moses' response.

Just as with your encounters with God, when Moses met God that day, it was not at Moses' initiative. As incredibly intriguing as Moses' life had been up to that point, it wasn't Moses who decided it was time to intervene in

Middle-Eastern history for the sake of the kingdom of God. On that fateful day in the desert, when God and Moses met over a burning bush, both had a history. The story of Moses up to that day is great drama—the reed-basket bobbing in the Nile, the young Jewish slave-boy morphing into a stately Egyptian prince, the hot-headed young man murdering his way into a desert oblivion. You could easily be tempted to misread the exodus account as Moses' encounter with God.

However, the God who is always achieving His unchanging purpose brought to that burning bush an even more compelling drama. Creation had started a great battle for the right to reign over the earth. Satan made his bid. Unfortunately, the first humans seized it. As people fell, God decreed a way of redemption. Through Abraham, God initiated a covenant strategy whereby He would reign as King over all kingdoms. Now, using a reluctant Egyptian pharaoh and a remarkably storied man named Moses, God would reveal just how intent He was in making that strategy known!

> **Is God inviting you to be on mission with Him? Describe a turning point in your life that you now recognize was God's way to involve you in His mission.** (*example: God worked through my job loss to develop my spiritual life and make me lean more on Him.*)

───

> *You could easily be tempted to misread the exodus account as Moses' encounter with God.*

═══ DAY 2 ═══

GOD SPEAKS TO YOU INDIVIDUALLY

4. God speaks to you by the Holy Spirit through the Bible, prayer, circumstances, and the church to reveal Himself, His purposes, and His ways.

Although God speaks in many ways, He used a burning bush only once! When Moses answered the burning-bush call that day, God had more in mind than just freeing the Hebrew slaves—although their plight surely deserved His attention. He was on mission—a mission that stretched back to a promise made to Abraham some 430 years earlier.

> **Read Exodus 3:6 in the margin. How did God introduce Himself to Moses?**

───

"He said, 'I am the God of your father, the God of Abraham, the God of Isaac and the God of Jacob.' At this, Moses hid his face, because he was afraid to look at God" (Ex. 3:6).

The bush was not burning to invite Moses to help free the Hebrew slaves. It was burning to invite Moses to join God on the mission that God had declared to Abraham. God's purpose has never changed! His mission is no different today than it was 50 years ago or 2,500 years ago. It does not differ from individual to individual or from church to church or from nation to nation.

God speaks by the Holy Spirit through the Word of God, prayer, and circumstances. God speaks, and yet each of us in different ways perceives how God speaks to us. In the Bible God is always speaking. As you go through the Word, you read, "The Lord said," "God said," and "Thus saith the Lord." Interestingly, no matter how He spoke, people in the Bible always knew it was God. They understood who was speaking, and they knew what He was saying.

Moses clearly knew what God was saying; he just didn't want to agree. God speaks to you uniquely, but He's always speaking. He's always showing you His purpose and inviting you to experience His glory. He wants to involve you in what He's doing.

Read Hebrews 6:17 in the margin. Check all that apply.
☐ God wants to make the nature of His purpose clear.
☐ The nature of God's purpose is unchanging.
☐ God made an oath so that "the heirs of what was promised" would understand how serious He was about accomplishing His purpose.

You are correct if you checked all three. God is determined to make His purpose clear and to show that it is unchanging. To understand exactly what God is doing in your world today, come back to this central point: He is determined to fulfill an oath he made to Abraham. The very essence of His character—His holiness, His righteousness, His justice, His power—hangs on the fulfillment of that covenant. Because He has sworn with an oath that the Abrahamic covenant will be fulfilled, anything less means that He is unreliable.

You cannot put that covenant, or the God who made it, in the box of ancient history. The God of history is meeting you as the I AM, inviting you to join Him as He accomplishes His purpose, even as He did that day with Moses. The history of God's mission is actually the history of the Bible itself. His mission has played out over thousands of years, among thousands of peoples, involving countless kings and kingdoms. He is headed to a definite conclusion with clearly explained outcomes. Throughout this study you will examine that mission—the theme that weaves the Bible narratives together.

When was the last time you clearly heard God speaking? _____

How did He speak to you? _____

What did He ask you to do? _____

Are you doing what He asked? ☐ Yes ☐ No

If not, when will you start? _____

As you meditate on the way God has connected your life to His, you can see that the Bible itself is a remarkable record of moments when God encountered men, women, nations, and peoples. He still encounters people today, and He wants to encounter you to join Him on His mission to the world.

God speaks to you uniquely, but He's always speaking.

"Because God wanted to make the unchanging nature of his purpose very clear to the heirs of what was promised, he confirmed it with an oath" (Heb. 6:17).

The history of God's mission is actually the history of the Bible itself.

5. God's invitation for you to work with Him always leads you to a crisis of belief that requires faith and action.

Moses responded to God's call with the words: " 'Who am I, that I should go to Pharaoh and bring the Israelites out of Egypt?' " (Ex. 3:11). In effect, God replied to Moses, "It's My identity, not yours, that will make the difference."

God then revealed His identity in the promise of His presence. He said, "I will be with you. And this will be the sign to you that it is I who have sent you. When you have brought the people out of Egypt, you will worship God on this mountain" (v. 12). What kind of promise is that? In a way it's after the fact. God said, "I am giving you a vision that My promise is true and will be fulfilled when all the people of Israel meet Me on this mountain."

In my own experience I find that God often leads by Bible promises. He leads as we apply His Word to very specific situations. That happened to Moses here. God said, "It's on this very mountain where you are standing, with the burning bush, that I'm going to reveal myself to the children of Israel." The possibility must have encouraged Moses. Without that promise Moses might never have done what he did. He would have quit many times except for God's promise that this was going to happen.

"Moses said to God, 'Suppose I go to the Israelites and say to them, "The God of your fathers has sent me to you," and they ask me, "What is his name?" Then what shall I tell them?' God said to Moses, '"I AM WHO I AM." This is what you are to say to the Israelites: "I AM has sent me to you" ' " (Ex. 3:13-14).

Read Exodus 3:13-14 in the margin. How was Moses instructed to introduce the God of Abraham, Isaac, and Jacob to the children of Israel?

_____

God revealed to Moses a new name—I AM WHO I AM. The bush wasn't just about the God of history but the glory of His presence in all ages. God made a new, deeper revelation about His purposes as He declared His identity to Moses.

From mere curiosity in turning aside to see the burning bush, Moses' faith developed steadily from crisis to crisis. By the end of his life, he had prepared Israel to enter the Promised Land.

As with Moses, God reveals Himself to you to increase your faith. Then God reveals His purposes to you so you will do His will. Once you know who He is and what He wants to do, He desires that you seek to do His will to accomplish His purpose for His glory.

Describe a crisis of faith you now face as God speaks to you.

_____

6. You must make major adjustments in your life to join God in what He is doing.

Part of the miracle of God's connection with your life is that He does not come just one time and then vaporize back to heaven. When you meditate on Scripture, pray, and join your life with other believers, God continues to encounter you and require adjustments in your life to join what He is doing.

If you see God's purpose as a mighty, rushing river headed to the very throne, you realize that standing against that force will either knock you down or wash you onto the shore. To be in line with God's purpose, align your life with the direction of the river of His will, and you will experience His glory.

How many signals of what He is about to do does God have to give you to make you curious enough to follow them up? How does God speak to you? I look back on my life and wonder how many times I have missed what God intended for me. I'm so thankful for the times I did listen. Sometimes you think God occasionally works in your life, but He is actually working all the time. God doesn't just speak when a bush burns. Be alert so that you can always be ready to say, "Lord, help me know when You are speaking."

Many times when I'm discontented, I realize God is getting ready to speak to me. When something I don't understand stirs in me, that's God trying to get me ready to listen to Him. God uses many ways to capture our attention.

The experience with God at the burning bush caught Moses' attention. But don't get so caught up in the encounter that you forget the point of the experience. Your version of a burning bush is never the culmination of your faith. The opportunity to meet with the God who is on mission will always involve an obligation to respond.

Read Exodus 3:8 and 10 in the margin. Answer this question:
Who is on mission? ☐ God ☐ Moses

God determined that His glory will fill the earth, and He will accomplish that mission through Moses. God determines to use ordinary people but to do extraordinary things through them. Why? So that God will get the glory. God is looking for a people who will give Him the glory.

Did Moses remember that early burning-bush experience? It was etched on his memory forever. Will you remember your burning bush? Only if you recognize God speaking to you through it. Be assured, however, that He *is* speaking, inviting, working, and accomplishing His purpose. If you listen with the perspective that He is indeed accomplishing His mission, you will find new ways to pray and minister in situations that come before you. For every event that slams full force into you, remember that the God of the universe is at work.

Write a major adjustment that you think God is asking you to make.

---

7. *You come to know God by experience as you obey Him and He accomplishes His purpose through you.*

Experiences with God are not just random encounters when God happens to drop into the stream of life to pluck someone from peril. Rather, God's unswerving plan permeates every encounter with His people. When God meets you, He is always headed in the same direction—that all peoples of the earth glorify Him! Through Moses, God revealed Himself as I AM WHO I AM, whose plan is to show His glory through His people, who are to be a kingdom of priests to all peoples—an amazing revelation to Moses and perhaps to you, too!

If you were to tell me your story, you would probably relate a series of encounters with God. Perhaps you were a child when you first encountered the

To be in line with God's purpose, align your life with the direction of the river of His will.

" 'I have come down to rescue them from the hand of the Egyptians and to bring them up out of that land into a good and spacious land, a land flowing with milk and honey—the home of the Canaanites, Hittites, Amorites, Perizzites, Hivites and Jebusites' " (Ex. 3:8).

" 'Now, go. I am sending you to Pharaoh to bring my people the Israelites out of Egypt' " (Ex. 3:10).

Somewhere along the course of your life, you have met with God.

living God. Maybe your first encounter was born in a moment of personal despair when you had nowhere else to go for help. But somewhere along the way, you met with God. You have sensed His presence at the birth of a child or felt His saving power when you confessed Him as Lord of your life. These very experiences with God have shaped not only the way you live, but also who you are.

Reflect on your experiences with God. Describe a time when you remember experiencing God in your life when you obeyed Him.

_____

_____

Most assuredly, we are going to come back to your story, because God is doing something specific and definable—something that has not changed from the days of Abraham, something that will end only at the throne when people from every nation, tribe, and tongue join in one loud and persistent chorus of praise—has connected your life to His purposes!

DAY 3

HAVE FAITH AND TRUST IN GOD

1. God chooses you to be on mission with Him to reconcile a lost world to Himself.

When God chose Moses, He knew all of Moses' weaknesses, even though Moses insisted on reminding God about them. The Lord answered every excuse.

Read Exodus 3:11—4:17. List God's answers to Moses' excuses.

Moses' Excuse	God's Answer
1. Who am I to go to Pharaoh?	_____
2. What if the Israelites ask me Your name?	_____
3. What if they won't listen or believe me?	_____
4. Lord, I'm not eloquent. Send someone else.	_____

Moses insisted in holding on to one specific fear—he could not speak plainly. This unwillingness to trust God to do whatever was required to mold Moses into a man God could use would cause Moses a great deal of grief.

God finally sent Aaron to be the mouth for Moses, but the price was high. It was Aaron who made the golden calf. God desired to use Moses directly, but he wouldn't agree. At the very least, this scenario should make you hesitant to make excuses to God! In His grace He has decided He will use ordinary people through whom He will do extraordinary things—so that He will get the glory. God is looking for a people who will give Him the glory!

Even in the seemingly hopeless situations we see in the world today, God has chosen someone to intercede. As bad as situations may be, God has not left them dangling. How can you be sure? For one thing, He has put it on your heart. The circumstances God brings before you help you realize He has chosen you to do something about them.

> The circumstances God brings before you help you realize He has chosen you to do something about them.

Will you pray about a specific situation in the world that you sense God is working in now? Name the situation here.

_____

_____

Because God will establish His kingdom, He has set in motion a strategy to redeem humanity. He has chosen to use a holy priesthood, a chosen people, who will represent His glory and love to the nations. God will bring the people of those nations before His throne to worship Him throughout eternity.

2. God calls you to Himself to be on mission with Him.

You cannot escape the obligation brought by this opportunity to be on mission with God. Just as you cannot escape His kingdom's inevitability, you also cannot escape His kingdom's call. To be allowed to behold His glory and to benefit from His blessings calls for a commitment to His purpose. God cannot—will not—show His power in your life only to have you sully His reputation with indifference, fear, or complaints.

When God calls people, He does not seek leaders—because *He* is the Leader. He seeks servants who will follow. Moses said, "I'm not worthy, Lord, to do this." God says, "I know, but I'm calling you to follow Me." Scriptures say Moses was the meekest man in all the earth—a servant. Having abilities to lead is not important, but knowing who the Leader is and letting Him lead is vital.

> Having abilities to lead is not important, but knowing who the Leader is and letting Him lead is vital.

Read Psalm 103:7 in the margin. Answer the following questions.

Israel knew God's _____ . Moses knew God's _____ .

> *"He made known his ways to Moses, his deeds to the people of Israel"* (Ps. 103:7).

God wants an intimate relationship with you through which you know His ways and know where He is going next. Anyone can see God's works, but God showed Moses His ways. Consider with me some of the ways of God.

Read Exodus 4:1-11 in your Bible. Study the ways of God with individuals as revealed by this experience.

Way of God #1: He takes very ordinary things and people and does extraordinary things with them. What God was about to tell Moses to do didn't make sense, but Moses obeyed. He threw the staff on the ground. It turned into a snake. God said, "Pick it up by the tail." You never pick up a snake by the tail, because it will bite you. After 40 years in the desert Moses could have lectured God on how not to pick up snakes!

When God tells you to do something, He expects you to do it whether or not it makes sense. Then He said, " 'Reach out your hand' " and take it by the tail. Moses did. When it turned back into a staff, Moses probably breathed a sigh of relief. " 'This,' " said the Lord, " 'is so they may believe that the Lord, the God of their fathers—the God of Abraham, the God of Isaac and the God of Jacob—has appeared to you' " (v. 5). God was saying, "I'm going to show My wonders to people through you so that they will know who I am and glorify Me!"

Way of God #2: He expects you to obey His instructions, whether or not they make sense. God said, " 'Put your hand in your cloak.' " When Moses pulled his hand out, it was leprous (see v. 6). He expects you to obey even if you don't understand. Obeying Him builds your faith. If you understood it, it wouldn't be faith. God uses your obedience to move you into what He is doing.

> God uses your obedience to move you into what He is doing.

Way of God #3: When you obey, things won't always turn out the way you thought they would. When you obey and things get worse, start praising God, because God is about to reveal or do something far beyond what you can imagine! You may be right at the center of God's will when things get worse. God said to Moses, " 'Put your hand back in your cloak.' " Moses might have said, "If I put my hand in the first time and got leprosy, what will I get the next time?" When Moses put his hand back in his cloak, his hand was restored (see v. 7).

> When you obey and things get worse, start praising God.

Way of God #4: God tells you just enough to know what to do next. In verses 8-9 Moses had another concern: " 'What if they don't believe these signs?' " God said, "Well, beyond these signs I have just shown you, you will take water out of the Nile and turn it to blood." Moses did that in Egypt.

> **How many plagues occurred in Egypt?** _____
> **How many signs did God show to Moses in this passage?** _____

God usually doesn't tell you all that will happen. Of the 10 plagues God only showed Moses 3. He develops you so He can lead you step-by-step to do exactly what He wants you to do. That is the glory of His presence in your life. He tells you only what you need to know. Then He says, "I will give you the ability to do whatever I ask, even though you've never been there before."

Today God moves in unprecedented ways. A precedent may not exist for what God calls you to do. God's call disturbed Moses. You also may struggle with it. What will the Lord have to do to get your attention?

> A precedent may not exist for what God calls you to do.

> **Check the item that reflects the way God responded to a time when you refused to move out on mission with Him.**
> ☐ He called you more emphatically.
> ☐ He troubled your mind daily.

☐ He moved other believers to support the call.
☐ He withdrew the call after a time and removed the possible blessing.
☐ He disciplined you to bring you back in line with His purpose.

God took the only thing Moses had—his staff—and parted the waters of the Red Sea, led the Israelites out of Egypt, and brought forth water from the rock. Give back to God whatever He has given you, and He will use it for His glory!

Give back to God whatever He has given you, and He will use it for His glory!

3. God initiates a covenant of promise and obedience with you.

Read Exodus 2:23-25 in the margin. As the Hebrew people groaned for relief from their plight, what did God remember that caused Him to intervene in the history of both Egypt and Israel? Underline it.

When Moses saw his people suffering, he wanted to end their slavery. God looked on His people and wanted to end their slavery because their prayers caused Him to remember His covenant. Could they have been praying not just: "Please help us get free. Please stop our suffering. Please do something" but rather, "God, You have a promise to fulfill. God, we have a mission to complete in the promised land. Help us fulfill our destiny"?

Read Exodus 6:2-8 in your Bible. Circle the word *covenant* each time it is used. Below write God's promises to His people.

I will bring you out _____.

I will free you _____.

I will redeem you _____.

I will take you _____, and I will be _____.

I will bring you to _____.

"During that long period, the king of Egypt died. The Israelites groaned in their slavery and cried out, and their cry for help because of their slavery went up to God. God heard their groaning and he remembered his covenant with Abraham, with Isaac and with Jacob" (Ex. 2:23-25).

If you were not impressed with God's heart of compassion before you read these words, surely you are now. Psalm 105 is a hymn praising God's work in history to fulfill His mission. The purpose behind all of the glorious acts listed in that Psalm is His covenant with Abraham and its reaffirmation to Moses.

Read Psalm 105:8-10 in the margin. Circle words or phrases that show the eternal significance of the covenant with Abraham.

"He remembers his covenant forever, the word he commanded, for a thousand generations, the covenant he made with Abraham, the oath he swore to Isaac. He confirmed it to Jacob as a decree, to Israel as an everlasting covenant" (Ps. 105:8-10).

"Forever," "for a thousand generations," and "everlasting" show that God took a long view of His promise to Abraham. Perhaps you even circled words like "the oath he swore" or "decree" or the word "covenant" itself. The driving purpose of the exodus was God's covenant and His determination to see it fulfilled.

The key to understanding the Bible and what God is doing is to understand His mission: people are free to do as they will, but God works in all situations to lead people to His ultimate purpose: He will be acknowledged as Lord of all!

Read Exodus 9:13-17 in your Bible. Write in the blanks below the purpose of each of the following events of the exodus.

Let my people go so that _____

I will send the full force of my plagues against Egypt so that

_____

_____

I have raised you up for this very purpose so that _____

and so that _____

5 "'Do not come any closer,' God said. 'Take off your sandals, for the place where you are standing is holy ground.'"
6 "Then he said, 'I am the God of your father, the God of Abraham, the God of Isaac and the God of Jacob.' At this, Moses hid his face, because he was afraid to look at God."
7 "The Lord said, 'I have indeed seen the misery of my people in Egypt. I have heard them crying out because of their slave drivers, and I am concerned about their suffering.'"
8 " 'So I have come down to rescue them from the hand of the Egyptians and to bring them up out of that land into a good and spacious land, a land flowing with milk and honey—the home of the Canaanites, Hittites, Amorites, Perizzites, Hivites and Jebusites.' "
9 " 'And now the cry of the Israelites has reached me, and I have seen the way the Egyptians are oppressing them.' "
10 " 'So now, go. I am sending you to Pharaoh to bring my people the Israelites out of Egypt' "
(Ex. 3:5-10).

God wanted the Hebrew slaves released so they could worship Him. He sent plagues against Egypt because He wanted the most powerful ruler of the day to know that no comparable god existed in all the earth.

Why were the Hebrews delivered? What is the reason for this and every account in Scripture? That the name of the Lord be proclaimed in all the earth. God orchestrated the exodus so that the world would know and glorify Him! Egypt's position as one of the world's leading nations guaranteed that other nations would hear of a God who could deliver slaves from its bondage.

In the presence of International Mission Board President Jerry Rankin, a missionary in Central Asia thanked God for Marx and Stalin. Jerry asked how the missionary could pray such a prayer. The missionary answered, "I praise God that the Soviet Union has dominated these people groups for 70 years! … This was the stronghold that has been propagating the Islamic faith for generations, but in a mere 70 years of Communist domination with its atheistic ideology that stronghold has been emasculated, leaving the people … open to the gospel." Although millions died in the purges of China's Mao Tse Tung, his regime wiped out ancestor worship and many family ties that kept many Chinese from Christ. Because Communists have been in power in China beginning in 1949, the Christian population has grown from 750,000 to a reported 75 million!

≫━ DAY 4 ━≪

GOD PREPARES HIS PEOPLE

4. God prepares and equips you for His mission.

Because of His promise to Abraham, God began to seriously prepare Moses for his task at the burning bush.

Match the five truths from Exodus 3:5-10 (in the margin) by writing the number of the verse beside the corresponding truth.

Verse ____ God is holy.   Verse ____ God is personal.
Verse ____ God is faithful.   Verse ____ God is eternal.
Verse ____ God is concerned.

If Moses didn't know it before, that day he learned God's holiness demanded his respect. The unquenched fire in the bush—the real eternal flame—showed him that God is eternal. His statement "I am the God of your father" demonstrated that God is personal. God showed His concern for His people, who cried out to Him in their bondage. God demonstrated His faithfulness by telling them He would give them the promised land. God continues to reveal Himself to you just as He did to Moses. He is the I AM of the present, past, and future. He reveals Himself to you, not only as holy God, personal God, and historical God but also as everlasting God. "I AM," He says.

Once as I landed in Cyprus, I began to wonder how God looks at Cyprus. I remembered, *Cyprus is the first place missionaries went when the Holy Spirit sent Paul and Barnabas on their first mission trip. It was the first place a leader of government accepted Christ as Savior. It was just south of that island Paul went on his way to prison in Rome.* I had just read the psalm that says, "A day is as a thousand years to the Lord, and a thousand years is as a day." The Lord said to me, "Avery, do you realize that from My perspective, it was just day before yesterday when Paul and Barnabas were coming here, and it was just two days before that when Moses led the children of Israel out of Egypt, and tomorrow is AD 3000?" Wow! God is the everlasting "I AM!"

Moses' ongoing preparation included repeated challenges from Pharaoh and the people of Israel. Unfortunately, he grew discouraged and complained to God—just as the Israelites complained to Him. The Lord patiently encouraged him as He prepared him to act to fulfill the promise to free God's people.

In the midst of his continuing preparation, Moses asked the Lord for a great gift. Read about it in Exodus 33:13-18 in the margin.

Write your personal request to the living God.

_____

"'If you are pleased with me, teach me your ways so I may know you and continue to find favor with you. Remember that this nation is your people.' The Lord replied, 'My Presence will go with you, and I will give you rest.' Then Moses said to him, 'If your Presence does not go with us, do not send us up from here. How will anyone know that you are pleased with me and with your people unless you go with us? What else will distinguish me and your people from all the other people on the face of the earth?' And the Lord said to Moses, 'I will do the very thing you have asked, because I am pleased with you and I know you by name. Then Moses said, 'Now show me your glory'" (Ex. 33:13-18).

5. *God sends you to the place where He can best work through you to accomplish His mission.*

In Exodus 3:9-10 God said, " 'Now the cry of the Israelites has reached me, and I have seen the way the Egyptians are oppressing them. So now, go. I am sending you to Pharaoh to bring my people the Israelites out of Egypt.' " Moses couldn't stay and still go with God. God moved him to where He could best use him. God sent Moses to Egypt so that He could move His people to the promised land.

In the margin write your memory verse. Circle each of three action verbs in this verse. Apply God's words to Pharaoh to your own life.

God has raised you up so that you _____

That He may show you _____

That you may proclaim_____

6. God guides you on His mission.

In dealing with the most powerful ruler on earth, Moses needed God's guidance at every step. The Lord knew Pharaoh would harden his heart, so He prepared Moses for the response. Why did God send Moses 10 times to Pharaoh? Each plague was God's testimony of power against a specific Egyptian deity. By the time the plagues were finished, Pharaoh and the Egyptians had seen Jehovah confound the power of every deity they worshiped. Israel should have been convinced forever that their God was the only One to worship. However, our hero repeatedly hit bottom and wanted to give up as he faced the following obstacles:

- Pharaoh reacted by making the task harder after each plague.
- The Israelites faced the Red Sea when Pharaoh pinned them between the mountains, the sea, the desert, and his army.
- After victory the Israelites wanted to lynch Moses and return to Egypt.
- Israel worshiped a golden calf, breaking the first two commandments.
- The people refused to trust God enough to take the promised land.

Unfortunately, throughout their wilderness wanderings, the Israelites mirrored Moses' weakness of not trusting God. As a result of their lack of faith and obedience, the whole generation of which Moses was a part was not permitted to enter the promised land. Under such trying circumstances you might have complained and become as angry as Moses did. How would you have fared as leader of such a large group of people upon whom God passed judgment and told them that everyone over 20 years of age would die without reaching the promised land?

The Lord repeatedly sent tests and tragedies to curb the prideful spirit of His people.

Because they were His children, God had both the right and the obligation to discipline Israel. The Lord repeatedly sent tests and tragedies to curb the prideful spirit of His people. Only Joshua and Caleb wholeheartedly followed God and were rewarded accordingly. Sadly, it took a whole new generation to obey God and to conquer the land He had promised to His people.

> **Stop and ask God to make you obedient to His guidance so that you may experience the glory of His presence day by day. Check here ☐ when you finish.**

7. God uses you to bring glory to His name through His mission.

The final act of God's deliverance of Israel from bondage was about to be played out on Egypt's stage. Every Egyptian home echoed with weeping and wailing when the firstborn was found dead—fathers, sons, husbands, brothers, even the male animals. The Israelites must have been awed that God had spared them. In fleeing from Pharaoh's regime, they plundered the Egyptians of articles of silver, gold, and clothing.

God's final showdown with Egypt was under way!

Amid the mourning, Pharaoh suddenly realized what he had done—every one of the slaves was gone! Meanwhile the Israelites, led as God displayed His glory in a pillar of cloud by day and a pillar of fire by night, hastily moved to ultimately encamp where God directed on the Red Sea shores. God's final showdown with Egypt was under way!

In your Bible read Exodus 14. Answer *T* (true) or *F* (false).

____ 1. Israel wandered around in confusion, hemmed in by the desert.

____ 2. God knew that Pharaoh would pursue the Israelites.

____ 3. The Lord wanted to gain glory for Himself through Pharaoh's army.

____ 4. Pharaoh left the best chariots and warriors at home.

____ 5. Israel was not the least bit worried when it saw the Egyptians.

____ 6. Moses told the Israelites to be still—the Lord would fight for them.

____ 7. Using Moses' staff, the Lord parted the waters of the Red Sea.

The Egyptians did not understand—the great I AM was in control. Pharaoh's chariots reached the middle of the Red Sea as the last of the Hebrews stepped out on the opposite bank. God released the waters, drowning all of Pharaoh's horses and charioteers. God decisively intervened in the history of one of the world's greatest nations, proving Himself greater than any king or kingdom. Numbers 1, 4, and 5 are false.

Read the Scriptures in the margin. Underline the ultimate reason God worked through Moses on this mission.

As you look back over today's lesson, remember that your life is connected to God not just so that you will experience His glory but also so that you can participate in His purposeful mission. In your own words, describe that mission.

_____

_____

The ancient world was crisscrossed by caravans of merchants; traders; ambassadors of nations; and people from Africa, India, and China. On the trip back home, these people told of the Egyptian events, attributing them all to Israel's God, Jehovah. God's deeds became known everywhere.

God never just works with one individual when He is on mission. Not Moses. Not you. He uses individuals to influence His people to be on mission with Him. Moses was God's instrument to awaken His people and to equip them.

God reveals Himself by His acts. The creation, the flood, and the confusion of tongues at Babel revealed to early people that God was powerful and involved with their daily lives. The Egyptians learned God's power by His triumph over their gods. After the exodus, Israel understood her chosen status as a treasured nation. The plagues and the parting of the Red Sea revealed that God could change the course of history on behalf of His people.

God set out to plant this treasured possession to be a showcase to the world. Israel was to be a kingdom of priests and a holy nation, thus connecting people to God. An attention grabber in the exodus drama is the way God revealed that He would go about gaining worldwide recognition. During the exodus itself Israel first became conscious of its role in God's unfolding world plan.

Even in its privileged spiritual position, Israel did not perceive God's ways. As Moses prepared to end his earthly journey, he told Israel the ways of God

"'I will harden Pharaoh's heart, and he will pursue them. But I will gain glory for myself through Pharaoh and all his army, and the Egyptians will know that I am the Lord.' So the Israelites did this" (Ex. 14:4).

" 'The Egyptians will know that I am the Lord when I gain glory through Pharaoh, his chariots and his horsemen' " (Ex. 14:18).

"When the Israelites saw the great power the Lord displayed against the Egyptians, the people feared the Lord and put their trust in him and in Moses his servant" (Ex. 14:31).

" 'You yourselves have seen what I did to Egypt, and how I carried you on eagles' wings and brought you to myself. Now if you obey me fully and keep my covenant, then out of all nations you will be my treasured possession. Although the whole earth is mine, you will be for me a kingdom of priests and a holy nation.' These are the words you are to speak to the Israelites" (Ex. 19:4-6)

*"The Lord's portion is
  his people.
  Jacob his allotted
  inheritance.
In a desert land he
  found him,
in a barren and howling
  waste.
He shielded him and cared
  for him;
  he guarded him as the
  apple of his eye,
like an eagle that stirs up
  its nest
and hovers over its young,
  that spreads its wings to
  catch them
and carries them on
  its pinions"* (Deut. 32:9-11).

with His people in terms they could remember. Both Exodus 19:4-6 and Deuteronomy 32:9-11 (in the margin) describe God's ways with the image of an eagle training its young to fly. We will explore this image of an eagle's care for the rest of today's lesson, and we will continue it tomorrow.

Way of God with His people #1: He stirs up their nests to get them on His agenda. When an eagle gets ready to build its nest, it finds a crag or a ledge where wild animals cannot get to it. There the eagle weaves such a large, solid nest out of sticks, branches, briars, or bones that even the high, swirling winds cannot blow it down. Then it lines that nest with feathers, cloth, papers, or anything soft for comfort. The little eaglets hatch in that cozy environment. As a baby eagle, you are safe.

The mother eagle knows that these eaglets were not born to sit in a nest all their lives. When the time comes for them to fly, she reaches into the nest, pulls out all the soft down and paper, and sits the little eaglets down on the briars, sticks, bones, and branches. They begin to cry out because everywhere they turn, they get stuck. That is what God says He did to Israel; He stirred up its nest. God had given the Israelites the choicest part of Egypt. For four hundred years Israel was nurtured in this nest. Now God stirred up their nest. When you get stuck in one of the stages of development, one of God's ways is to make you uncomfortable by stirring your nest, readying you for His next move.

These free people who had been assured a promised land found themselves building storehouses for Pharaoh. That was not what they were meant to be! God had to get them where He wanted them to go, so He let them fall into the hands of Pharaoh, who enslaved them and made their lives miserable. They began to cry out to the Lord. God works with His people this way: He stirs their nest so that they cry out to Him.

God may be stirring your nest to help you and your church wake up to His mission. He may be asking you to take a step of faith. If you don't respond to Him, you will be miserable and make those around you miserable. God is stirring His people all over the world to join Him on mission. As I write this, I conclude trips to every part of the world to meet with leaders of Great Commission Christian organizations and leaders of Baptist conventions. God is stirring them in unprecedented ways to join Him in taking the gospel to every people group in the world and in establishing churches among them.

Read Hebrews 12:5-13 in your Bible. Think of evidence that you are God's child by the way He disciplines you and His church.

Describe a circumstance in which God has stirred up your church's cozy nest or is now stirring your nest.

_____

_____

DAY 5

ON EAGLES' WINGS

Way of God with His people #2: He demonstrates His power by hovering over His people. After the eagle stirs the nest, she hovers over it with her wings to show the eaglets how big she is. She seems to say to the eaglets, "Never fear; Mother is here. I know you sit on briars. I know you are crying. But I have everything under control." God sent Moses to the people to demonstrate His power. The 10 plagues were God's hovering over Israel. He showed how mighty and powerful He really is so that the Israelites would, in faith, leave their nest for the promised land.

When the eagle hovers over the nest, the eaglets realize how big their mother is—with a wingspan of from 5 to 12 feet. She hovers to free them from worry. After God stirs your nest, He hovers over you, showing you He's all you need. God wants you to see He is big enough to accomplish His mission. Realizing this, how can you say you would rather sit in the nest than do by faith what He wants you to do? When He stirs your nest, God shows you His power in unusual ways. His hovering is not to make you comfortable but to cause you to believe Him for the next thing He wants to do in your life.

> **List some ways that God (perhaps even through this study) has been showing Himself and His power to you and/or His church.**

_____

_____

_____

Way of God with His people #3: God leads you to take the next step on mission with Him by bearing you on His wings and then shaking you off. God's way is to stir you up, hover over you, and then bear you up on His wings. The mother eagle places her wing on the edge of the nest and says to the eaglets, "Get off the briars and get on the wing." If they won't do it, she starts beating them until they do. Even their mother has turned against them, it seems! Sometimes God has to let you get beaten by circumstances until you say, "I'll take anything but this." At that point you get on the wing.

Once the eaglets get on her wing, the mother lurches off the cliff and begins to fly. For the first time they experience the ecstasy of flight. They soar through the air and enjoy it. They begin to understand the reason for which they were born. The mother eagle takes them back to the nest. After jumping into the briars, they jump right back onto her wing. Again she takes them high above the earth. This time while they enjoy their flight, she shakes them off. They tumble down. Some fly and some don't. She dives under those that can't fly and catches

> Sometimes God has to let you get beaten by circumstances until you say, "I'll take anything but this."

"If this is so, then the Lord
knows how to rescue
godly men from trials and
to hold the unrighteous for
the day of judgment,
while continuing their
punishment. This is
especially true of those who
follow the corrupt desire of
the sinful nature and
despise authority.
Bold and arrogant, these
men are not afraid to
slander celestial beings;
yet even angels, although
they are stronger and more
powerful, do not bring
slanderous accusations
against such beings in the
presence of the Lord"
(2 Pet. 2:9-11).

"And has made us to be a
kingdom and priests to
serve his God and
Father—to him be glory
and power for ever and
ever! Amen" (Rev. 1:6).

them. Again, she takes them up to the heights, lets them relax, and shakes them off again until they learn how to fly. Sometimes instead of taking them on her wings, she takes them to the edge of the cliff and pushes them over. That is how God gets his people to fly. To fulfill the purpose for which He created you, He puts you in a faith-creating situation.

Recall a circumstance in which you felt that God "pushed you off the cliff" or when God shook you into the air to cause you to fly by faith.

_____

_____

_____

God bore Israel on eagles' wings. When the Hebrews flew by faith, He repeatedly demonstrated that He was sufficient. In the miracles in Egypt, in the parting of the Red Sea, in providing manna and quail, in supplying water from the rock, God showed that He wanted the Israelites to step out in faith. If they fell, He picked them up and took them up again and again to teach them to fly.

In the margin read Exodus 19:4-6. Underline what Israel is to be.

At the beginning of God's covenant with Israel, He promised the people they would be a holy nation and kingdom of priests, reflecting His glory. At the close of the age God has decreed that His people will be called "priests of the Lord" and "ministers of our God." God never wavers in His purpose (read 2 Pet. 2:9-11 and Rev. 1:6 in the margin). He chose the tribe of Levi to be priests and models of what the nation was to become. Old Testament priests brought Israel before God to worship and experience the glory of His holiness. Although having many duties, priests had two key functions: (1) representing God to people and (2) representing people to God. God intended Israel to perform these two functions in relation to the nations.

If the entire nation were to function as priests, to whom were they to be priests? Certainly not just to themselves but to the nations. God's intention seems clear. But Israel misunderstood, misinterpreted, or rejected it. At this stage God did not intend for the Israelites to take the initiative in converting the nations to God but to be faithful and to become His people so that they could reflect His glory. At the right time Israel was to proclaim salvation to the whole world. Unfortunately, Israel rebelled, never living up to its missionary potential.

God expects His people today to be priestly and suffering people, willing to lay down their lives for others. We are to love, serve, suffer, and minister as God does. We are to take the salvation message to all the world.

In the column "Old Testament," using a scale of 1 to 10 (with 10 highest), indicate how you believe Israel scored in terms of being the kind of people God wanted in that day. In the column "Your Church" indicate how you believe your church rates in this manner.

	Old Testament	Your Church
An obedient people	_____	_____
A holy people	_____	_____
A disciplined people	_____	_____
A priestly people	_____	_____
A servant people	_____	_____
A missionary people	_____	_____

As He did with Israel, God brings His people to a decision point. He brings you to the place where you must choose about exercising faith—stepping out on a limb that you don't know will hold you up. But the end of the limb is where the fruit is. In stepping out in faith, you find that God provides wings—the wings of faith. You begin to fly and fulfill the glorious purpose for which God has designed you! God's people today are at this point. We will believe and follow God, or history will record the story of our bleached bones in the desert.

Stop and pray. Ask God to show you how He wants to use you and His church for His glory in the heart of His world. Record your prayer.

_____

_____

_____

_____

God deserves glory and honor.
For Moses and the Hebrew people, the exodus and its attending miracles deeply impressed on their hearts God's exalted position. Exodus 15 records the song of deliverance as Israel left Egypt. The Hebrews realized that all these great acts of God pivoted on one central truth: the God they knew was like no other (see Ex. 15:11 in the margin). In comparison to all other gods, the God of Abraham, Isaac, Jacob—and now the Hebrews—was alone worthy of worship. This is Moses' eternal contribution to our understanding of God's mission.

1. God is on mission so that the knowledge of His glory will cover the earth as the waters cover the sea.

You cannot fully understand God's mission without understanding why He insists that all the earth acknowledge him as Lord. He expects you to give Him the glory due because He is God—to bow before Him as Lord above all and to serve Him (see Ex. 33:15-16 and Isa. 48:9-11 in the margin).

We will believe and follow God, or history will record the story of our bleached bones in the desert.

"Who among the gods is like you, O Lord? Who is like you— majestic in holiness, awesome in glory, working wonders?" (Ex. 15:11).

"Then Moses said to him, 'If your Presence does not go with us, do not send us up from here. How will anyone know that you are pleased with me and with your people unless you go with us? What else will distinguish me and your people from all the other people on the face of the earth?' " (Ex. 33:15-16).

"For my own name's sake I delay my wrath; for the sake of my praise I hold it back from you, so as not to cut you off. See, I have refined you, though not as silver; I have tested you in the furnace of affliction. For my own sake, I do this. How can I let myself be defamed? I will not yield my glory to another" (Isa. 48:9-11).

Here you come face-to-face with the core issue of redemption. Make no mistake about it: what God does, He does for His Name's sake—not just for your good or your salvation. Yes, He reigns and redeems with love, and you certainly gain both salvation and incredible good from His reign. But reign He does, and He expects our worship, our adoration, and our praise, because He alone is God. His own glory is at the epicenter of all that He does! Exodus 15 captures Israel's awe and adoration of our incredible God, who reigns supreme over all that is, was, and ever will be.

Underline the three aspects of God's greatness in Exodus 15:11 (p. 73).

God is majestic in holiness.

God's holiness manifests at least three things—He is the standard of holiness, He is other (meaning different in kind), and He is love. God is so majestic that He towers above all gods and religions, philosophies, cultures, and people—the greatest kings, presidents, and generals. He is the standard for truth, righteousness, and faithfulness. He is different from His creation, humans, and all other gods. He shows His majestic love by His mercy in forgiving our sins and giving us eternal life.

God is awesome in glory.

Everyone who has come into God's presence has been overwhelmed (see Ex. 33: 18-21; 34:5-7). Moses saw only the back side of God, but he saw more than anybody else ever had! When Ezekiel saw God's glory, he was overwhelmed with God. Isaiah said, " 'Woe to me! I am ruined. For I am a man of unclean lips, and I live among a people of unclean lips' " (Isa. 6:5). Read in your Bible what Job said at the end of his complaining, dialogue, and debate (see Job 42:1-6).

> **Consider the glory of the things of this world—athletic success, political power, or human achievement, for example—compared with the glory of God as you know Him. Stop and worship God as you think of the comparison.**

2. God's glory is His presence among His people.

When the Israelites made a golden calf to worship, God told Moses He would not go with them into the promised land. Moses interceded, saying that if God's presence did not go with them, He must not send them to the promised land.

> **Read Exodus 33:12-18 in your Bible. Check Moses' chief reason for asking God not to send them to the promised land unless His presence went along.**
> ☐ It would show God's favor—that He was pleased with them.
> ☐ God's presence would distinguish them from all other peoples.
> ☐ He wanted to see God's glory.

Although Exodus 33:12-18 mentions all three, Moses' chief reason was that God's presence would distinguish Israel from other peoples. Does God's presence distinguish you and your church from other people?

3. God's glory involves our going on mission with Him.

Once you understand that God's purpose to see His glory proclaimed among the nations is the mission that drives His every encounter with you, you begin to see what an incredible blessing you have to participate in God's mission. To join God on His mission is to be assured that your life will be eternally successful!

Repeatedly, I hear stories of people who give up successful careers and lifestyles to answer the missionary call overseas. To the uninformed, their actions may seem foolish, but they, like Moses, see the eternal blessings yet to come from proclaiming the glory of God to others. His presence distinguishes them from all the peoples who don't know God through Christ.

What does God want more than anything else? _____

_____

What does God want His people to be? _____

_____

What is the most important revelation God has given you during this

week's study? _____

_____

How will you respond to it? _____

_____

God wants all peoples to worship and glorify Him. He expects His people to be a holy kingdom of priests to bring all peoples to Him.

DAVID

ON MISSION WITH GOD: ESTABLISHING A KINGDOM WITHOUT END

Heart Focus

"Ascribe to the Lord, O families of nations, ascribe to the Lord glory and strength, ascribe to the Lord the glory due his name. Bring an offering and come before him; worship the Lord in the splendor of his holiness" (1 Chron. 16:28-29).

This Week's Lessons

Day 1: An Individual Encounter
Day 2: God's Plan Is Always Better
Day 3: God's Plan Includes All His People Reigning with Him
Day 4: Promises and Obedience
Day 5: An Eternal Kingdom for All Peoples

This Week's Learning Focus

You will be able to understand and describe how through David God revealed that all His seed would rule all nations and His Kingdom would be for all peoples.

DAY 1

AN INDIVIDUAL ENCOUNTER

Listening to Nigerian President Olusegun Obasanjo speak during the 150th anniversary celebration of Baptist work in his country, I could hardly believe how God had raised up this man from anonymity and imprisonment to be president of the largest country in Africa. While a student at Abeokuta Baptist Boys High School in his hometown, Obasanjo experienced Jesus Christ as Lord and Savior.

His father, previously a successful farmer, had suffered financial hardships and left the family just before his son began high school. After graduation the younger Obasanjo worked in a clerical position and then taught religion and science at the African Church Modern School. Though he wished to attend college he could not afford it, so he joined the army.

He moved up the army's ranks until, as commander of the Third Marine Commando Division, he accepted the Biafran surrender ending the Nigerian Civil War in 1970. In 1975, General Murtala Muhammed and Obasanjo led a bloodless coup after which Muhammed became head of state and named Obasanjo Nigerian army chief of staff. In 1976, Muhammed was assassinated. Obasanjo assumed leadership of Nigeria, becoming the first Yoruba president. Obasanjo challenged British colonialism in Africa and in 1978 adopted a new constitution guaranteeing some basic human rights. He held free elections in

1979 as he promised, but lost narrowly. He became the only military ruler in the nation's history to step down voluntarily. He then started a farming company, raising chickens and pigs and growing bananas.

In 1993, General Sani Abacha became head of state in yet another coup, and accused Abiola, who apparently had won the presidency in an election, and Obasanjo of treason and plotting a coup. They were both jailed for life, along with about 40 others, some of whom received death sentences for charges that were never revealed. After an international outcry, Abacha reduced the sentence, but Obasanjo spent three years in prison. After Abacha's sudden death, elections were held. Obasanjo won the presidency by a 62 percent vote.

During an interview with him at the dedication of the first protestant chapel on the presidential grounds, I presented him a Nigerian copy of *Experiencing God* and and the *Experiencing God Bible*. I said, "Your story parallels much of the story of King David, who went through 10 very difficult years before he finally became king." He replied, "I love David, and I wrote a book in prison that I call *The Youth of God*. David is one of my 'miracle children.' " The president told about how he had begun to study *MasterLife* in prison and then had been moved to another prison, where he recommitted his life to Christ and wrote four Christian books.

Do you ever feel as though you are a nobody in God's eyes? You compare yourself to others and believe you come up short. *You think, I don't have any special abilities. I'm just an ordinary person. How can God use me?* Most important biblical figures began their walk with God in much the same way. David was a little person—the underdog—in one of the greatest dramas of the Bible. Yet God used David to accomplish mighty things for Him. From giant killer to sweet psalmist of Israel, David was a remarkably skilled servant of God who reveled in God's glory.

However, the truly mighty thing David did in his encounter with Goliath was much more significant than simply toppling a wicked giant. God's purpose for David involved all the peoples of the world.

> **Read 1 Samuel 17:45-47 in the margin. State what God's purpose was locally and globally.**

Locally (for the immediate people involved) _____

_____

_____

Globally (for the wider group of people involved) _____

_____

_____

God's purpose locally was to show the Philistines and Israelites that the battle was the Lord's and that He would win it. His purpose globally was that through the telling of the story, the whole world would know God and His glory. God was making Himself a name through David.

"David said to the Philistine, 'You come against me with sword and spear and javelin, but I come against you in the name of the Lord Almighty, the God of the armies of Israel, whom you have defied. This day the Lord will hand you over to me, and I'll strike you down and cut off your head. Today I will give the carcasses of the Philistine army to the birds of the air and the beasts of the earth, and the whole world will know that there is a God in Israel. All those gathered here will know that it is not by sword or spear that the Lord saves; for the battle is the Lord's, and he will give all of you into our hands'" (1 Sam. 17:45-47).

*"O Lord, you have
searched me and you
know me.
You know when I sit and
when I rise;
you perceive my thoughts
from afar.
You discern my going out
and my lying down;
you are familiar with
all my ways.
Before a word is on my
tongue you know it
completely, O Lord.
You hem me in—behind
and before; you have
laid your hand upon me.
Such knowledge is too
wonderful for me,
too lofty for me to
attain"* (Ps. 139:1-6).

*"The Lord said to Samuel,
'Do not consider his
appearance or his height,
for I have rejected him.
The Lord does not look
at the things man looks at.
Man looks at the outward
appearance, but the Lord
looks at the heart'"*
(1 Sam. 16:7).

*"Yet you brought me out
of the womb;
you made me trust
in you
even at my mother's
breast.
From birth I was cast
upon you;
from my mother's womb
you have been my God"*
(Ps. 22:9-10).

1. God is always at work around you demonstrating His presence.

In Psalm 139:1-6, in the margin, David acknowledged that God was involved in everything he did, said, or thought. He experienced God's glory in every aspect of life. David's words can be your words, too.

In Psalm 139:1-6 underline the words or phrases that show how God is at work around you and pursuing you with His love.

2. God pursues a continuing love relationship with you that is real and personal.

We first meet David when Samuel is told to anoint one of the sons of Jesse whom He had chosen to become Saul's successor (see 1 Sam. 16:1). People often overlooked David because he was the youngest and was a shepherd. Often the one God uses is the one others overlook. See what God said to Samuel when Samuel thought the first son, Eliab, was to be anointed king (read 1 Sam. 16:7 in the margin). Finally, David was called in to meet Samuel, who saw that he was also "ruddy, with a fine appearance and handsome features" (v. 13). Still Samuel realized that he could not depend on outward looks. "Then the Lord said, 'Rise and anoint him; he is the one.' "

God had special plans for David even before he was born in Bethlehem. In Psalm 22:9-10 in the margin, David reflected on his knowledge of this. David was born into a nation of people experiencing God's judgment for desiring to have a king like their neighbors instead of having the Lord reign over them. God permitted them to have Saul, who started out well but was of a totally different character than David. To replace Saul, God looked for someone whose heart would be turned toward Him. He found that quality in a little nobody who had a mundane job—shepherding—that slaves or females usually did. But David's time spent outdoors with the sheep gave him opportunities to talk to God and to listen to Him. David's psalms showed that he experienced God's glory through a long-term, intimate relationship with God.

You may believe you are a nobody and that your daily life is made up of ordinary activities. You may even think all your mundane tasks do not relate to God's glory and to His mission. Look again! God has had His eye on you since before you were born. He has particular plans for you. God is always at work around you, and He initiates an experience in which His glory is revealed in His real and personal love relationship with you.

Name one way you have seen God at work around you demonstrating

His love. _____

_____

In Psalm 139:1-6 which you just read, David acknowledged that the love relationship God had for him involved everything he did, said, or even thought. David's words can be your words, too. Underline the words or phrases that show how God pursues you with His love.

3. God invites you to become involved with Him in His work.

As soon as Samuel anointed David, "From that day on the Spirit of the Lord came upon David in power" (1 Sam. 16:13). No doubt David understood some of the implications of this anointing by the famous prophet Samuel. We have no details about the way David responded to this invitation of God except for David's expressions of humility and praise in his psalms. However, word apparently got out that the Spirit of God was on Him (1 Sam. 16:18). Later, when David took supplies to his brothers on the battlefront, David heard Goliath and immediately asked about the giant who defied the armies of God. In 1 Samuel 17:32 (in the margin) read David's first response to Saul. Then, in 1 Samuel 17:36-37 (also in the margin) see David's stirring statement that followed.

David responded positively to the invitation of God to join Him on His mission. David knew God's heart. He knew that God wanted to show His glory and that "the whole world will know that there is a God in Israel" (v. 46). David understood what was at stake for God's name, which he revered.

The David and Goliath story is more than that of a young boy defeating a giant. God was fulfilling His mission through David. Today this record of David's defeating the giant is still being told all over the world, to the delight of people from thousands of people groups and to the glory of God's name, which is just being introduced in many places.

"David said to Saul, 'Let no one lose heart on account of this Philistine; your servant will go and fight him'" (1 Sam. 17:32).

" 'Your servant has killed both the lion and the bear; this uncircumcised Philistine will be like one of them, because he has defied the armies of the living God. The Lord who delivered me from the paw of the lion and the paw of the bear will deliver me from the hand of this Philistine' " (1 Sam. 17:36-37).

Check any ways God is inviting you to join Him.
☐ A friend is asking me questions about God.
☐ I have an interest in people of other nationalities.
☐ The enemies of God are challenging Him.
☐ I am considering giving to a specific Christian ministry.
☐ Other_____

4. God speaks to you by the Holy Spirit.

The first detailed encounter of God's speaking to David occurred when David challenged Goliath. Although he came to the front lines only to bring supplies to his brothers, who mocked him, David's first response was " 'Who is this uncircumcised Philistine that he should defy the armies of the living God?' " (v. 26). God's Spirit was on David as he spoke. God worked in David's heart to cause him to be jealous for God's name and God's covenant people. David didn't see the giant as an invincible foe but as an opportunity for God to manifest His power.

David didn't see the giant as an invincible foe but as an opportunity for God to manifest His power.

How do you see challenges you face? ☐ problems ☐ opportunities

Pray that God will assure you by His Spirit the way you are to join Him in His mission. In the margin, write any confirmations you receive about this—in Scripture, prayer, circumstances, confirmation by the body of Christ, or the counsel of a trusted Christian.

5. God's invitation for you to work with Him always leads you to a crisis of belief that requires faith and action.

If God has invited you to join Him, you will either believe Him and act on it or fail to obey and sit on it. David did not hesitate or dwell on his weaknesses. He spoke with confidence to Saul and Goliath. He acted on faith by refusing Saul's armor and instead picked up five smooth stones for his slingshot. God had promised He would be with David, as He had been in the past. He could trust God. Some might call this naïveté or blind enthusiasm, but it was neither. It was faith in God, who had called him and had anointed him.

David did not hesitate or dwell on his weaknesses. He spoke with confidence to Saul and Goliath.

With what do you face your Goliaths? Below check all that apply.
- ☐ naïveté
- ☐ enthusiasm
- ☐ faith
- ☐ fear
- ☐ presumption
- ☐ apathy
- ☐ assurance of God's strength
- ☐ other _____

6. You must make major adjustments in your life to join God in what He is doing.

Perhaps David's major change began when Samuel anointed him. He went back to be a shepherd, but certainly he perceived the implications of the anointing. He must have wondered how he would become king. His brothers' reaction indicates that they saw him as different and envied him.

The obvious major adjustment occurred when David took supplies to his brothers. During that visit David went from being a shepherd, harpist, and delivery boy to being a soldier of the king. He went from being a nobody to being a national hero. Joining God on His mission changed David's identity. Although it was a change in David and in his life, it was not a change in God's plan for him. All along, God had planned that David would be on mission with Him and would fulfill a major part of God's revelation of Himself to the world!

All along, God had planned that David would be on mission with Him.

Check any major adjustments you have already made in order to be involved with God on mission.
- ☐ Changed jobs
- ☐ Refused to participate in a previous activity
- ☐ Spent more time in a regular quiet time/devotional period
- ☐ Contacted a missions agency about some kind of service
- ☐ Other _____

7. You experience God's glory as you obey Him and He accomplishes His purpose through you.

David knew God better as he experienced God working through him to defeat Goliath! David saw Goliath's challenge of Israel and God as a challenge to the name and power of Jehovah. David obeyed what he believed God had called him to do. Without obedience David would have missed God's plan for his life.

If you could see what you have missed by your disobedience, you would cry for one more opportunity to obey God and to fulfill His mission in your life. You will be surprised by what God will accomplish through you if you obey Him.

Has God asked you to do something you have not done yet?
If so, describe it here.

_____

_____

To delay obedience is disobedience. Perhaps you have already delayed obeying what you know the Lord wants you to do. Do not despair. Delayed obedience is better than no obedience at all. But don't delay any longer, lest you miss your intersection with God's purpose and an opportunity to be on mission with Him!

DAY 2

GOD'S PLAN IS ALWAYS BETTER

When he killed Goliath, David was just beginning a lifetime of walking with God. He was 71 years old when he finished his course as king and went to be with the Lord forever. In the interim God did tremendous things through David as he joined the Lord on mission for a lifetime.

1. *God chooses you to be on mission with Him to reconcile a lost world to Himself.*

David had been chosen for this moment in history, to do great exploits for God. The Lord was getting ready to exalt this God-honoring young man and to turn the course of history for His nation, the children of Israel.

> **Read Psalm 89:19-26 in the margin. Underline words and phrases that depict what God did for and with the young David.**

Looking at the words you underlined, you see that the Spirit of the Lord working in power through him was the secret to David's success. God found him, anointed him, sustained him, and exalted him. God crushed his foes and cut down his enemies. God's faithful love did all of this for His servant David. He knew that David would give God all the glory.

You are called on to fight many spiritual battles on your way through this world. The enemy will put obstacles in your path, but the Lord desires that you become an overcomer, as David was. When you rely on Him and not yourself and are willing to give the glory to Him, He will fight for you. Your anchor in these times of crisis is that God chose you for His purpose. He is faithful.

> **Read Psalm 139:13-16 in the margin on page 82. Underline phrases that indicate that God has chosen you and has a plan for you, as He did David.**

*"Once you spoke in
a vision,
to your faithful people
you said:
'I have bestowed strength
on a warrior;
I have exalted a young man
from among the people.
I have found David
my servant;
with my sacred oil I have
anointed him.
My hand will sustain him;
surely my arm will
strengthen him.
No enemy will subject him
to tribute;
no wicked man will
oppress him.
I will crush his foes
before him
and strike down his
adversaries.
My faithful love will be
with him,
and through my name
his horn will be exalted.
I will set his hand over
the sea,
his right hand over
the rivers.
He will call out to me,
"You are my Father,
my God, the Rock
my Savior" ' "*
(Ps. 89:19-26).

"Samuel took the horn of oil and anointed him in the presence of his brothers, and from that day on the Spirit of the Lord came upon David in power. Samuel then went to Ramah" (1 Sam. 16:13).

2. God calls you to Himself to be on mission with Him.

God's call comes in many disguises. David's call was dramatic and unexpected. On his way from the pasture he must have wondered why his father had called him in the middle of the day. When he arrived, he realized that the prophet of the Lord was there. You may think God's call comes in a dramatic experience. But, as with Elijah, you learn that God often speaks in a still, small voice.

Samuel had already consecrated David's brothers, who stood to one side confused because Samuel had not chosen them. Jesse was proud that one of his sons was going to be chosen, but he was perplexed that Samuel passed over his first seven sons. Before David could grasp the significance of what was happening, Samuel poured oil all over him. Immediately, David was aware that the Spirit of God was there (see 1 Sam. 16:13 in the margin).

Everyone knew that Samuel had anointed Saul as king in the same way. The significance of this act could not be missed. David evidently went back to tending the sheep. But the Spirit of the Lord began to speak to him and to help him understand what it meant to be chosen and called as the next king.

When you recognize that God has anointed you with the Holy Spirit, begin to ask Him what He has in mind. Have you sensed God anointing you, calling you, getting you ready for something?

Stop and pray. Ask God what He is calling you to do and be. Write what you think He is telling you.

_____

_____

_____

This young man whom God had chosen to be king had many exploits ahead of him. For defeating Goliath, he became a hero in the people's eyes. Later, they sang, "Saul has slain his thousands, and David his tens of thousands" (1 Sam. 18:7). That acclaim could have gone to his head, but David was eager to give God the glory. After all, he was on God's mission—not his own.

What has God called you to do that could cause you to become puffed up with pride instead of giving God the glory?

_____

_____

How can you use the same situation you just mentioned to glorify God instead of yourself?

_____

_____

3. God initiates a covenant of promise and obedience with you.

The Lord made a covenant with David when Samuel anointed him—that he would be king over Israel. In David's experience with Jonathan God gave him a living picture of what a covenant is. The first time Jonathan saw David, he "became one in spirit with David and he loved him as himself" (1 Sam. 18:1).

Read 1 Samuel 18:3-4 in the margin. Underline how Jonathan expressed his covenant with David.

David learned afresh by his experience with Jonathan that God takes the initiative in His love and covenant. He realized that God loved him with a totally unselfish love. The gifts Jonathan gave David symbolized the kingdom that Jonathan should inherit but that God would give to David. David began to realize the words that appear in 1 Samuel 18:14, in the margin. God made many promises to David, and David pledged his allegiance to God. However, God's covenant with David culminated when David wanted to build a house for God where the ark of the covenant could reside. Through the prophet Nathan God told David he wouldn't build the temple because he had shed blood. Then God turned the tables on David and promised to build him a house!

Read 2 Samuel 7:8-16 in your Bible. Underline at least nine promises God made to David in this covenant.

David also committed himself to God and His glory. He gave God the glory for all his victories. He worshiped Him only. When the time came, he gave lavishly for the building of the temple and prepared the plans God gave him so Solomon could build it.

In the Bible God makes more than three thousand promises to His people. He makes many of these personal promises for you. As you read His Word, His Holy Spirit communicates that a particular promise is for you. John 3:16 and Matthew 28:20 are two promises all believers can claim.

Write one or more promises that you sense God has made to you in Scripture. Then stop and pray, pledging that you'll be faithful to do your part and trust God to keep His promises.

_____

_____

_____

"Jonathan made a covenant with David because he loved him as himself. Jonathan took off the robe he was wearing and gave it to David, along with his tunic, and even his sword, his bow and his belt" (1 Sam. 18:3-4).

"In everything he did he had great success, because the Lord was with him" (1 Sam. 18:14).

GOD'S PEOPLE WILL REIGN WITH HIM

From the time you are called until you fulfill that call lies a valley of testing. God must develop your character to match your assignment. When young preachers have a flush of success and receive accolades from their friends, they think they have arrived. God has just begun His work in them so that He can work through them.

God prepared David all his life. He chose him before his birth, called him from the sheep pasture, anointed him, and covenanted to bless him. God gave him physical abilities, intellectual knowledge, wisdom, emotional sensitivity, and spiritual perception and awareness. But it took time and experience for God to develop all of these characteristics in David.

4. God prepares you for His mission.

If you looked at David as a boy, you would have never guessed what God had in store for him. If you could compare your life with God's original plan, you would be elated by what He has planned and disappointed by what you have accomplished thus far. If you could step back and look at your whole life, you would be amazed at what God is still prepared to do through you!

David might have expected that he was ready to be the king when Samuel anointed him. However, he would experience two more anointings before he became the king over all Israel—first, as the king of Judah and then as the king of Israel. In between he experienced 10 grueling years while God prepared him for his assignment. When God calls you and makes a covenant to bless you, prepare for training, testing, and tribulation. That's what happened to David. He experienced Saul's jealous rages and attempts to kill him, as well as many other hardships.

> **What have you experienced that has helped prepare you in your effort to follow God's leadership in your life? Check any that apply.**
> ☐ Failure of heroes ☐ Life-threatening situations
> ☐ Jealousy of others ☐ Disapproval of family
> ☐ Frequent moves and uprootings ☐ Other _____

David developed many God-given skills. God prepared him as a brave warrior to fight Goliath, as a musician to play the harp for Saul and write psalms, as a leader to defeat the Philistines, and as a king to rule.

As a missionary I discovered that God used not only skills I had developed but also abilities I didn't know I had. God helps you develop your skills. God uses missionaries from hundreds of occupations. Secular skills allow lay people to work and witness among residents of restricted countries, where traditional missionaries are not allowed. On the other hand, God teaches you that without

If you could step back and look at your whole life, you would be amazed at what God still is prepared to do through you!

Him, you can do nothing. Sometimes He moves you in a direction the opposite of your skills so that you will totally depend on Him. Success depends not so much on your ability as your availability and willingness to accept responsibility.

What skills do you have that God could use? _____

_____ **What are some abilities you**

have seen God call forth from you that you didn't realize you had?

_____

Sometimes He moves you in a direction the opposite of your skills so that you will totally depend on Him.

5. God sends you to the place where He can best work through you to accomplish His purpose and bring glory to God.

David couldn't remain a shepherd and be used of God as king. God had to get him out of his father's household to the king's palace and then to the battlefield in order to prepare him for his important role. What if David had said, "No, thanks. I'm comfortable here. I like being a shepherd. I like staying near my family. Find someone else who is restless and ambitious"? Then God could not have sent David to the place He could best work through him to fulfill God's mission.

Is God moving you out of your comfort zone to better serve Him? If so, what are some indications?

_____

_____

_____

Following God's guidance always demands a willingness to deny yourself, take up your cross daily, and follow Christ (see Luke 9:23). God sent David to the place where He could best prepare him for the next step in His plan. When God beckons you to leave where you are and go anywhere He leads, make your obedience immediate and absolute.

God sent David to the place where He could best prepare him for the next step in His plan.

6. God guides you on His mission for His glory.

God used many means to guide David. God was willing to show him step-by-step as he followed Him obediently. David's heart was so in tune with God that he was able to be guided by Him on His mission.

Read 2 Samuel 11:2-10 in your Bible.

One evidence that the Bible is true is that it reveals the weaknesses and failures of its heroes. Failure comes from not following God's guidance. The Bible passage describes a time when David did not follow God's guidance and instead followed his own lusts. In this familiar circumstance David—

- should have led his army instead of remaining home;
- should have looked at the stars and worshiped God (see Ps. 19) instead of watching Bathsheba bathe;
- should have thanked God for His goodness instead of forgetting His covenant with God and thus falling into adultery with Bathsheba and engineering the murder of her husband, Uriah.

David's choice to reject God's guidance gave the Lord's enemies a chance to blaspheme his God instead of bringing glory to God. Do you find yourself being tempted? Today pornographic material is readily available on TV, the Internet, and elsewhere. It is easy to become involved in a sexual relationship. The greatest protection is a love relationship with God and strict adherence to His command to flee "evil desires" (2 Tim. 2:22).

Realize that anyone can fall if he or she doesn't depend on God. As a young preacher, I remember reading David's story and thinking, *I'll never do anything like that.* Dr. Herschel Hobbs, a renowned Christian leader, once took some of us young "preacher boys" aside and told us about a pastor who had fallen. Then Dr. Hobbs shocked me by saying, "I can't say that that won't ever happen to me. The heart is deceitful above all things and desperately wicked. Who can know it? First Corinthians 10:12-13 says, 'If you think you are standing firm, be careful that you don't fall! No temptation has seized you except what is common to man. And God is faithful; he will not let you be tempted beyond what you can bear. But when you are tempted, he will also provide a way out so that you can stand up under it.' "

How could such a mighty leader admit—especially in public—that he might fall? Many times since then, I have thanked God for Dr. Hobbs's openness. He helped me realize that if I thought I was strong enough to resist temptation on my own, I was vulnerable to fall. His honesty with people, as well as God's hand on him, may well have been the key that kept Herschel Hobbs faithful to the end of his life—some 40 years after the comment was made.

In what ways has Satan tempted you to fall?

☐ Arrogance   ☐ Lust
☐ Quest for material possessions   ☐ Control needs
☐ Addiction   ☐ Other _____

God was faithful to convict David of his sin by sending His prophet Nathan. David could have hardened his heart against God, but instead, his heart was broken. He repented of his sin and was restored to full fellowship with God.

Stop and pray Psalm 51 as a personal prayer for your sins. Underscore phrases that show David's repentance. Ask God to help you repent of your sins as David did.

Although David repented of his sin and God forgave him (see Ps. 32), God stated eight consequences of David's sin that he reaped. In the margin read eight consequences of David's sin.

1. Before David's eyes someone close to him would commit adultery with David's wives (2 Sam. 12:11).

2. While David sinned in secret, the above desecration would be before all Israel (2 Sam. 12:12).

3. David gave the enemies of the Lord an opportunity to show utter contempt for (blaspheme) God (2 Sam. 12:14).

4. The baby Bathsheba bore died (2 Sam. 12:18).

5. David's son Amnon raped his sister, Tamar (2 Sam. 13:1-15).

6. David's son Absalom killed Amnon (2 Sam. 13:29).

7. Absalom led a rebellion against his father to take the kingdom from him and desecrated his wives before all Israel (2 Sam. 15).

8. Absalom was killed, and David wept brokenheartedly (2 Sam. 18:32-33).

When you miss God's guidance, it is usually because you are not in a proper relationship with Him. The key is not how God guides you but how you respond to Him. God does not give you a road map of life but a relationship for life. You don't need a road map when you have the Road Maker beside you!

7. God uses you to bring glory to His name.

God not only used David in his day but also continues to use him today. Probably more people read David's writings than those of any other person, especially the psalms where he bared his soul.

Check ways God used David. Add others in your own words.
- ☐ To establish His kingdom
- ☐ As a forefather of Jesus
- ☐ To unify His people
- ☐ To show people how to worship
- ☐ To establish worship
- ☐ To show how to repent of sin
- ☐ To prepare for the temple to be built
- ☐ Other _____

You may not have the same gifts David had, but if you have a willing heart that is in intimate fellowship with God, He will use you to go on mission with Him and to bring great glory to His name!

When David killed Goliath, which was most important? Check one.
- ☐ His skill with the slingshot
- ☐ His heart to glorify God and make Him known among the nations

When David wrote and sang psalms, which was most important?
- ☐ His ability to compose songs and play the harp
- ☐ His open heart to God and others to express his deepest feelings

If David had not had the musical ability to compose and play songs, they might not have been preserved. But what makes them so precious to millions of people is that David was able to open his heart to God and to people and let us see his deepest feelings in the midst of trials and temptations—in confession and in worship. God used him to give us a timeless message of hope and abiding faith!

Stop and pray that God will make you a man or a woman after God's own heart who seeks God's glory more than anything else in life.

DAY 4

PROMISES AND OBEDIENCE

You do not live or die to yourself. You influence the people around you for good or bad. Like a pebble thrown into a lake, your life sends out ripples to touch distant shores.

1. God chooses His people as His instruments to reach the world.

God took the concept of kingdom that people understood and used it to help Israel see that He alone is King of kings and that they are to obey Him. He took their limited concept of kingdom and expanded it to include the whole world.

David and his son Solomon were part of God's plan to teach Israel about Himself and His kingdom. However, Israel mistook God's blessings for His approval and equated her earthly kingdom with God's eternal kingdom. She saw herself as God's chosen reservoir of His grace to which the rest of the world must come rather than the river of God's grace that flows to the world. Because Israel failed to understand her role in establishing God's kingdom, God destroyed her earthly power. He sent prophets to proclaim her decline and fall. The Babylonian exile was a 70-year object lesson to teach Israel that God alone is God and that she must obey Him.

Unfortunately, even then Israel learned the wrong lesson. Instead of returning to the personal relationship, Israel's faith turned to legalism. By New Testament times—more than 400 years later—the law itself was hardened into a legalistic mold, and the concept of Israel as God's favored people had narrowed to shut out the rest of the peoples of the world. Other peoples were not allowed to worship God unless they became Jews. Israel perverted her responsibility for the nations by presuming that she alone was the object of God's love.

God's people today often make the same mistake Israel made. We try to shape ourselves to reflect the world rather than proclaim the kingdom of God to the world. When this happens, churches either close down, linger on the brink of death, or mask their problems with vigorous social activity. God's plan is for churches to be houses of prayer for all peoples to reconcile a lost world to Himself.

> **What evidence can you give that your church is being used to fulfill its calling by reconciling lost people to God?** *(example: My church sponsored a mission trip to Uganda, where participants were able to share Christ with hundreds of people, many of whom were dying of AIDS.)*

_____

_____

2. God calls all His people to be on mission with Him.

God called Israel out of Egypt, delivering her people and establishing them so that they would follow Him and worship Him. God developed His relationship with Israel so that her people would follow Him as Lord. When they rejected Him and asked for a king like other nations around them, God accommodated and gave them Saul. Samuel was crushed.

> **Read 1 Samuel 8:4-9 in the margin. Whom does it say the people of Israel rejected?**

_____

Margin notes

Israel failed to understand her role in establishing God's kingdom.

Israel perverted her responsibility for the nations by presuming that she alone was the object of God's love.

"All the elders of Israel gathered together and came to Samuel at Ramah. They said to him, 'You are old and your sons do not walk in your ways; now appoint a king to lead us, such as all the other nations have.' But when they said, 'Give us a king to lead us,' this displeased Samuel; so he prayed to the Lord. And the Lord told him: 'Listen to all that the people are saying to you; it is not you they have rejected, but they have rejected me as their king. As they have done from the day I brought them up out of Egypt until this day, forsaking me and serving other gods, so they are doing to you. Now listen to them; but warn them solemnly and let them know what the king who will reign over them will do'" (1 Sam. 8:4-9).

The people rejected God as their king. Although He warned them of the consequences of having an earthly king, God had David waiting in the wings to lead them in the paths of righteousness. The Lord was not caught by surprise when Saul—the people's choice—failed. God planned to raise up a king who would be a "man after my own heart" (1 Sam. 13:14) to reveal Him and His purposes to the world.

Today God again calls His church to follow Him and not to imitate Israel, who rejected Him as their leader. He longs for a close, intimate fellowship with His children. He desires that we live in unity under His leadership. The Lord also wants us to share the good news of the gospel throughout the world—not grasp a special relationship with Him for our own benefit, as Israel did.

Every church is called to a specific ministry to further the kingdom. What role do you think God has called your church to play?

_____

_____

_____

3. God initiates with His people a covenant of promise and obedience that will bless the nations.

More than anything else, God wanted His people to love and worship Him. Soon after they arrived in the promised land, the children of Israel forgot their covenant with God to be a holy, separate nation. Even this extreme act of defiance did not thwart God's ultimate purpose. He chose David and made a covenant with him to establish His kingdom forever. David demonstrated patience and perseverance before he came to the promised throne. Finally, after the death of Saul the Lord led David to settle in Hebron, where his own tribe, Judah, covenanted together with him as king to rule over them (see 1 Chron. 11:1-3, in the margin).

David was so sure of God's covenant with him that he stood firm under incredibly difficult circumstances.

In your Bible read 1 Chronicles 16:7-36. Underline any words relating to the nations, the entire earth, or all peoples.

Under David, God graciously gave Israel another opportunity to return to Him and to respond obediently to the covenant relationship He desired. David reminded Israel of her special status as God's people and of her obligation to obey Him and be His instrument to the nations. He returned the ark of the covenant to Jerusalem and established the worship of God there, setting an enthusiastic personal example in public. Later, he gathered materials for a magnificent temple that his son would build. He also put in place the musicians and instruments for temple worship. He even planned the court of the Gentiles. God's covenant with Israel and His kingdom always included all the peoples of the world.

"All Israel came together to David at Hebron and said, 'We are your own flesh and blood. In the past, even while Saul was king, you were the one who led Israel on their military campaigns. And the Lord your God said to you, "You will shepherd my people Israel, and you will become their ruler." ' When all the elders of Israel had come to King David at Hebron, he made a compact with them at Hebron before the Lord, and they anointed David king over Israel, as the Lord had promised through Samuel" (1 Chron. 11:1-3).

Evaluate your church and its fulfilling of God's covenant with the nations. Is it dedicated to the nations? Write two actions you think your church could take to fulfill God's covenant. *(example: My church could adopt an unreached people group and pray for it regularly.)*

1. _____

2. _____

4. God prepared His corporate people for His mission.

God shaped David to be like Him and to respond as He would. David spent his lifetime preparing God's people to worship and serve Him. Likewise, God shapes various components of the corporate body of Christ for His purpose. When churches go through severe trials and distress, God is able to develop perseverance in the church's character.

Often things appear to get worse before they get better because God is preparing a church for what He wants to do through it (see Jer. 12:5 in the margin). In difficulty be encouraged that God will use your church in much greater responsibilities as it develops perseverance.

"If you have raced with men on foot and they have worn you out, how can you compete with horses? If you stumble in safe country, how will you manage in the thickets by the Jordan?" (Jer. 12:5).

Recall a time when your church has persevered in difficult circumstances, through which God has prepared it for greater usefulness.

_____

_____

5. God sends His corporate people to the place where He can best work through them to accomplish His mission.

Long before Jerusalem existed, the Lord determined that it would be the place where a temple to honor Him would be built as the centerpiece of Israel. He put that desire into David's heart and sent him to accomplish His mission. Once David became king of all Israel, he worked to establish a united kingdom that would honor God. One of the first things he did was attack Jebus, a city on Mount Moriah, where Abraham had gone to sacrifice Isaac. David and his army captured the city and made it the capital of his kingdom, naming it Jerusalem.

Also known as Zion, Jerusalem was situated between the northern and southern tribes of Israel, thereby becoming an important unifying factor in the nation. It would later be the site of the temple Solomon built at the Lord's instruction. Jerusalem attracted rulers of other nations to come and see what the Lord had done for His people and to experience His glory (see 2 Chron. 9:4).

Today God places His people in strategic places where He desires His name to be glorified. Missionaries and other Christian workers are making thrusts into populous gateway cities. These are exciting days on the Last Frontier of missions when Christ's body, the church, is being stirred to go to places where God can work through His people! Missionaries are segmenting cities like Mexico City into clusters of one million people each and asking U.S. churches to adopt individual segments because they cannot reach them with the present number of missionaries. Other missionaries enlist U.S. churches to partner with local churches in South America to reach unreached people groups of fewer than 25,000 in population that have no missionaries. Advocates are seeking churches to adopt the 150 cities in China with more than one million in population each.

If David had preferred to stay with his father in Bethlehem, he would never have established what God desired in Jerusalem. You may have been born in the country or a small town and do not care much for the cities. In 1950 fewer than 30 percent of the world's people lived in cities. At the beginning of the 21st century almost 50 percent live there. By 2025 two-thirds will be urban inhabitants. Already more than 70 percent of Latin America's people live in cities.

What does your church do to reach any great city of the world? *(example: We sent a mission team to the ghettos of New York.)*

_____

_____

6. *God guides His people as they go on mission with Him.*

Apart from Christ's body, a believer cannot experience God in all the dimensions God has for him or her. As you think about being involved in God's passion for the world, coordinate your pursuits with your local church's life. Stay accountable to His people, and God will guide you.

In chapter 10 of *Experiencing God: Knowing and Doing the Will of God* Henry Blackaby describes the importance of functioning within the body of Christ: "Something is different about the way a church comes to know God's will and the way an individual knows God's will. A church is the body of Christ. A body functions as one unit with many members. All the members are interdependent—they need each other. No one individual can know all of God's will for a local church. Each member of the body needs the other members of the body to fully know God's will."[1]

Even before the church existed, David grasped this concept for the people of Israel. He understood the importance of the relationship believers have with God and with each other in corporate worship.

Write what you would say to a person who says he or she doesn't need the church and can worship God just as well alone.

_____

_____

Stay accountable to His people, and God will guide you.

7. *God uses His corporate people to fulfill His mission.*

God's promises to David were fulfilled as He used him remarkably during his lifetime. Acts 13:36 says, "When David had served God's purpose in his own generation, he fell asleep." This amazing epitaph emphasizes a fact you can overlook—you can serve only your own generation! God can multiply that service in the future but not if you don't do what you can in your generation.

As a young man, David would never have guessed how God would use his life to influence his own generation and generations afterward. Today God desires to use you and His corporate body to fulfill His mission in the world.

Today God desires to use you and His corporate body to fulfill His mission in the world.

Check below all the ways God has used your church to fulfill His mission in the world.
- ☐ Adopting a missionary unit
- ☐ Giving to special offerings to minister to the peoples of the world
- ☐ Presenting programs to make people aware of needs around the world
- ☐ Conducting special ministries to those in need
- ☐ Sending youth on missions trips
- ☐ Other _____

〰️〰️ ~ DAY 5 ~ 〰️〰️

AN ETERNAL KINGDOM FOR ALL PEOPLES

God not only worked through David and Israel to reveal His glory and mission, but He also communicated to everyone His reign's eternal nature. The eternal message that God revealed through David was twofold: He was establishing His kingdom, which would have no end, and this kingdom would surpass all this world's kingdoms. Today you'll consider four meanings of this eternal message.

1. The kingdom is the REIGN OF THE SOVEREIGN LORD in His people's lives. Through them He extends His rule to the world.

"The Lord is King for ever and ever;
the nations will perish from his land"
(Ps. 10:16).

Modern meanings of the word *kingdom* as a political entity pale in comparison to the original terms in Scripture that refer to the sovereignty, dominion, authority, and rank a king exercised. The Bible describes God as an eternal King (read about this in Ps. 10:16 and Ps. 103:19 in the margin). Throughout the universe God is in complete control. An accurate view of His sovereignty is the bedrock of a proper perspective on His kingdom.

"The Lord has established his throne in heaven, and his kingdom rules over all" (Ps. 103:19).

In your Bible look up the Scripture references printed in the margin. Match aspects of God's kingdom with the appropriate Scripture.

a. Psalm 145:10-13
b. Romans 16:25-27
c. Daniel 7:27
d. Psalm 22:27-28

____1. All peoples will bow down to the Lord. He will rule over them.
____2. The saints will tell of the glory of God's everlasting kingdom.
____3. The saints will participate in the established merit of the everlasting kingdom, where all rulers will worship and obey God.
____4. God will make it possible for all nations to hear the proclamation of the gospel, believe, obey, and glorify God.

The correct order above is *d, a, c,* and *b.*

If all of these aspects of God's kingdom are true, how can the world be so wicked? God's archenemy is Satan, the "adversary" who wanted to be "like the Most High" (Isa. 14:14). He rebelled against God and formed a rival kingdom of his own. Unfortunately, Satan succeeded in tempting Adam and Eve to rebel against their Creator, plunging the whole human race into spiritual darkness.

God has not abdicated His throne because of this universal rebellion but works to redeem the human race and restore His rule. Because He is sovereign, He has not relinquished His power and dominion over the rebellious but has demonstrated His purpose to reestablish His rule by love. David's kingship began the unfolding of His plan to restore God's kingdom to its right place in the hearts of people.

What pockets of rebellion to God's rule are still evident in your life?

_____

Read Mark 12:30-31 in the margin. Stop and pray. Ask God to remove all rebellion from your heart so that you might love and obey Him as you go on mission with Him.

What is the first eternal truth about the kingdom?

_____

" ' "Love the Lord your God with all your heart and with all your soul and with all your mind and with all your strength." The second is this: "Love your neighbor as yourself." There is no commandment greater than these' " *(Mark 12:30-31).*

2. The kingdom is a DISCIPLING MOVEMENT OF GOD that brings total devotion and obedience to God's will among His people.

God chose Abraham to be the father of a nation that was to be God's peculiar people through whom He would bless all nations. God used Moses to show the principles of His righteous rule of His people. Then God raised up David to be the king to further reveal His sovereignty. With each, God instituted a critical element in His eventual reign. God used Abraham to establish faith as the basic means of relating to Him and obeying Him. He used Moses to establish obedience to the law to indicate the way His kingdom was to function. He used David to establish worship as the response to His sovereignty as Lord over all.

Beside the name of each person below, write a key element God used to disciple His people and to establish an ideal for the kingdom.

Abraham _____

Moses _____

David _____

Faith, obedience to God's law, and worship of God in His sovereignty over all were demonstrated and taught in the lives of these three characters.

Even though the Israelites had rebelled against Him, God eventually brought them into the promised land and gave each tribe an inheritance there.

He desired to establish a sphere in which His rule would be acknowledged. Again, His people rejected Him in asking for a king to rule over them, the first of whom was the ungodly Saul. God redeemed that situation by giving them David, whom He knew would fulfill His will. David's influence for good in the life of the nation was very great. Every king after David was compared to the standard David set. Under his son Solomon the nation reached its zenith before spiraling downward into division and corruption under the rule of evil kings.

When the Old Testament prophets saw the kingdom of God in tatters, they might have despaired of its restoration. However, the Lord prophesied through them the hope of His kingdom's rising again through a faithful remnant who would be cleansed in fiery judgment and used for God's purpose. The hope was the beginning of an eternal kingdom composed of the King's obedient children. The key to kingdom restoration was the Descendant of Abraham and David (see Isa. 9:6-7; Obad. 21; Dan. 2:44; 7:27).

Can the kingdom of God possibly coexist with the kingdom of darkness or other kingdoms of this world? Christians have an edge on the rest of the world—God has shared the future with us. We know the secret—no matter how dark the situation may appear, God's kingdom will triumph! The sovereign Lord made it clear that His eternal kingdom will eventually destroy all others.

During David's lifetime God promised him a kingdom without end. Through prophets God showed that David's offspring would be the one to restore the kingdom and reign and rule over it. The Davidic dynasty was designed to further God's mission in His world.

"One of the elders said to me, 'Do not weep! See, the Lion of the tribe of Judah, the Root of David, has triumphed. He is able to open the scroll and its seven seals' " (Rev. 5:5).

Read Revelation 5:5; 22:16 in the margin. Underline the titles Jesus took that were related to David.

Revelation reveals the triumphant One to be "the Lion of the tribe of Judah, the Root of David" (Rev. 5:5). Jesus says of Himself, " 'I am the Root and the Offspring of David, and the bright Morning Star' " (Rev. 22:16). Could David, who started as a nobody, have looked down the centuries of time, he would have been amazed at the way God used his life. Not only was his leadership crucial in his lifetime, but the Lord would also eternally bless his life by making him the ancestor of God's only begotten Son! You would also be amazed at how God intends to use your life to help establish His eternal kingdom.

" 'I, Jesus, have sent my angel to give you this testimony for the churches. I am the Root and the Offspring of David, and the bright Morning Star' " (Rev. 22:16).

Using the phrases in capitals, write the first two eternal truths about God's kingdom.

1. _____

2. _____

3. The kingdom is the PRESSING REALITY OF GOD'S PRESENCE impacting everything and everyone in the world through His Son, Jesus Christ.

Matthew began the New Testament by tracing Christ to David and Abraham, two key figures from whose seed would come the Messiah: "A record of the genealogy of Jesus Christ the son of David, the son of Abraham" (Matt. 1:1). God arranged it so that Jesus was born in David's birthplace—Bethlehem. People referred to Christ as the Son of David.

The pressing reality of God's presence was experienced when Jesus came announcing the kingdom and calling people to repent. The kingdom reigns in people's hearts when they accept the King. It continues to spread each time someone believes the gospel. It will culminate when every knee bows and every tongue confesses Jesus as Lord.

When Jesus' followers asked Him to teach them to pray, at the heart of His prayer were the words " 'Your kingdom come, your will be done on earth as it is in heaven' " (Matt. 6:10). Toward the end of His ministry Jesus promised that He would return in glory with His angels to bless them with their inheritance, the kingdom prepared for them since the creation of the world (see Matt. 25:31-34). He comforted His disciples on the eve of His betrayal by conferring on them a kingdom in which they might eat and drink at His table and sit on thrones, judging the 12 tribes of Israel (see Luke 22:29-30 in the margin).

"And I confer on you a kingdom, just as my Father conferred one on me, so that you may eat and drink at my table in my kingdom and sit on thrones, judging the twelve tribes of Israel" (Luke 22:29-30).

The Jewish people and even the disciples of Jesus expected the Messiah to destroy the power of Rome. Instead, the kingdom of God in the person of Christ attacked the power behind all earthly kingdoms—the kingdom of Satan. Jesus came to destroy the works of the devil (see 1 John 3:8). Christ first restored God's kingdom in the spiritual realm rather than in the physical, political order. The kingdom of God came quietly, like a grain of mustard seed planted in the ground or yeast in a batch of dough (Matt. 13). As Christ submitted to the Father's sovereignty over His life, the victory was won. By His death and resurrection He broke the dominion of Satan, sin, and death over the human race.

Does that mean that all is accomplished in this world and nothing is left to do? See Christ's answer in Matthew 28:18-20, in the margin. Rather than all being accomplished, Christ says His authority is the basis on which He commands you to make disciples of all nations.

"Jesus came to them and said, 'All authority in heaven and on earth has been given to me. Therefore go and make disciples of all nations, baptizing them in the name of the Father and of the Son and of the Holy Spirit, and teaching them to obey everything I have commanded you. And surely I am with you always, to the very end of the age'" (Matt. 28:18-20).

Read the statements below. Mark the one that impacts you most. Then on the lines following, write why it impacts you this way.

1. He reigns in heaven and manifests His reign on earth in and through His corporate body, the church.
2. The kingdom of God is present within people's hearts.
3. Only when the gospel has been preached to all peoples will Christ return (see Matt. 24:14).
4. As the kingdom of God expands, the kingdom of darkness diminishes.
5. When He has finally accomplished His mission, He will return and establish His kingdom in glory!
6. When all things are put under Christ's feet, He will present this reclaimed kingdom to the Father (see 1 Cor. 15:24).
7. The kingdom's perfect blessings will be realized when sin, Satan, and death are banished forever and His is the kingdom, power, and glory.

_____

_____

God alone establishes His kingdom. He has done His part up to now and is ready to finish the job. However, He gives you every chance to partner with Him. He wants you to reign with Him someday. The time of Christ's coming and complete victory is hidden from you so that you will be about your Father's business. You have had the gospel revealed to you so that you can reveal it to the world before judgment day.

Write the kingdom's first three eternal aspects that you have studied.

1. The kingdom is the _____ in people's lives.

2. The kingdom is a _____ of God that brings total devotion and obedience to God's will among His people.

3. The kingdom is the _____ impacting everything and everyone in the world through His Son, Jesus Christ.

4. The kingdom is the MISSION OF GOD that culminates in Christ's victory in the world to the glory of God.

Christ's kingdom came humbly and unobtrusively, bringing the miracle of spiritual life and the blessings of God's rule in the hearts of people. The blessings of the coming age are with you now in the presence of God all around you. God's kingdom moves forward as Jesus' disciples take the gospel into all the world.

What is God's instrument to accomplish this? When Christ's redemptive work was finished, the divine purpose shifted from Israel to the church. Jesus told the unbelieving Jews, " 'The Kingdom of God will be taken away from you and given to a people who will produce its fruit' " (Matt. 21:43). Christ's church is "a holy nation" (1 Pet. 2:9). God's redemptive purpose in history is now being worked out through His corporate body, the church. The conflict still rages, but as God's people carry the gospel of the kingdom into all the world, the kingdom of Satan is being assaulted and thrown down.

God has entrusted you with a part of continuing and completing that task! Your responsibility is to be faithful as He completes it. As long as Christ has not returned, your work is incomplete. As you obey Him, He will complete His mission through you. Christ's disciples asked when the end of the age would come (see Matt. 24:3). The Lord's answer is your mandate as you go on mission with Him (see 1 Cor. 15:24-25 in the margin).

Pray the Lord's Prayer. Then conclude this study of David by praying to God the words from David's last psalm, Psalm 72:17-20 (in the margin).

You are living in the last days. The last days began at Pentecost and will end when Christ offers to God all the kingdoms of the world. The kingdom's urgency relates to both the impending judgment of God on people's sin and the promise that God will deal in mercy with those who believe in Him. You have only two alternatives to the kingdom tension: (1) give up all hope and responsibility for this world, retire from it, and let it go its suicidal way to hell or (2) by aggressive witness, fulfill your stewardship in God's establishing of the kingdom.

"The end will come, when he hands over the kingdom to God the Father after he has destroyed all dominion, authority and power. For he must reign until he has put all his enemies under his feet" (1 Cor. 15:24-25).

"May his name endure forever;
* may it continue as long as the sun.*
All nations will be blessed through him,
* and they will call him blessed.*
Praise be to the Lord God, the God of Israel,
* who alone does marvelous deeds.*
Praise be to his glorious name forever;
* may the whole earth be filled with his glory.*
* Amen and Amen.*
This concludes the prayers of David son of Jesse" (Ps. 72:17-20).

You are part of a generation of priests chosen to reign with the King. If you are to reign with Him in the coming kingdom, you must serve during its rise to power.

What one statement or Scripture affected you most in today's study?

_____

Meditate on its meaning to you and to the kingdom of God. Write the truth you see revealed.

_____

_____

Apply the statement or Scripture to your own life by writing what you will do in response to it during the next seven days.

_____

_____

---

[1] Henry Blackaby, *Experiencing God: Knowing and Doing the Will of God* (Nashville: LifeWay Press, 1990), 165.

JESUS

ON MISSION WITH GOD:
A SAVIOR FOR ALL PEOPLES

Heart Focus
"The Word became flesh and made his dwelling among us. We have seen his glory, the glory of the One and Only, who came from the Father, full of grace and truth" (John 1:14).

This Week's Lessons
Day 1: Jesus Is God's Glory in Person
Day 2: Called to Join God on Mission
Day 3: Letting God Work Through You
Day 4: Your Generation on Mission with God
Day 5: Jesus, the Only Way

This Week's Learning Focus
You will be able to explain how Jesus brings glory to God by reconciling the lost, and you will be able to defend the position that He is the only way to salvation.

 DAY 1

JESUS IS GOD'S GLORY IN PERSON

Each Saturday during my first full year of missionary service after a year of language study, I read to my Moslem secretary the sermon I had composed in Indonesian to see if it was grammatically correct and understandable before I preached it on Sunday. Often, the concepts, not the language, were difficult for her to understand.

One day I remarked off-handedly, "I love God." She responded, "How do you love God? I don't love God." I told her, "I love God because He first loved me. Why don't you love God?" She said she was "afraid of him because of my sins." I then told her "I love God because He sent His Son to save me. If I didn't love him, I wouldn't be in Indonesia." "But how can I love him? We have no *penjelmaan*," she exclaimed. "I'm glad you used that word *penjelmaan*," I replied. "That's the Indonesian word for incarnation. Now I understand why you can't love God. If God had not come in Christ, I could not love Him either. But since He first loved me and sent His Son, it's easy to love Him." Like her, millions around the world have no understanding of the incarnation. Jesus has come in human form, but they don't know it.

Just as Mount Everest towers above the mountains surrounding it, the life of the Lord Jesus Christ towers above all persons who have ever lived. The glory of God is 100 percent present in Jesus 100 percent of the time. That did not mean Jesus glowed with glory all the time as He did on the mount of transfiguration.

Jesus manifested God's presence many ways. He said, " 'Anyone who has seen me has seen the Father' " (John 14:9). We see God's glory manifested in His character, His attitude, His teachings, His actions, and His ways. He is the pattern for our lives. Through His only begotten Son, God revealed His love and His purpose to reconcile the world to Himself.

1. God is always at work around you.

God was at work around Jesus all His life. God was pleased with His Son. Scripture indicates that the Father was at work around Jesus in His early years.

Check the ways that God revealed His glory as He prepared for His Son's arrival.

☐ He was busy working throughout Old Testament times to foretell and prepare for His Son's arrival on earth.

☐ He foretold that Jesus would be born in Bethlehem (see Mic. 5:2), that He would go down into Egypt (see Hos. 11:1), and that He would settle in the town of Nazareth (see Matt. 2:23).

☐ An angel was sent to Mary to tell her she would be Christ's mother.

☐ The Father sent a dream to Joseph to announce Jesus' name and tell about His work of saving His people from their sins.

☐ An angelic choir gave glory to God as it announced Jesus' birth to simple shepherds.

☐ A bright star guided wise men from the East to where Jesus was.

☐ Wise men announced to Herod who Jesus' parents were.

☐ An angel told Joseph to flee to Egypt so Herod couldn't kill Jesus.

God was certainly busy getting ready for this earth-shaking event, announcing it to all concerned, and guiding explicitly its every detail! All the above are true except the next-to-last statement.

Read Luke 1:26-38 in the margin. Underline five facts Mary discovered about her unborn Son.

In this first meeting with the angel, Mary learned that Jesus would be born of a virgin, would be named Jesus, would be called the Son of the Most High, would reign as the Son of David forever, and would be called the Son of God. The Scripture doesn't tell us much about the childhood years of Jesus. The next glimpse you see of Jesus in Scripture is at age 12, when sons would normally accompany their parents on their annual trip to Jerusalem for the Passover. He lingered in the temple at Jerusalem for three days before Mary and Joseph realized He was not with them.

Although Jesus was doing His Father's work, notice that He went back to Nazareth and obeyed His parents. Luke 2:52 reports He also grew in wisdom (mentally), in stature (physically), and in favor with God (spiritually) and others (socially). What a wonderful pattern for us!

From the time of Christ to the present, many people have experienced God at work around them. How did you first become aware of the fact that God was working in your life?

"In the sixth month, God sent the angel Gabriel to Nazareth, a town in Galilee, to a virgin pledged to be married to a man named Joseph, a descendant of David. The virgin's name was Mary. The angel went to her and said, 'Greetings, you who are highly favored! The Lord is with you.' Mary was greatly troubled at his words and wondered what kind of greeting this might be. But the angel said to her, 'Do not be afraid, Mary, you have found favor with God. You will be with child and give birth to a son, and you are to give him the name Jesus. He will be great and will be called the Son of the Most High. The Lord God will give him the throne of his father David, and he will reign over the house of Jacob forever; his kingdom will never end.' 'How can this be,' Mary asked the angel, 'since I am a virgin?' The angel answered, 'The Holy Spirit will come upon you, and the power of the Most High will overshadow you. So the holy one to be born will be called the Son of God. Even Elizabeth your relative is going to have a child in her old age, and she who was said to be barren is in her sixth month. For nothing is impossible with God.' 'I am the Lord's servant,' Mary answered. 'May it be to me as you have said' " (Luke 1:26-38).

Describe your first awareness that God is at work around you.

_____

_____

_____

When and how did you first realize that God has a purpose for your life?

_____

_____

_____

Sadly, almost one of every three persons in the world has never heard of Christ. He wants you to help finish His work by telling people around the world about God's great love for them!

a. " 'The Father loves the Son and shows him all he does. Yes, to your amazement he will show him even greater things than these' " (John 5:20).

b. " 'I have made you known to them, and will continue to make you known in order that the love you have for me may be in them and that I myself may be in them' " (John 17:26).

c. " 'Father, I want those you have given me to be with me where I am, and to see my glory, the glory you have given me because you loved me before the creation of the world' " (John 17:24).

2. God pursues a continuing love relationship with you that is real and personal.

The Son of God was aware that the Father loved Him.

Match the verses in the margin marked a, b, and c with the ways Jesus revealed His relationship with the Father.
____ 1. He wanted the Father to show His relationship with Him before creation.
____ 2. He stated that the Father showed Him everything He does.
____ 3. He revealed the Father and His love to the disciples.

You can know that the Lord loves you because of what He did for you on the cross (Rom. 5:8). You have felt His presence as He revealed Himself to you and drew you to Himself. He has communicated His love to you through persons who know Him and who introduced Him to you. If you have not yet had a personal experience with God through Christ, be assured that He pursues you even as you read this. Even if you know Him as well as the disciples did, He has more of Himself that He wants to reveal to you. The correct order in the above matching exercise is *c, a,* and *b.*

List ways or persons through whom God has communicated His love to you.

_____

_____

_____

3. God invites you to become involved with Him in His work.

Before the world was created, the Father invited Jesus to be involved in His work. John 1:1-3 clearly states that Jesus created the world. At age 30 He knew what that work entailed and was ready to embark on public ministry with might and zeal. At His baptism Jesus was aware that God was present and at work.

Read Matthew 3:16-17 in the margin. Check the ways God demonstrated His relationship with Jesus.
☐ John announced God's love for Jesus.
☐ God showed His approval by sending a dove to light on Jesus.
☐ The people acclaimed God's love for Jesus.
☐ God said He was pleased with Jesus.

"As soon as Jesus was baptized, he went up out of the water. At that moment heaven was opened, and he saw the Spirit of God descending like a dove and lighting on him. And a voice from heaven said, 'This is my Son, whom I love; with him I am well pleased'" (Matt. 3:16-17).

The Father declared His approval of His Son when the Spirit of God descended like a dove and lighted on Him.

Every revelation of God and every assurance of His love is His invitation. He beckons you to join Him. When did God last speak to you through Scripture? Stop and reread the Scripture you read when you last realized He spoke to you. Ask God why He spoke to you and what this could have to do with your joining Him in His mission.

Write why you think God revealed Himself to you in that way.

_____

_____

_____

4. God speaks by the Holy Spirit through the Bible, prayer, and circumstances to reveal Himself, His purposes, and His ways.

Although Jesus constantly communicated with the Father, God still used the same ways to speak to Him as He does to you. The Father spoke directly to Him through the Holy Spirit. John 3:34 (in the margin) says the Holy Spirit was given to Jesus without limit. Jesus said His words came from the Father. In John 14:10 He said, " 'Don't you believe that I am in the Father, and that the Father is in me? The words I say to you are not just my own. Rather, it is the Father, living in me.' " He listened to the Father and limited His teaching to what He heard.

" 'The one whom God has sent speaks the words of God, for God gives the Spirit without limit' " (John 3:34).

Although you may not have the continual, perfect communication Jesus had with the Father, Jesus promised in John 16:13, " 'When he, the Spirit of truth, comes, he will guide you into all truth. He will not speak on his own; he will speak only what he hears, and he will tell you what is yet to come.' " God uses the same methods to speak to you that He used to speak to Jesus. Are you listening as Jesus did? Are you taking advantage of the communication tools God uses to speak to you?

A. The Father spoke to Jesus through the Bible.

Jesus often said that what He did was a fulfillment of Scripture. The Father spoke directly to Jesus through the Scriptures. Today He does the same with you.

Write the memory verse for the week. If necessary you may refer to the beginning of today's study where the verse appears.

_____

_____

B. The Father spoke to Jesus through prayer.

Jesus' prayer life was so compelling that His disciples asked Him to teach them to pray (see Luke 11:1-4). His communication with His Father came to a heart-rending culmination as Jesus prayed in the garden of Gethsemane (see Matt. 26:36-46). Again on the cross Jesus cried out to His Father. He may have comforted Himself with the words of Psalm 22 as He hung between earth and heaven, giving His life for the world's sin. In difficult days, when you seem to be alone, know that God's Word can be your comfort and strength as you pray.

In difficult days know that the Word of God can give you comfort and strength as you pray.

C. The Father spoke to Jesus through circumstances.

Jesus responded to God's prompting through circumstances. He was even attentive to seeming interruptions of His activity.

In your Bible read Matthew 9:14-25. Answer the following questions.

1. To whom was Jesus ministering at first? _____

2. Who interrupted this session? _____

3. Who interrupted this interruption? _____

In the midst of the circumstances surrounding Him, Jesus realized that the Father was at work. He joined Him immediately. Thus, when He taught John's disciples, He responded to the synagogue ruler's dilemma. On the way to solve Jairus's problem, He realized that the Father had inspired faith in the woman who had touched the hem of His robe. He redirected His attention to the woman with the issue of blood. He healed and released her from this plague, which had rendered her unclean for 12 long years!

When He arrived at Jairus's house, Jairus's daughter was dead. Jesus prayed for the Father to raise her from the dead, and He did. How often are you so focused on one thing that you miss the opportunity God is presenting you through circumstances? Interruptions may be divine appointments.

How often are you so focused on one thing that you miss the opportunity God is presenting you?

Write ways Jesus has been using the following to speak to you about joining His mission to reconcile the peoples of the world to Himself.

1. Bible _____

2. Prayer _____

3. Circumstances _____

5. God's invitation for you to work with Him always leads you to a crisis of belief that requires faith and action.

You may have difficulty understanding the faith Jesus exercised because you tend to concentrate on His divine nature more than on His human nature. I believe Jesus did His miracles by faith.

Read Hebrews 12:2 in the margin. Circle words showing that Jesus acted by faith.

Jesus believed the Father was leading Him throughout His earthly ministry and was willing to do what He asked. In His final act of trust in God, He faced death with faith that the Spirit would resurrect Him. As you read the Bible, realize that Jesus is your model. He lived by faith and acted completely by faith.

Describe a crisis of faith you face because of what God is revealing to you.

_____

_____

_____

6. You must make major adjustments in your life to join God in what He is doing.

You may think that because Jesus was God's Son, He didn't have to make major adjustments when the Father revealed His will to Him. The opposite is true.

Read Matthew 26:37-43 in the margin. Highlight the phrases that show the adjustments Jesus made under incredibly difficult circumstances.

The Son of God was willing to put aside His desires and adjust to the Father's will as He emptied the bitter cup for you and me and all the peoples of the world. Willingness to make the kind of adjustments Jesus made will be worked into your character only as you obediently surrender to the Father and allow His Holy Spirit to transform you into the image of Christ.

What adjustment is God asking you to make to join Him on His mission?

_____

_____

"Let us fix our eyes on Jesus, the author and perfecter of our faith, who for the joy set before him endured the cross, scorning its shame, and sat down at the right hand of the throne of God" (Heb. 12:2).

"He took Peter and the two sons of Zebedee along with him, and he began to be sorrowful and troubled. Then he said to them, 'My soul is overwhelmed with sorrow to the point of death. Stay here and keep watch with me.' Going a little farther, he fell with his face to the ground and prayed, 'My Father, if it is possible, may this cup be taken from me. Yet not as I will, but as you will.' Then he returned to his disciples and found them sleeping. 'Could you men not keep watch with me for one hour?' He asked Peter. 'Watch and pray so that you will not fall into temptation. The spirit is willing, but the body is weak.' He went away a second time and prayed, 'My Father, if it is not possible for this cup to be taken away unless I drink it, may your will be done.' When he came back, he again found them sleeping, because their eyes were heavy. So he left them and went away once more and prayed the third time, saying the same thing" (Matt. 26:37-43).

The Lord requires major adjustments from you to bring you in line with His will. Even when you follow Him day by day, you will often be surprised at how He wants to lead you forward. He may require an adjustment in what you are doing or how you are doing it. Often a major change in attitude is required. As you reflect on the invitation He extends to you, look at the faith step He asks you to make. Realize that if you don't make it, you will not be able to join Him in what He wants you to do next for His kingdom and personally experience His glory.

7. *You experience God as you obey Him and He accomplishes His work through you.*

The Bible clearly reveals that Jesus learned obedience by the things He experienced during His brief lifetime on earth. Not only did He learn by experience, but He also suffered temptations during His life so that He can help those who are being tempted (see Heb. 2:18). Hebrews 4:15 says He "has been tempted in every way, just as we are—yet was without sin." Jesus lived a perfect life on this earth and then tasted death for every person.

Ask God to reveal anything that may be standing in the way of your complete obedience to Him. Then describe it below. As you ask Him to eradicate it from your life, draw a line through it.

_____

_____

_____

_____

═══⋙ DAY 2 ⋘═══

CALLED TO JOIN GOD ON MISSION

Jesus lived 33 years—not a long life by today's standards. In that short span of time, however, He finished the work the Father gave Him to do. He said on the cross, " 'It is finished' " (John 19:30). In some of His final hours on earth, Jesus said, " 'I have brought you glory on earth by completing the work you gave me to do' " (John 17:4). You have no idea how long God has given you to live on this earth. Only the Lord knows the total plan for your life. As you seek to align your life with God's mission, realize that you will be enabled to experience God all your life by following the lessons you learn from the life of Jesus. Today you will review how the Father used Jesus and worked through His entire life to accomplish His mission. As you do so, ask God to reveal how He wants your whole life to accomplish His mission.

1. God chooses you to be on mission with Him to reconcile a lost world to Himself.

Only God could have thought up the incarnation. The concept of God's becoming a living human being is so incredible that you may struggle to understand it. Thousand of years before it occurred, God revealed His plans about His inheritance and possession.

Read Psalm 2:7-8 in the margin. Complete the statement below.

The Father promised to answer the Son's request to give Him the nations

as His _____ and the ends of the earth as His _____.

Peter declares that Jesus "was chosen before the creation of the world, but was revealed in these last times for your sake" (1 Pet. 1:20). God chose not only Jesus but also you before the world's foundation.

Underline the words in Ephesians 1:4,11 in the margin showing that God had a plan in creating you.

How reassuring to realize that God planned your life as well as the life of Jesus before the creation of the world! God's initiative calling you to Himself was not a spur-of-the-moment decision. Neither did you take the initiative to choose Him. You may not understand how He chose you before you were born, but once you are in the kingdom of God, He reveals that He made the initial choice. That means He has a purpose to fulfill in you. Will you do what He chose you to do?

Read Jeremiah 1:4-9 in your Bible. Ask God why He chose you. Describe what you think He is telling you.

_____

_____

_____

2. God calls you to accompany Him on His mission.

The Father's calling of Christ is an important concept in Scripture. The word *called* is used of Jesus in Matthew 2:15: " 'Out of Egypt I called my son.' " Early in His earthly life Jesus sensed the Father's call. At the age of 12 He said He must be about His Father's business.

"I will proclaim the decree of the Lord:
He said to me, 'You are my Son;
today I have become your Father.
Ask of me,
and I will make the nations your inheritance,
the ends of the earth your possession' "
(Ps. 2:7-8).

"He chose us in him before the creation of the world to be holy and blameless in his sight. In him we were also chosen, having been predestined according to the plan of him who works out everything in conformity with the purpose of his will" (Eph. 1:4,11).

Jesus also sensed God's call at the time of His baptism and insisted that His cousin John baptize Him. After that encounter with the Father, Jesus sensed the Spirit's call to go into the wilderness for Satan to tempt Him.

Think back on God's call to you. God's call was not only for salvation but also for service. His call to follow Him did not mean just down a church aisle or in baptism. His call is to be like Jesus and to let Jesus live His life through you. Read Luke 9:23 in the margin to see what Jesus said.

"He said to them all: 'If anyone would come after me, he must deny himself and take up his cross daily and follow me'" (Luke 9:23).

Describe any struggles you are having in joining God on His mission to save the peoples of the world.

_____

_____

_____

3. God initiates a covenant of promise and obedience with you.

Jesus fulfilled all the Old Testament covenants. As Abraham's seed, Jesus fulfilled the prophecy given to Abraham. Galatians 3:16 specifically states, "The promises were spoken to Abraham and to his seed." The Scripture does not say "and to seeds," meaning many people, but "and to his seed," meaning one person—Christ. Jesus' primary covenant was with the Father. He was the lamb slain before the foundation of the world. Jesus declared His willingness to fulfill the covenant of redemption by sacrificing Himself for the world's sins.

"First he said, 'Sacrifices and offerings, burnt offerings and sin offerings you did not desire, nor were you pleased with them' (although the law required them to be made). Then he said, 'Here I am, I have come to do your will.' He set aside the first to establish the second. And by that will, we have been made holy through the sacrifice of the body of Jesus Christ once for all" (Heb. 10:8-10).

Read Hebrews 10:8-10 in the margin. Bracket [ ] Jesus' commitment to fulfill the Old Covenant and establish the New Covenant.

Christ's awareness of His covenants with the Father and God's covenants with His people kept Him focused on His purpose. During His earthly life, He operated on the basis of God's working through Him to fulfill His mission in the world.

Fill in the blanks for the memory verse of this week: "The Word became

_____ **and made his dwelling among us. We have seen his**

_____ **, the** _____ **of the One and Only, who came**

from the Father, full of _____ **and** _____ **"**

(John ___:____).

⟫ DAY 3 ⟪

LETTING GOD WORK THROUGH YOU

4. *God prepares you for His mission.*

Through the struggles you endure, you are prepared to do God's will. The Father prepared Jesus before He came on His mission to redeem the world. The Father continued to prepare Jesus throughout His life to fulfill His mission. God's directive that He grow up in a faithful Jewish family helped Him understand the mission. His participation in the rigorous synagogue training given young men of His day further prepared Him. His baptism and the Father's loving affirmation prepared Him for the wilderness temptations. You may marvel that God's loving Spirit led Jesus into temptation. Jesus, the Hero of all time, had no weakness, but the unexpected event of the temptation proved that point for all eternity!

> The Father prepared Jesus before He came on His mission to redeem the world.

Read Luke 4:1-13 in your Bible. Circle or underline Jesus' reply to each question, as described below.
1. Satan questioned Jesus' identity as the Son of God and dared Him to prove it by changing stones into bread for His own use.
2. Satan questioned the way Jesus would accomplish His mission and lead people to follow Him.
3. Satan questioned the means by which Jesus would become King over all the kingdoms of the earth.

Jesus may have been face-to-face with the devil, but His focus was on God! Quoting words from Deuteronomy 6—8, Jesus remained true to the Father's revealed will. Through the power of the Holy Spirit, He resisted Satan's temptation to seduce Him from His Father's purpose.

Perhaps you have struggled in a similar way. You have felt God inviting you to follow Jesus and get involved in His work, but the pull in other directions has been strong. By now you realize that your salvation is not only to benefit you but also to fulfill His mission to the whole world!

Jesus is recruiting an army. He rescued you from the tyrant who has abused you all your life. He wants to enlist you to join Him to save others from the tyranny of the tempter. Every revelation of Himself is an invitation for you to join His mission. He wants you to be aware of His vision for all peoples to know Him (see Phil. 1:29 in the margin).

> *"It has been granted to you on behalf of Christ not only to believe on him, but also to suffer for him"* (Phil. 1:29).

Satan may tempt you in ways similar to the ways he tempted Jesus. How would you answer these temptations if Satan said them to you?

1. "If you are really a child of God, then show it by exposing yourself

to_____ (your greatest temptation) and then resist it."

How would you respond?

_____

2. "You don't really need to deny yourself to be on mission with God. Just do a spectacular work that people can see, such as … "_____

How would you respond?

_____

3. "If you will take my shortcut to success, you can have anything you want."

How would you respond?

_____

Satan continued to test Jesus throughout His earthly existence. He even induced Peter to rebuke Jesus for predicting that He would die (see Matt. 16:22). The Gethsemane experience of asking the Father to let this cup of suffering pass further equipped Christ to pay the ultimate price of redemption. All His life He was being equipped to accomplish His mission. When the time came for Him to die, God's Son did not falter.

Each trial you face prepares you for further testing to become equipped to accomplish your mission with God. You may not understand why you must go through one more trial when you think you are already prepared for anything. The Father, however, knows what further character development you need to match the assignment He has for you.

Name what you think God wants to develop in you through a test or trial you are now facing.

_____

_____

_____

Through faith steps God leads you along the path of His perfect will for your life.

God asks you to take steps of faith and action. Through faith steps God leads you along the path of His perfect will for your life. The experience you have is His continuing love relationship with you drawing you after Him throughout your lifetime. You will gain insight into your own preparation for being on mission with God as you read the Bible and realize that Jesus lived and acted by faith.

Quote the memory verse for the week. Practice saying it until you can quote it. Check here ❑ when you have it memorized.

5. God sends you to the place where He can best work through you to accomplish His mission.

In the past you may have struggled to know the place God has chosen for you. No question existed as to the place the Father chose for His Son's mission. If He was to totally identify with people, Christ had to live among them. The quest required that He come as the lowliest of people—a servant. Nothing God asks of you can compare with the sacrifice He made to be in the place God desired.

Read Philippians 2:5-8 in the margin. Check the boxes that indicate how the Father sent Jesus and ways you think He may be sending you.

	Jesus	Me
Humility	☐	☐
Poverty	☐	☐
Servanthood	☐	☐
Obedience	☐	☐
Death	☐	☐

For God to use you fully, get to a place where He can bless others through you. Check the possibilities you believe represent God's intention for you.

_____1. Your same geographical location but in a servant role

_____2. Another part of the geographical area surrounding you

_____3. A different job than you are now doing

_____4. A different people/racial group from your own

_____5. Another people group/country where the gospel isn't known

6. God guides you to join Him on mission.

The Father always guided Jesus to do what He desired. Because He loved the Father and had an intimate relationship with Him, Jesus never disappointed Him. As you have seen, the Holy Spirit was active in Christ's life on earth. The Word He had learned in His youth, prayer in every perplexing situation, and the circumstances in which He found Himself all guided Jesus. The Father took the initiative and showed Him what He was doing. One instance of particular importance in this regard is outlined in Mark 1:35-38, in the margin.

Complete these statements, based on the verses in the margin.

1. Jesus got up very _____ in the morning while it was still _____.

2. He went off to a _____ place where He _____.

3. The disciples thought He would yield to _____ looking for Him.

4. Jesus had heard from the Father that He should go instead _____ else

   to a nearby village so that He could _____ there.

"Your attitude should be the same as that of Christ Jesus: Who, being in very nature God, did not consider equality with God something to be grasped, but made himself nothing, taking the very nature of a servant, being made in human likeness. And being found in appearance as a man, he humbled himself and became obedient to death—even death on a cross!" (Phil. 2:5-8).

"Very early in the morning, while it was still dark, Jesus got up, left the house and went off to a solitary place, where he prayed. Simon and his companions went to look for him, and when they found him, they exclaimed: 'Everyone is looking for you!' Jesus replied, 'Let us go somewhere else—to the nearby villages—so I can preach there also. That is why I have come'" (Mark 1:35-38).

" 'The Counselor, the Holy Spirit, whom the Father will send in my name, will teach you all things and will remind you of everything I have said to you' " (John 14:26).

" 'I will not leave you as orphans; I will come to you' " (John 14:18).

" 'Teaching them to obey everything I have commanded you. And surely I am with you always, to the very end of the age' " (Matt. 28:20).

After Jesus said this, he looked toward heaven and prayed: Father, the time has come. Glorify your Son, that your Son may glorify you. For you granted him authority over all people that he might give eternal life to all those you have given him. Now this is eternal life: that they may know you, the only true God, and Jesus Christ, whom you have sent. I have brought you glory on earth by completing the work you gave me to do (John 17:1-4).

While the human response would be to go to the people seeking Him, Jesus said He must go to other towns and villages because "That is why I have come." God's will won out over others' appeal and counsel!

Following Jesus' example, be sure you receive your guidance from the Father through the Holy Spirit rather than from people around you.

Read the promises for guidance (John 14:26; 14:18; Matt. 28:20) in the margin. Write Jesus' promises that He will guide you.

1. _____

2. _____

3. _____

7. God uses you to bring glory to His name through His mission.

The Father must have delighted daily in using Christ to reveal His nature, demonstrate His glory, and accomplish His ultimate purpose in the world. In the margin read what Jesus said in John 5:30. Because He obeyed and was willing to deny Himself and please the Father, Jesus accomplished great things through His brief life on earth. Satan and death were defeated on the cross, new life became possible through the resurrection, and victory was ensured through His ascension and enthronement.

Read John 17:1-4 in the margin. Below note the ways Jesus glorified the Father. Write a similar way you could glorify God.

1. By glorifying the Father when He was glorified

_____

2. By giving eternal life to all those the Father has given Him

_____

3. By finishing the work the Father had given Him to do

_____

You and I are not to be concerned about how God will use others. When Jesus told Peter to follow Him and feed His sheep instead of fishing, He revealed that in his old age others would carry him where he did not want to go. Peter wanted to shift the subject to someone else (John 21:20-22). Don't shift attention to someone else or do what they do. Allow the Lord to use you as He chooses!

══════ ～ D A Y 4 ～ ══════

YOUR GENERATION ON MISSION WITH GOD

Jesus could have won the world by Himself, but He was not content to do that. Instead, He realized that it was in the Father's plan to recruit His generation to take the gospel to the ends of the earth.

1. God chooses His people in your generation to be on mission with Him to reconcile a lost world to Himself.

As you have seen, Christ spent much time praying before He selected the twelve disciples. He took more than three years to teach and train them for the global task for which He had carefully chosen them. Then after His resurrection He commissioned them for worldwide mission, using the words from Matthew 28:18-20, in the margin. God calls you to the same task.

> **In the margin, read Acts 1:8, which records Jesus' final words to His disciples as He was received back into heaven.**

The disciples might have tried to reach the whole world by themselves, but that would not demonstrate God's glory. The Holy Spirit, working in and through them, daily added to the church those who were being saved (see Acts 2:47). Christ was building His church from the chosen people of that generation (see Matt. 16:18). The plan was that each believer would be a witness, believing with the heart and confessing with the mouth that Jesus is Lord (see Rom. 10:9-10).

The game plan has not changed. Just as the disciples were empowered then, the Holy Spirit empowers you in this century to be His witness to people in your city, in your state, in your country, and around the globe.

God has not only chosen you, but He also has chosen the church, which means the called-out ones. Everyone in His body is chosen for His purpose. Think about the church of which you are a member. For what purpose has God chosen you? Each church is to be a world-mission strategy center. Each church has distinctive local and global roles to play.

What role(s) do you think God wants your church to play in

1. your Jerusalem?_____

2. your Judea?_____

3. your Samaria?_____

4. your uttermost?_____

"Jesus came to them and said, 'All authority in heaven and on earth has been given to me. Therefore go and make disciples of all nations, baptizing them in the name of the Father and of the Son and of the Holy Spirit, and teaching them to obey everything I have commanded you. And surely I am with you always, to the very end of the age' " (Matt. 28:18-20).

" 'You will receive power when the Holy Spirit comes on you; and you will be my witnesses in Jerusalem, and in all Judea and Samaria, and to the ends of the earth' " (Acts 1:8).

Each church is to be a world-mission strategy center. Each church has distinctive local and global roles to play.

2. God calls His people to Himself to be on mission with Him.

Daily the disciples saw Jesus fulfill the calling His Father had placed in His life. His ministry was so incredibly effective that the disciples must have felt inadequate as they faced the task of winning the world to Jesus. Because He had chosen them, they knew they were called to leave their former pursuits and to pursue the goals of God's kingdom. Because they obeyed, the Holy Spirit worked powerfully through them to turn the world upside down (see Acts 17:6, KJV).

> The disciples must have felt inadequate as they faced the task of winning the world to Jesus.

Beginning with the Jews in Jerusalem and moving on to the Gentiles in Samaria and surrounding areas, the disciples took the message of Christ's crucifixion, resurrection, and ascension to pagan peoples, knowing it could turn their world right side up (see Acts 11:19-21).

The wicked and perverse generation Rome ruled became so permeated with the good news of the gospel that its pagan gods came crashing down and Christianity was proclaimed the religion of Rome by A.D. 313. Seventeen hundred years later, the gospel and the mandate have not changed! God's church is called to go with the good news to our generation, where mammon and materialism and false religions hold sway in many sectors of the globe.

As the Father called Jesus, so He calls His people to follow Christ. God's general call is to be a holy people, a kingdom of priests to the peoples of the world. We have applied the word *call* to individuals so often that we miss that it first primarily applied to all the people of God.

> Jesus did not give the Great Commission just to the apostles or to a certain class of people. He gave it to every Christian and every church.

Jesus did not give the Great Commission just to the apostles or to a certain class of people. He gave it to every Christian and every church. All of Christ's followers are called to be involved in His mission.

Read Acts 8:4 in the margin. Circle the word that indicates who preached the Word wherever they went.

> *"Those who had been scattered preached the word wherever they went"* (Acts 8:4).

Philip went to Samaria, and the Spirit used him to bring multitudes into the kingdom. Next we see him in the desert witnessing to the Ethiopian. God may choose to use you to win the multitudes, but He also wants you and your church to witness to individuals around you.

Name places your church is witnessing to the world around you.

_____

Name a people group(s) your church has adopted.

_____

Name a missionary (or missionaries) your church has adopted.

_____

Name a missionary who has gone from your church.

_____

3. God initiates a covenant of promise and obedience with your church and generation.

Imagine being raised under the rules and regulations of the old covenant, then suddenly being released to share the glorious freedom of the new covenant with your generation. This is what the disciples experienced. Through their intimate, personal relationship with the Son of God, they were miraculously transformed. These men had to be amazed to be part of a major transition that affected the very roots of their former religion. Instead of sacrificing bulls, goats, and lambs, they now celebrated, in the bread and wine, the broken body and shed blood of Christ, with whom they had walked and talked (see Luke 22:14-20).

The same excitement the disciples must have felt in telling the world that the Lamb of God, whom they knew personally, takes away sins can be yours today through the new covenant God has made with you through the blood of His Son. Read 2 Corinthians 5:17 in the margin and remember the timeless message you have to share with the world.

Read Hebrews 8:8-12 in the margin. Underline the differences the first Christians must have felt in the new-covenant age.

4. God prepares His people in your generation for His mission.

Just as the Father took great pains to prepare His Son for the ministry to which He was called, Christ carefully prepared His disciples for the work of the kingdom. The Lord spent many hours teaching them, using simple parables to drive home the truth.

Today, by His Holy Spirit the Lord is willing to spend time with your church, preparing you for an outreach as great as—if not greater than —that of the early apostles. That preparation takes place during the difficulties you experience as you submit to God's will during your life.

Jesus demonstrated what it means to be on mission. When Satan, His disciples, His brothers, or His townspeople tried to divert Him, Jesus remained on course because He was always aware of His mission to redeem the lost world. He had a passion to fulfill His mission. Since He believed the results of His mission were sure, He endured whatever it took to finish His task. Adopt that same mind-set today as you rise above the outlook of your affluent culture.

God performed miracles in the midst of the first-century church to show that He was the One taking the initiative to win the world to Himself. Today on foreign frontiers we hear about modern-day miracles God performs to bring people who have never heard the gospel to faith in His Son. You and your generation can join God as He reaches out in mighty power to the unreached of your day.

5. God sends His people today to the place where He can best work through them to accomplish His mission.

Since Babel (see Gen. 11) the world has never been more of a global village than it is today. Migration from all over the world has integrated the peoples of the world. Disasters have dispersed refugees everywhere. Education has attracted

"God found fault with the people and said: 'The time is coming, declares the Lord, when I will make a new covenant with the house of Israel and with the house of Judah. It will not be like the covenant I made with their forefathers when I took them by the hand to lead them out of Egypt, because they did not remain faithful to my covenant, and I turned away from them, declares the Lord. This is the covenant I will make with the house of Israel after that time, declares the Lord. I will put my laws in their minds and write them on their hearts. I will be their God, and they will be my people. No longer will a man teach his neighbor, or a man his brother, saying, "Know the Lord," because they will all know me, from the least of them to the greatest. For I will forgive their wickedness and will remember their sins no more' " (Heb. 8:8-12).

scholars from all over the world to the centers of learning. World economics has caused all nations to emphasize learning English as a second language. Business people travel by the millions to other countries. Why has globalization occurred at this time in history?

Do you think it is possible that God is doing a special work to send us to the nations and the nations to us in order to get the gospel to all people in our day?   ☐ Yes ☐ No

What do you think God is doing in your life and in your church to send you to the place where He can best work through you to accomplish His mission?

—— DAY 5 ——

JESUS, THE ONLY WAY

"What I received I passed on to you as of first importance: that Christ died for our sins according to the Scriptures, that he was buried, that he was raised on the third day according to the Scriptures" (1 Cor. 15:3-4).

From eternity Jesus invaded time. What He did in time affected eternity. He established the gospel. What are the facts of the gospel?

Read 1 Corinthians 15:3-4 in the margin. List three facts of the gospel that the passage mentions.

1. _____

2. _____

3. _____

Paul says the facts of the gospel are that Jesus died, was buried, and rose from the dead. One other fact implied is the incarnation of Christ. When you look at the eternal results of Christ's life, focus on His incarnation, crucifixion, and resurrection. Each of these must be believed and acted on for salvation. These facts make Jesus unique in all history. Each makes Jesus the only way to God. No other religion can claim that its leader came, died, and rose from the dead for the world's sins. " 'There is no other name under heaven given to men by which we must be saved' " (Acts 4:11-12). Today we will explore the meaning of God's glory being manifest explicitly through Christ's incarnation, crucifixion, and resurrection for God's mission.

The Incarnation
To the Muslim, it is absurd to think the transcendent, all-powerful God would limit Himself to become a human being. To the Hindu, the distinctiveness of the incarnation as a once-for-all coming of an only true God into history is preposterous. To the Buddhist, to even exist is evil. He cannot imagine God becoming a person and living in the world. To the animist, if God is believed in at all, He is far removed from the earth and pays little attention to people and their plight.

No wonder Jesus is the stumbling block to those who will not accept Him as God's revelation. Only God could think up the incarnation. Religions of human invention exalt people to god status; only the Bible teaches that God became a person. No person's life is complete until he or she has a real-life encounter with the God who invaded history. Christians can't rest until all persons know that God visited earth to bring them into a right relationship with their Creator and experience God's glory in person.

Answer the following questions about the incarnation.

Do you believe that the Word became flesh and dwelt with us? ❑ yes ❑ no

If so, what does this mean to you personally? _____

_____

_____

How does Christ's incarnation obligate you to those who don't know about it or have not experienced it in the new birth?

_____

_____

_____

"But made himself nothing, taking the very nature of a servant, being made in human likeness" (Phil. 2:7).

In Philippians 2:7 (in the margin) the Greek word for "made himself nothing" (*kenoo*) means simply *to empty, to make void or of no effect.* To be in God's form means that Jesus was no less God when He took human form. To be in human likeness means that He was no less human because He was God in the flesh. Jesus was not half God and half human but fully God and fully human.

We focus on the divine signs of God's glory in Jesus' birth and forget the humanness of it. Often we fail to realize that Jesus was born in a stable to a woman who conceived before she was married. Perhaps God reassured her, "He is in your lap, Mary, as much as He is in heaven." How overwhelming the thought that the God who created all the universe limited himself to a human form, some 18 inches long and weighing approximately 7 pounds! No wonder other religions find believing the incarnation so difficult!

In using the metaphor "he emptied himself," the Bible expresses the completeness of Christ's self-renunciation. Scholars debate what it meant for Christ to empty Himself. Nevertheless, you cannot ignore New Testament evidence that Jesus laid aside His advantages as God to face life as you do. His identification with you is complete.

Jesus had to grow in wisdom and in physical stature (see Luke 2:52). He had to learn obedience (see Heb. 5:8). He knew actual hunger and thirst. He experienced the emotions of anger and compassion; He endured pain. He had to live by faith that He was the Son of God and constantly retreat to the place of prayer to receive the Father's knowledge and wisdom. Yes, Jesus was really human.

To be in human likeness means that He was no less human because He was God in the flesh.

Check the following items that help you identify with Christ.
- ☐ He had to learn obedience.
- ☐ He got angry.
- ☐ He was hungry.
- ☐ He experienced pain.
- ☐ He was thirsty.
- ☐ He lived by faith and prayer.
- ☐ He got tired.

A graphic picture of His servant role occurred when Jesus washed His disciples' feet.

Almost as startling as the incarnation was the fact that Jesus became a servant. A graphic picture of His servant role occurred when Jesus washed His disciples' feet. God, who became a person, stooped to serve people so that we might catch the vision of serving. Jesus experienced and reflected God's glory.

The Crucifixion

The self-emptying of Christ culminated with Gethsemane and Golgotha. Philippians 2:8 in the margin moves directly from Christ's incarnation to His crucifixion. Jesus was the Suffering Servant and fulfilled Isaiah's divine prophecy. The cross was unavoidable.

"Being found in appearance as a man, he humbled himself and became obedient to death—even death on a cross!" (Phil. 2:8).

The crucifixion did not catch the Father or the Son by surprise. God did not have to change His plans suddenly. Jesus, the Lamb of God, was slain before the foundation of the world (see Rev. 13:8). Since He came to earth for that purpose, He resolutely and purposefully directed His steps toward Calvary.

In Gethsemane as the horror of death pressed on Jesus, the Father was His only resource. He enlisted Peter, James, and John to pray for Him, but they slept and left Him to face it alone. The battle of Gethsemane raged. Jesus wanted only to please the Father, but He sought a way to do it other than having to bear the sin of humankind and face death for every person. No wonder He spoke the words of Matthew 26:38, in the margin. The raging battle during the wilderness temptation reached fever pitch. Satan assaulted Jesus' humanity to tempt Him to shrink from His impending sacrifice. Jesus' human and divine nature seemed to clash. See Luke 22:44 in the margin.

"He said to them, 'My soul is overwhelmed with sorrow to the point of death. Stay here and keep watch with me' " (Matt. 26:38).

Jesus was not role-playing. The battle was real. Yet Jesus completely surrendered to the Father's will. Jesus' will, always submissive to the Father's, overcame both the physical reality and satanic presence when He uttered, " 'Father, if you are willing, take this cup from me; yet not my will, but yours be done' " (Luke 22:42). At that moment Jesus won the war of the ages! He arose with a confidence that never wavered in the face of soldiers, suffering, and death. For Him, to know the Father's will was to do it.

"Being in anguish he prayed more earnestly, and his sweat was like drops of blood falling to the ground" (Luke 22:44).

Jesus' death was an act of atonement, which in the Old Testament meant the covering of sin through God's own provision. On this basis Jesus reconciled people to God (see 2 Cor. 5:14—6:2). By His death Jesus satisfied the Father, subdued Satan, and reconciled people to God. Forgiveness was made available to those who believe in Christ as Savior on the basis of His sacrifice.

Complete the following sentences by using a synonym for the words used in the preceding paragraph.

Jesus' death _____ the Father.

Jesus' death _____ Satan.

Jesus' death_____ humanity.

Since Christ died for the world, every person has a right to choose salvation. People may choose not to respond to Christ's offer, but if they are not given a chance to respond, we have robbed them of the opportunity Christ died to give them.

People are lost for only two reasons: first, they have never adequately heard the message of salvation, or second, they have rejected God's offer of reconciliation in Christ.

Complete the following.
What can you do about the first reason—that they haven't heard?

_____

_____

What can you do about the second reason—that they reject Him?

_____

_____

You can't affect the second reason, but you are obliged to eliminate the first. After Satan failed to eliminate Christ, he tried to falsely convince people that Christ's redemptive acts are unnecessary for salvation. Satan says other ways to be saved exist outside of Christ.

What a paradox! Just at the time we try to take the gospel to everyone, Satan's philosophy now adopted by the post-modern world has permeated the life-stream of the church and sapped our spiritual strength. Thought patterns growing out of universalism, humanism, and secularism have robbed many Christians of the verve and audacity to proclaim Jesus Christ as Savior and Lord to every person. People daily hear this insidious, worldly philosophy in these expressions.

Write your answer to the following arguments based on universalism.

1. "Other peoples have their own religions; leave them alone."

_____

_____

_____

2. "Be tolerant of others and not so bigoted that you tell them that they are wrong if they don't accept Christ as the only way to God."

_____

_____

_____

3. "We haven't done so well ourselves; we should clean up our own back doorstep before we go to other nations to tell them how to live."

_____

_____

_____

Be prepared to share your answers with your group members.

Focus on the following statements and pray about their meaning to you.
- Our task as priests is not to offer a sacrifice for sin but to proclaim the sacrifice Jesus has made.
- Our priestly role is to make the cross real to people at the crossroads of their lives.
- When we cease to believe that Jesus is the only way of salvation, we disqualify ourselves to be on mission with God.

The Resurrection

Had Jesus stayed in the grave, the incarnation and the crucifixion would have been a dead-end street for God's mission. Without prophecy and Jesus' own predictions, Satan might have appeared to have won the battle. But God's counteroffensive, the resurrection, gained the victory.

Jesus' physical, bodily resurrection firmly established God's invasion of history. The empty tomb and His appearances to the believers authenticated it. Jesus actually ate, was touched by, and transformed believers. Jesus' resurrected body was more than His physical body. God's glory shone through Him. He walked through locked doors, disappeared, and appeared at will, but He was the same Jesus the disciples had seen, heard, and felt.

When Jesus emerged from the tomb, a new age dawned on the world! Humanity had a new King! Jesus revealed through the resurrection that He had gained all authority in heaven and earth (see Matt. 28:18). He ruled over sin, death, and every created power. He had reconciled the world to God (see 2 Cor. 5:18-19; Col. 1:20).

Jesus' resurrection proved that Satan's evil forces had been conquered. In His death and resurrection Jesus, "having disarmed the powers and authorities, … made a public spectacle of them, triumphing over them by the cross" (see Col. 2:15). The decisive battle has been won over Satan. Satan may continue to defeat Christians and to retard kingdom progress, but the outcome is no longer in doubt.

The greatest creative act of all time was the resurrection of Jesus. Its power is manifested most clearly for us in the new birth (see 2 Cor. 5:17). The resurrection revealed the nature of God. His love, power, presence, and purpose took on added meaning.

The resurrection became the touchstone of gospel proclamation. Before the resurrection the gospel was not preached to the nations. The good news had not all come to pass. The resurrection brought new meaning and glory to the incarnation and death of Christ. Now the whole gospel could be preached and was preached by the first-century Christians. It revealed that God had brought salvation to people in Jesus Christ. The resurrection ushered in the last days. We live between the resurrection and the return of Christ. During these times the gospel is to be preached to all nations (see Matt. 24:14 in the margin).

The resurrection cut across all national and racial lines to present us with a universal, spiritual, omnipotent, and omnipresent Christ. No wonder your memory verse for this week says, "We have seen his glory, the glory of the One and Only, who came from the Father, full of grace and truth" (John 1:14).

" 'This gospel of the kingdom will be preached in the whole world as a testimony to all nations, and then the end will come' " (Matt. 24:14).

People of all nations identify with Him and claim Him as their own. Christ's resurrection demands worldwide proclamation that "Jesus is Lord!"

Go back to page 111 and circle each "all" in Matthew 28:18-20, in the margin. Ask God to help you obey all He commanded.

In your own words write the way God manifested His glory in Christ and what you think you should do about it as you join God on mission. Be prepared to discuss your answer in the group session.

_____

_____

_____

Women on Mission

MARY
ON MISSION WITH GOD

Your role in God's mission may take you down a lonely, puzzling path that causes you to feel that others misunderstand you and that yields profound heartache for you. If so, you are in good company. Mary, the mother of Christ, was on mission in this manner. Yet God did more through her than she could have ever imagined, and all humankind has benefited from her obedience. The Son she bore is the Savior of the world! Sometimes your role in God's mission, like Mary's, may be to parent one who will make a greater contribution on mission with God than you will. Obviously, that child could not be on mission without you! Are you playing the role God has in mind for you?

1. God chooses to involve you in His mission to reconcile the world to Himself.

For centuries young Jewish virgins hoped they would be selected to be the mother of the Messiah. What a surprise it was for Mary to discover that God had chosen her to bear His Son! What if God has chosen you to give birth to and/or rear one of His choice servants? Suzanne Wesley faithfully prayed one hour each day, not knowing that her 24th and 25th children would be John and Charles Wesley, who would play a significant part in the Great Awakening and who would start the Methodist church! Your first reaction may be to shrink back when you realize all it means to respond to God's call, whatever that call may be. Mary was greatly troubled when the angel said to her, " 'Greetings, you who are highly favored! The Lord is with you' " (Luke 1:28). But she was willing to accept the role for which she was chosen. Are you?   ☐ **Yes** ☐ **No**

2. God calls you to Himself so that you can be on mission with Him.

Even when you realize that God has chosen you for a vital part in His mission, you may tend to say, as Mary did, " 'How will this be?' " (Luke 1:34). No matter what the question is, your answer to God's assignment for you can be the same as Mary's: " 'May it be to me as you have said' " (Luke 1:36). Accept God's call to be on mission with Him. Are you willing for God to do whatever He wants when He calls you?   ☐ **Yes** ☐ **No**

3. God initiates a covenant of promise and obedience with you in order to accomplish his mission.

When God calls you, He promises to bless you if you will obey Him. God promised Mary that her child would be called the Son of God. There was only one mother of the Messiah, but God commits to all parents, "Train a child in the way he should go, and when he is old he will not turn from it" (Prov. 22:6).

All God's promises have an "if" and a "then" or "when." The promises depend on your obeying His commands. You may experience a test of faith because your child is not walking in the way you taught him or her. If you did your part, will you still believe God's promise? Time may be required, but when he or she is old, the child will fulfill what God promised. The question is not whether God will fulfill His promise to you but whether you will obey and believe. Will you?

Write your commitment below.

_____

_____

_____

4. God prepares and equips you to be on mission with Him.

God has unusual ways to prepare people to be on mission with Him. Mary had to face the stigma of being an unwed mother or being accused of being unfaithful to the man to whom she was engaged. Joseph was ready to divorce her when God sent a dream to him to confirm what He had said to Mary. God sent her to visit her cousin, Elizabeth, three months later. If she had any doubts during those three months, Elizabeth's words answered those doubts. "When Elizabeth heard Mary's greeting, the baby leaped in her womb, and Elizabeth was filled with the Holy Spirit. In a loud voice she exclaimed: 'Why am I so favored, that the mother of my Lord should come to me? As soon as the sound of your greeting reached my ears, the baby in my womb leaped for joy. Blessed is she who has believed that what the Lord has said to her will be accomplished'" (Luke 1:40-45). Through Elizabeth's words Mary saw that what God promised her was being fulfilled. God even prepared her as "Mary treasured up all these things and pondered them in her heart" (Luke 2:19). Later, He prepared her with Simeon's words "Then Simeon blessed them and said to Mary, his mother: 'This child is destined to cause the falling and rising of many in Israel, and to be a sign that will be spoken against, so that the thoughts of many hearts will be revealed. And a sword will pierce your own soul too'" (Luke 2:34-35). Mary was warned of the cost. Are you willing to go through the difficult times for God to prepare you for the fulfilling of His mission?   ☐ **Yes** ☐ **No** ☐ **Not Yet**

5. God sends you where He can best work through you to accomplish His mission.

Mary must have had difficulty traveling from Nazareth to Bethlehem to have her son born soon after she arrived. It wasn't easy a few months later when the angel told Mary and Joseph to flee to Egypt, away from their homeland, so that Herod wouldn't kill Jesus. She easily could have said, "I'm ready to go back to Nazareth. I'll take my chances there." But she realized that she must go where God sent her because that was where He could best work through her to accomplish His mission. Perhaps you sense that God is calling you to go to a place you had rather not go. Will you go, trusting that He knows best?   ☐ **Yes** ☐ **No**

6. *God guides you step-by-step on His mission to glorify Him among all peoples.*

Sometimes Mary had difficulty knowing how to respond to what happened to her and to her Son. Her other children did not believe that Jesus was the Messiah, and her neighbors tried to kill Him. Once when she and Jesus' half-brothers went to take Jesus home with them because people were saying He was demon-possessed, Jesus even refused to see them and said, " 'Who is my mother, and who are my brothers?' " Pointing to his disciples, he said, 'Here are my mother and my brothers. For whoever does the will of my Father in heaven is my brother and sister and mother' " (Matt. 12:48-50). No matter how hurtful this was to Mary, she stayed faithful and did the will of the Father. Are you questioning God because of what is happening to you? Don't! Follow God and His leading to the end of the trail. You will see that you were on mission with God even when you felt ignored and mistreated. What is God guiding you to do now? Just do it.

7. *God uses you to fulfill His mission for your lifetime.*

Mary might have questioned whether Jesus was fulfilling the Father's mission when He was being tried and crucified. She remembered that Jesus, more than 20 years earlier, had told her in this same city, " 'Why did you seek Me? Did you not know that I must be about My Father's business?' " (Luke 2:49, NKJV). Mary lived to see her son stay on mission with the Father through the crucifixion and resurrection. As Jesus was dying on the cross, He expended His waning strength to tell John to care for His mother, who was at the foot of the cross, and to tell her to look to John as her son. After Jesus ascended to heaven, "They all joined together constantly in prayer, along with the women and Mary the mother of Jesus, and with his brothers" (Acts 1:14). Mary heard Jesus say, " 'It is finished' " on the cross and lived to see Him do His continuing work through His disciples in the first church. What joy she must have experienced as she told Luke all the things she had pondered in her heart when he wrote the Gospel of Luke and the Acts of the Apostles. Stay true to God and His mission for you (and your children) even to death. See God do more than you can ever imagine because you joined Him on mission. Are you on mission with God?   ☐ **Yes** ☐ **No**

PETER

ON MISSION WITH GOD: A CHURCH FOR ALL PEOPLES

This Week's Lessons

Day 1: God's Invitation
Day 2: Your Life from God's Perspective
Day 3: God Prepares You When He Calls You
Day 4: Influencing God's People
Day 5: God Fulfills His Purpose Through His People

This Week's Learning Focus

You will be able to explain how the Holy Spirit awakened and empowered the church to be a witnessing community of faith for all peoples.

Heart Focus

" 'I tell you that you are Peter, and on this rock I will build my church; and the gates of Hades will not overcome it. I will give you the keys of the kingdom of heaven; whatever you bind on earth will be bound in heaven, and whatsoever you loose on earth will be loosed in heaven' " (Matt. 16:18-19).

DAY 1

GOD'S INVITATION

When Communism fell in 1989, pastor Gary Hillyard and a few of his members in a small, Seattle, Washington, church began praying daily for God to work in their midst. One Sunday they set aside regular services to involve the whole church in a day of prayer. About 2:00 p.m. the pastor met a man at the door who said, "I'm a Baptist from the Ukraine. Can I worship with you here?" He brought other Ukrainians to church. One of them said, "A family who is emigrating from Luganz, Ukraine, owns a six-room house there that we want to give you for mission work."

Gary responded, "What can I do with a six-room house in the Ukraine?" He offered the house to his denomination's state convention and their mission boards, but they said they were not the answer to his prayer.

Gary had studied *Experiencing God*, so he called Henry Blackaby and asked, "What can I do with a six-room house in the Ukraine?" Henry replied, "Your question should be 'What can God do with a six-room house in the Ukraine?' Your church can be a world mission-strategy center. Ask God what to do."

Soon afterward Don English, a former schoolmate of Gary's, called to say, "Gary, I believe I've been called to go to the former Soviet Union." They prayed and talked together. Once again, Gary called Henry Blackaby and asked, "What do I do now? Our church can't support a missionary." Henry asked, "Have you asked the people to give?" Gary said, "No, we are just a little church with fewer than one hundred members. We are poor people. We can't send a missionary." Henry said, "Why don't you pray and then ask them to give what they can?"

The church prayed, and Gary invited people to leave money at the front to send the Englishes as missionaries. They got enough for a one-way ticket for the Englishes to go to the Ukraine. Don rented a theater. In a week more than two thousand people had come to Christ. Over time they were given a school, a camp, and land for a radio station that TransWorld Radio was able to use. Finally, Gary Hillyard, the pastor, resigned from his church in Washington and went to the Ukraine, where he began to help take care of new Christians. What can a little church of one hundred people do to influence the world? Whatever God can do! He wants to manifest His purpose and glory through every church.

How do you think Henry's statement "Your church can be a world mission-strategy center" applies to your church?

_____

_____

Perhaps you identify with Peter, too.

More people identify with Peter than with most of the other characters of the Bible. They say, "You know, I feel like this guy." Perhaps you identify with Peter, too. This rugged fisherman couldn't have had any idea of what the Lord had in mind when He first saw him. All his life was spent on the lake. His salty language probably matched his occupation!

1. God is always at work around you, whether or not you see Him.

Peter may not have realized all God was doing around him, but he was a seeker of truth. You first meet his brother, Andrew, a disciple of John the Baptist. When John said, " 'Look, the Lamb of God!' " (John 1:29), Andrew and another of John's disciples immediately followed Jesus. They asked, " 'Where are you staying?' " (John 1:38). Jesus invited them to spend the day with Him. After this exhilarating encounter Andrew was so excited that he located his brother, Peter, and said, " 'We have found the Messiah!' " (John 1:41). He introduced him to Jesus, but Peter didn't respond immediately. Jesus nicknamed him Cephas, the rock, but he was anything but a rock. He was more like sand. God knew what He would do with Peter's life, but Peter had no idea (see John 1:35-42).

What mission does God have in mind for you? He knows what it is. You may still not know what that is, or you may already be on that mission. Your mission is to be in the middle of God's mission. God's mission is like a great river. Your life is like a small boat that bobs on its surface. You launch your boat on His mission at a certain point, and eventually, you will disembark on the other shore. The kingdom will flow on like a river. You will either be caught up in God's mission, or you will fight the current, get caught in the backwater, or get drawn into a whirlpool. God is on mission. He wants to do His mission through you. God works with you as He worked with Peter.

God is on mission. He wants to do His mission through you.

Answer the following questions about your relationship with Christ.

Who first brought you to Jesus? _____

How did you first respond to Him?

_____

What did you think God wanted to do with your life?

_____

How has your concept of God's will for you grown since then?

_____

2. God pursues a continuing love relationship with you that is real and personal.

Peter next encountered the Savior in Capernaum. We don't know what happened between the time of Peter's first meeting with Jesus in Judea and this one. God was always at work around Peter. Jesus went to Peter's home, healed Peter's mother-in-law of a high fever, and then healed others (Luke 4:38-44). The next morning Jesus was praying in a solitary place when the disciples found Him. They said, "Hey, Jesus, guess what? Everybody is looking for You. Don't worry about setting up Your kingdom. The people are ready now." At least they suspected that He was the Messiah from God.

If you and I had been in Jesus' place, we would have responded positively to their appeal. But Jesus had been talking to the Father and said, " 'I must preach the good news of the kingdom of God to the other towns also, because that is why I was sent' " (Luke 4:43). In effect He said, "I must do that which is against human nature and do what My Father wants Me to do." Jesus demonstrated God's purpose through His obedience to preach to those who had not heard.

> *Jesus demonstrated God's purpose through His obedience to preach to those who had not heard.*

Evaluate a situation you now face. What do you think the Lord wants you to do? Do others advise you without considering how God is working around you and in your life?

_____

_____

3. God invites you to become involved with Him in His work.

After Jesus followed His Father's plan to keep preaching in the Judean synagogues, He taught the crowds by the Lake of Gennesaret, or Galilee (see Luke 5:1-11). Mobbed by people, He looked around and found a couple of fishing boats. Selecting Peter's boat was no accident. Jesus chose his boat to involve him in His mission! I wonder how Peter felt about that, since he was probably tired

Whether or not you recognize or expect it, God has a plan and a purpose for you.

from fishing all night. Jesus got in the boat with Peter and taught the multitude while Peter eavesdropped.

God wants to get into your boat. Whether or not you recognize or expect it, God has a plan and a purpose for you. He is at work where you work.

Do you believe that God is at work where you work? ☐ Yes ☐ No

What is God doing where you work? _____

_____

What do you think God is inviting you to do with Him at your work place?

_____

_____

Any revelation of God is His invitation for you to join Him on mission.

4. God speaks to you personally.

When Jesus finished addressing the multitude, He zeroed in on Peter right where Peter lived. He said, " 'Put out into deep water, and let down the nets for a catch' " (Luke 5:4). Peter respectfully addressed Jesus as Master but proceeded to give Him the experienced fisherman's point of view! Peter was probably tired and discouraged after working hard all night and not catching anything. He may have wanted to rest. But when he heard an authoritative voice from God, he obeyed.

Daily you face that choice: to listen or or not to listen. You may think you know what your job is—even in kingdom work—and may consider yourself an expert at what you do. Like Peter, you may have toiled diligently at a project, only to be discouraged. In such times listen for God's voice and avoid citing reasons for your failure. God is all-knowing and has the answer for every dilemma you face.

Recall the last thing God told you to do. Describe it below.

_____

_____

Write your response to His word to date.

_____

_____

5. God's invitation to be on mission for Him will lead you to a crisis of belief that requires faith and action. Your faith is a platform from which He will demonstrate His glory.

Peter protested, " 'Master, we've worked hard all night and haven't caught anything.' " What would you expect Peter to say next? Surprisingly, he added, " 'But because you say so, I will let down the nets' " (Luke 5:5). So often we say, "I have been doing this for so long. Nothing is going to happen." Or "I have tried to lead people to Christ. I have tried to live as a witness in my workplace or neighborhood. Why do it one more time?" The truth is, God still speaks. God still reveals His purposes.

> **Read John 16:12-15 in the margin. Explain the way the Holy Spirit brings glory to Jesus in our lives.**

_____

_____

God is in the business of saying what He will do in the future. God speaks to His servants—to get them to the place He wants them to be (see Amos 3:5-7). What you do next shows how much you really believe God. Peter obeyed because he believed!

I don't know how you feel about getting a word from God. In my own experience at every critical point in my life God led me by His word. Often I wasn't ready to receive that word. Often it was a difficult word. At times it was such a good word that I couldn't imagine what He said would happen. But God speaks in this manner and confirms it by the Holy Spirit. The result? God is glorified.

Peter obeyed. They caught so many fish that their newly mended nets began to break. They called their partners, "Come and help us!" When you believe and act on what God tells you to do, He will surprise you.

> **Read Ephesians 3:20 in the margin. Ask God to show you what He wants you to believe He will do in your life.**

6. You must make major adjustments in your life to join God in what He is doing.

When Peter realized what Jesus had done, he cried, " 'Go away from me, Lord; I am a sinful man!' " (Luke 5:8). Why did he say he was sinful? I think he said it because he had not really believed Jesus at first. Peter repented and admitted his sin. Jesus went a step further and added a challenge to his comforting words: " 'Don't be afraid; from now on you will catch men' " (Luke 5:10). That would involve a major adjustment in this fisherman's life!

God always gets involved in your life and in your work to get you involved in His work. You may think that a special blessing just for you when God intends it to go beyond you. Peter was learning that lesson as He obeyed and experienced God in this situation.

" 'I have much more to say to you, more than you can now bear. But when he, the Spirit of truth, comes, he will guide you into all truth. He will not speak on his own; he will speak only what he hears, and he will tell you what is yet to come. He will bring glory to me by taking from what is mine and making it known to you. All that belongs to the Father is mine. That is why I said the Spirit will take from what is mine and make it known to you. In a little while you will see me no more, and then after a little while you will see me' " (John 16:12-15).

"Now to him who is able to do immeasurably more than all we ask or imagine, according to his power that is at work within us, to him be glory in the church and in Christ Jesus throughout all generations, for ever and ever! Amen" (Eph. 3:20).

What major adjustment is God asking you to make to join Him?

_____

_____

_____

Study your memory verse phrase by phrase. Think about how your challenge would have affected Peter. Then fill in the blanks.

" 'I tell you that you are _____, and on this _____ I will

build my _____; and the gates of Hades will not _____

it. I will give you the _____ of the kingdom of _____;

whatever you _____ on earth will be _____ in heaven, and

whatever you _____ on earth will be _____ in heaven.' "

7. *You experience God's glory as you obey Him and He accomplishes His work through you.*

You see proof of Peter's life-changing encounter with Jesus in his words and actions. He could have just gone home after this experience, told his wife and mother-in-law what a great time he had with Jesus, and settled down to his daily routine. Or he could have asked Jesus to be his partner in his fishing business.

But faith without obedience is dead. The Lord got through to Peter with an analogy he understood. Jesus promised that Peter would catch many men, just as he had caught fish. The lesson was not lost on Peter and his friends (see Luke 5:11 in the margin). This was a costly decision, but they agreed to leave all to experience an intimate relationship with Christ. Thus, Peter and his partners went on mission with God and allowed Him to accomplish His work through them!

If you were to obey Christ fully what would you do now?

_____

_____

_____

"They pulled their boats up on shore, left everything and followed him" (Luke 5:11).

DAY 2

YOUR LIFETIME FROM GOD'S PERSPECTIVE

You have looked at early episodes in the life of Peter—when Jesus changed his name from Simon to Cephas (the Aramaic term for *rock*). Later, Jesus referred to him as Peter (the Greek term for *rock*). At that point Peter was anything but a rock. Jesus knew what He had chosen Peter to be and with this name gave him a hint of his mission. Look at Peter's life from God's perspective.

1. God chooses you.

God chose Peter before Jesus ever came to earth, but Peter had numerous faults—perhaps the worst being impulsiveness. This habit often got him into trouble. Even after following Jesus for a year and a half and uttering God-revealed, earthshaking revelations, he messed up.

> **Read Matthew 16:13-23 in your Bible. In the margin are some statements between Christ and Peter. Match them with the correct descriptions below.**
> _____ 1. Peter's answer to Jesus' question
> _____ 2. The source of Peter's answer
> _____ 3. The first name Jesus called Peter
> _____ 4. The second name Jesus called him
> _____ 5. Peter's response to Jesus's revelation that He would be killed and rise from the dead

a. " 'Never, Lord, this will never happen to you.' "

b. " 'You are the Christ, the Son of the living God.' "

c. " 'This was not revealed to you by man but by my Father.' "

d. " 'You are Peter and on this rock I will build my church.' "

e. " 'Get behind me, Satan.' "

God chose you knowing that you are not perfect. Peter exemplified that fact on this occasion. At one moment He was a mouthpiece for God; the next, He spoke Satan's words. The correct order of answers in the previous exercise is *b, c, d, e, a*. Imagine a human being rebuking the Son of God! He was so proud of the revelation that God had just given him that he thought he knew it all. Have you ever done the same thing by saying, "No, Lord" or "Never, Lord" or "Later, Lord" when He asks you to join Him on mission? God has great plans for you—just as He had great things in mind for Peter in spite of his weaknesses.

> **Check the answer you would give Jesus at this moment if He were to say to you, "Follow Me, and I will use you to bring glory to God."**
> ☐ "No, Lord."   ☐ "Never, Lord."   ☐ "Yes, Lord."
> ☐ "Later, Lord."   ☐ "I'll think about it."   ☐ "I could never do that."

2. God calls you to Himself to be on mission with Him.

Peter's call was very clear. He was one of the first Jesus called to be a disciple. Later, he would be called out and commissioned as an apostle. Peter's name is at the head of every list of the twelve Jesus called to be on mission with Him!

"As Jesus walked beside the Sea of Galilee, he saw Simon and his brother Andrew casting a net into the lake, for they were fishermen. 'Come, follow me,' Jesus said, 'and I will make you fishers of men.' At once they left their nets and followed him. When he had gone a little farther, he saw James son of Zebedee and his brother John in a boat, preparing their nets. Without delay he called them, and they left their father Zebedee in the boat with the hired men and followed him" (Mark 1:16-20).

"Jesus went up on a mountainside and called to him those he wanted, and they came to him. He appointed twelve — designating them apostles — that they might be with him and that he might send them out to preach and to have authority to drive out demons. These are the twelve he appointed: Simon (to whom he gave the name Peter); James son of Zebedee and his brother John (to them he gave the name Boanerges, which means Sons of Thunder); Andrew, Philip, Bartholemew, Matthew, Thomas, James son of Alphaeus, Thaddaeus, Simon the Zealot and Judas Iscariot, who betrayed him" (Mark 3:13-19).

Compare the two calls Jesus gave to Peter. The first, in Mark 1:16-20, was to follow Him as a disciple. The second, in Mark 3:13-19, was to follow and to be sent out as an apostle, meaning *sent one*. Compare the two passages in the margin and fill in the blanks.

Mark 1:16-20

1. Jesus walked by the Sea of _____.

2. Jesus called _____ disciples to follow Him.

3. Simon and Andrew left their nets _____ to follow _____.

4. James and John left their _____ to follow Him.

Mark 3:13-19

1. Jesus went up a _____.

2. Jesus appointed _____ apostles to be with Him.

3. He called them to be with _____.

4. Jesus sent them out to _____.

In the first call Jesus walked beside the Sea of Galilee, and in the second He called His apostles from a mountain. The first calling was to four disciples, but the second included all twelve. The first time, they left their nets to follow Him, and the second, to be with Him. The first time they left their occupation, and the second time they took up His mission to preach and to cast out demons. Note that Jesus called all of His disciples and apostles first to be with Him. Their intimate relationship with the Son of God would be the wellspring from which their ministry flowed to bless others—the key to their being on mission with Him, as they were sent out as apostles to preach with His authority.

Today God calls you to Himself so that you can walk intimately with Him. Your mission may be in your neighborhood or in the inner city. It may involve leaving behind your occupation or family. Whatever He asks you to do will result in your being appointed and anointed to join Him on an exciting kingdom mission that results in your experiencing God's glory!

3. God initiates a covenant of promise and obedience with you.

The Lord made a covenant with Peter. He said, "Follow me, and I will make you a fisher of men. I promise you, Peter, it's going to be better than what you just saw when the nets were breaking. You will fish for men." Jesus saw the day when Peter would cast the net with one sermon and see three thousand people come into the kingdom! Peter couldn't see that yet.

What does God have in mind for you that you haven't believed yet? You may say, "I'm sinful, God; You know that. I don't have great faith. I can't do things others can do." Peter was like that. But Jesus promises, "You follow Me, and I will make you a fisher of men." That word of promise from God demands obedience.

Write a Scripture reference God has given you as a life verse, a verse for the year, or a verse for a particular situation.

_____

The first word I remember God's giving me was Matthew 6:33 (in the margin). The second word He gave me, Psalm 71:17-18 (also in the margin), was even more of a challenge to me. From my youth I had declared His marvelous deeds. I could not imagine what it meant for me to declare His power to the next generation and His might to all who would come. For 25 years I didn't share that verse with anyone because it sounded both frightening and presumptuous. However, I truly believed that God had given me this promise because the Holy Spirit had so impressed it on my heart. I decided to apply this verse to my life and see what God would do. I now see how God is fulfilling His promise to me through my writing *MasterLife* and other books, my ministry in Indonesia and America, and now my work all over the world with the International Mission Board. Repeatedly, God has reminded me of this promise or challenged me with a word that said, "This is what I will do through you, an ordinary person, for my glory."

Have a vision for your life. View the term *vision* differently than the business world does. In business terms that word means "Dream as big as you can and go for it." But Peter saw that visions from God involve three things:

A. Life visions must be God-revealed, not humanly conceived.
If you thought it up, it might not be from God. Through His Word, prayer, circumstances, and other Christians' counsel, God helps you understand His vision for your life. He may not tell you everything now. He gives you enough insight to respond with the next step.

B. Life visions from God are so big that you cannot accomplish them yourself.
If you can accomplish them yourself, then they are probably not from God. God wants to give you a vision that will make you depend on Him for its accomplishment so that He is glorified.

C. Visions that come from God are life-arrangers.
When your priorities are arranged correctly, other decisions become easier. As a Christian youth I committed, "God, I want to keep myself pure for my future wife." A friend responded, "That sounds stupid." But that commitment helped me say no when faced with tough decisions. Because I had committed this to God, the other decisions became easier. When you make the right commitments, you narrow your focus to concentrate on what God really wants to do in your life. Be alert for a life vision from God as you read His Word.

What vision has God given you for your life?

_____

_____

" 'Seek first his kingdom and his righteousness, and all these things will be given to you as well' " (Matt. 6:33).

"Since my youth, O God, you have taught me, and to this day I declare your marvelous deeds. Even when I am old and gray, do not forsake me, O God, till I declare your power to the next generation, your might to all who are to come" (Ps. 71:17-18).

Be alert for a life vision from God as you read His Word.

DAY 3

GOD PREPARES YOU
WHEN HE CALLS YOU

Peter needed the Lord to prepare him for an entirely new mission in life. From fearful fisherman to fearless apostle was a long stretch for Peter. God knows how much preparation is required in your life to get you to the point that you are equipped to be an effective colaborer with Him.

4. God prepares you for His mission.

God will take you through a lot to develop your character to match your assignment.

"He said to them, 'This is what I told you while I was still with you: Everything must be fulfilled that is written about me in the Law of Moses, the Prophets and the Psalms.' Then he opened their minds so they could understand the Scriptures. He told them, 'This is what is written: The Christ will suffer and rise from the dead on the third day, and repentance and forgiveness of sins will be preached in his name to all nations, beginning at Jerusalem. You are witnesses of these things. I am going to send you what my Father has promised; but stay in the city until you have been clothed with power from on high' " (Luke 24:44-49).

The 3 years of preparation must have seemed like 30 to Peter. When you first commit to God's call, this often occurs. In your zeal you think, *I'm going out and win the world.* God will take you through a lot to develop your character to match your assignment. In the beginning you are not the kind of person God can use to give Him glory.

Remember the experience of the Seven you have studied so far. Abraham waited 25 years for the promise. Moses spent 40 years becoming the person to lead the children of Israel. David was probably just a teenager when he was anointed to be the king. During the next 10 years Saul hounded him, he was forced to hide in caves, and he was tempted to kill Saul. Meanwhile, he developed a heart for God. At least 10 years after he was anointed, he became the king. For Paul it was at least 13 years from the time he was called until the time that Barnabas came back to Tarsus to involve him in missionary work.

How many years has God been preparing you for your mission? _____

God has to build the character in you that makes you what He really calls you to be and to do. In this case *rock* was used to describe Peter. Much concrete was added to the sand to make Peter a rock. God mixed tough times with the good times to accomplish His will in Peter's life. Often you become more like God during the tough times than you do during the good times. He prepares you to make right choices and live according to His values.

Describe one difficult experience God has used to develop your character for His mission.

_____

_____

_____

_____

Christ took many corrective measures as He walked with Peter. After the resurrection one major event changed Peter and the other apostles' lives forever—the coming of the Holy Spirit at Pentecost.

Part of God's preparation involves empowering you for the work He has for you. Something dramatic happened to Peter between John 21 and Acts 1. After Christ gave the Great Commission and ascended to heaven, Peter joined 120 of Jesus' followers who were obediently waiting in the upper room. During 10 days of prayer God arranged and rearranged their thinking as they waited for the Holy Spirit to come. First, He grounded them in the Word (see Luke 24:44-49; Acts 1:15-22). Peter began to lead. Using the Scriptures, he led those present to replace Judas on the apostolic team. Before Pentecost you never hear the disciples quoting Scripture. After Pentecost they quoted Scripture in every message. Second, God prepared their hearts through prayer. As they prayed, God brought them to a great unity. Third, God prepared them to wait expectantly in faith for the Father's promise—the Holy Spirit.

What was to happen in the church first had to happen to Peter. He had to experience the power of God before he could demonstrate it. The Lord wants to empower His church. To do that, He empowers its members as individuals. Do you embody what God wants to do with the people with whom you associate—your family, your church, and your ministry team? Is your prayer "O God, make me the person You want me to be so that You can accomplish what You want through my life"?

Suddenly it happened—not only to Peter but also to all the apostles at Pentecost. They were all filled with the Holy Spirit. They would never be the same again. Peter was transformed from fearful to fearless, from faithless to faithful. Have you been filled and are you being filled daily with the Spirit? To be filled with His Spirit means a continual relationship with Him. Nothing else will suffice for the task to which He has called you!

Read Luke 24:44-49 in the margin on page 132. Ask yourself whether you are continually being filled with the Holy Spirit.

Read Ephesians 5:18 in the margin. Ask God to fill you and empower you for the work He has called you to do.

5. *God sends you to the place where He can best work through you to accomplish His mission.*

Peter was privileged to be at the hub of things with Jesus—one of three in His inner circle, along with James and John. The trio represented the only ones allowed to experience several life-changing situations.

Read the three sets of Scriptures in the margin. Below write the letter of the set of Scriptures that matches each of the following experiences.
____ 1. Being asked to pray during the Lord's agony in Gethsemane
____ 2. The raising from the dead of Jairus's daughter
____ 3. Christ's transfiguration

"Do not get drunk on wine, which leads to debauchery. Instead, be filled with the Spirit" (Eph. 5:18).

a. *"He did not let anyone follow him except Peter, James and John the brother of James" (Mark 5:37).*
"When he arrived at the house of Jairus, he did not let anyone go in with him except Peter, John and James, and the child's father and mother" (Luke 8:51).

b. *"After six days Jesus took with him Peter, James and John the brother of James, and led them up a high mountain by themselves. There he was transfigured before them. His face shone like the sun, and his clothes became as white as the light" (Matt. 17:1-2).*

c. *"He took Peter and the two sons of Zebedee along with him, and he began to be sorrowful and troubled" (Matt. 26:37).*
"He took Peter, James and John along with him, and he began to be deeply distressed and troubled" (Mark 14:33).

Write the appropriate letter that matches Jesus' revelation.
_____ 1. glory _____ 2. prayer life _____ 3. power

The Lord wanted these three disciples to experience His prayer life, His power, and His glory at close range so that they would remember these extraordinary events after He appointed them to lead the early church (see Gal. 2:9). Peter was also trained along with the other disciples through the special missions Christ sent them on during His earthly ministry. The correct order in the first exercise is *c, a, b*. The correct order in the second exercise is *b, c, a*.

Have you ever believed you have failed the Lord so badly that He would never send you on another mission? Even then, God does not give up on you. Peter fell terribly far when he denied his Lord three times. After this Peter must have believed that any ministry for him was over. But the Lord had not given up on Peter. He allowed him to be the first disciple to witness His resurrection from the dead (see Luke 24:34; 1 Cor. 15:5). Later, when Jesus met with Peter at the Sea of Galilee, He allowed Peter to affirm his love for Him three times to counter those three dreadful denials. Peter wasn't finished at all. Instead, Jesus wanted to send a humbled, repentant Peter to feed His sheep. The result of that conversation was that Peter was commanded to follow Him.

Getting things in the proper order when Jesus meets you is important. Read John 21 in your Bible. Number the following statements in proper sequence.
_____ 1. Peter jumped in the water and swam.
_____ 2. Jesus told Peter to follow Him.
_____ 3. Peter went fishing.
_____ 4. Jesus asked Peter if he loved Him.
_____ 5. Peter and the other disciples didn't catch any fish.
_____ 6. Peter climbed on board the boat and dragged the net ashore.
_____ 7. Peter and the other disciples caught a bunch of fish.
_____ 8. Jesus asked Peter to feed His sheep and lambs.

Note interesting similarities between Peter's initial call to follow Christ and this postresurrection encounter with the risen Lord. Jesus seems to want to give Peter a fresh start in all the areas where he had failed to live up to his "rock" potential. Today if you sense that you have failed the Lord, He wants to restore you to full fellowship with Himself. Then, like Peter, He can send you on a new assignment—to feed His lambs and tend His sheep and not just to catch fish. The correct order in the above exercise is *4, 8, 1, 6, 2, 5, 3, 7*.

6. God guides you on your mission with Him.

Would you like to have walked with Jesus when He was here on earth and experienced the glory of His physical presence? Peter was so privileged. Peter experienced God's glory many ways, and all of them dramatically changed his life. In 2 Peter 1:16-18 (in the margin) he gives an eyewitness account. For three years he experienced one-to-one, personal guidance from Jesus. After Christ's ascension Peter enjoyed the glory of the Holy Spirit's personal presence and guidance, sometimes under very trying circumstances. What an incredible

"We did not follow cleverly invented stories when we told you about the power and coming of our Lord Jesus Christ, but we were eyewitnesses of his majesty. For he received honor and glory from God the Father when the voice came to him from the Majestic Glory, saying, 'This is my Son, whom I love; with him I am well pleased.' We ourselves heard this voice that came from heaven when we were with him on the sacred mountain" (2 Pet. 1:16-18).

experience that must have been for Peter to experience God's glory in the personal guidance of these two members of the Godhead! In the margin (Luke 22:31) read Jesus' prayer for Peter before he denied Jesus. Even as Peter prepared to hit bottom, Christ foresaw the day when Peter would strengthen the church. Only through the Holy Spirit's power would Peter be so transformed that he could assume this leadership role.

" 'Simon, Simon, Satan has asked to sift you as wheat. But I have prayed for you, Simon, that your faith may not fail. And when you have turned back, strengthen your brothers' " (Luke 22:31).

Read Acts 3:1-10 in your Bible. Answer *T* (true) or *F* (false).

_____ 1. Peter and John were going to the temple to pray.
_____ 2. The man at the gate had been crippled in an accident.
_____ 3. Peter and John ignored the crippled beggar at first.
_____ 4. John said to the beggar, "Look at us."
_____ 5. Peter decided to give the beggar silver and gold.
_____ 6. The crippled man was healed through Peter's name.
_____ 7. He limped into the temple as his ankles gained strength.

In this fascinating incident Peter obviously tried to figure out what the Lord wanted him to do. As Peter intently looked at the crippled man, the Holy Spirit guided the next step. Peter commanded him, in Jesus' name, to walk! He was also led to take the man by the right hand and help him to his feet. When an astonished crowd gathered around, Peter realized that the Lord had given him a perfect platform for preaching the gospel. The next day, after spending the night in jail for this act of mercy, Peter was filled with the Holy Spirit and spoke powerful words before the rulers, elders, and teachers of the law. In the previous exercise only the first statement is true.

If you've ever been in a situation as Peter was, you will appreciate how helpless he would have felt without the Lord's guidance. Having experienced his own limitations, now he totally depended on God. He became transformed as he went on mission with God and allowed the Lord to work through him.

7. God uses you to bring glory to His name through His mission.

Everyone remembers Peter's failures, but in history he is known for his role at Pentecost and for leading the first church. You cannot start a spiritual awakening, nor can you start a Church Planting Movement. Neither could Peter, but God used him to do both. God has a purpose for your life to be a part of His work among His people. See what Acts 5:15 in the margin says about Peter. Through his example and his writings Peter's life still casts a shadow today.

"As a result, people brought the sick into the streets and laid them on beds and mats so that at least Peter's shadow might fall on some of them as he passed by" (Acts 5:15).

Write a brief sentence that you want to be part of a spiritual will you would like to leave as a legacy.

_____

_____

INFLUENCING GOD'S PEOPLE

What a makeover God did in Peter's life! Meeting him before and after Pentecost, you would not believe he was the same person. God had more in mind than just changing Peter. He intended to launch a church for all peoples. He chose Peter to be the leader through whom He would work. Jesus knew that strong leadership was required to launch a church for all peoples. That's why He spent so much time discipling Peter and the other apostles. Christ wanted a firm foundation for His church as it faced a hostile, pagan world.

1. God chooses His people to be on mission with Him.

"Brothers, think of what you were when you were called. Not many of you were wise by human standards; not many were influential; not many were of noble birth. But God chose the foolish things of the world to shame the wise; God chose the weak things of the world to shame the strong. He chose the lowly things of this world and the despised things— and the things that are not—to nullify the things that are, so that no one may boast before him. It is because of him that you are in Christ Jesus, who has become for us wisdom from God—that is, our righteousness, holiness and redemption. Therefore, as it is written: 'Let him who boasts boast in the Lord'" (1 Cor. 1:26-31).

If you were to choose church leadership for today, you would probably be tempted to choose people with the best personalities, abilities, and gifts. The group Jesus chose lacked in most of those areas.

Read 1 Corinthians 1:26-31 in the margin. Below circle the kind of people God has chosen to overcome the world.

wealthy	wise	well-educated	physically attractive
despised	weak	influential	lowly

James and John were called Sons of Thunder. Matthew was a hated publican who collaborated with the Roman government. Simon the Zealot was a revolutionary trying to overthrow the Romans. Doubting Thomas was an unlikely overcomer, as were most of the disciples whom we know only by name. Peter, the usual leader, seemed to have some of the worst warts! But each disciple was chosen to fulfill the Father's purpose.

If you think you are foolish, weak, lowly, and despised, you are exactly what the Lord is looking for. God can use you and other "misfits" to disable the mighty empires of this modern age. Even if you and others in your church are highly educated, wealthy, wise, and respected, recognize that without God's working in you, you can do nothing of eternal value. He looks for humble people to join Him on mission! When He does it through you, He gets the glory.

2. God calls His people for His purposes.

Have you ever considered that you might be called to lead in Christ's church, as Peter was? You might reply, "No way!" I'm sure Peter was surprised at the great changes the Lord would make in His life and the catalyst He would become in the body of Christ. Through Peter's weaknesses God demonstrated how the Holy Spirit empowers His people to be His witnesses to all peoples.

As you experience God on mission, you will be amazed at His aims for you, the shame you will feel at your failures, and the fact that He will reclaim you and that people may even acclaim you as a leader. But that is how God works among His people to influence the world. Empowered by the Holy Spirit, Peter was fearless and courageous before the authorities of his day (see Acts 4:13 in the margin). Above all, that is what the world needs to know: "Have you been with Jesus?" The educated elite took note that Peter and John had been with Jesus!

God's purpose is to use all of His people—not just some of His people or just His leaders. God wants to use you and your church the way He used Peter and the first church—as world-changing catalysts. You are called to stand before the world's authorities and boldly witness about Christ. He calls all His people, even those with great weaknesses, to be on mission with Him!

"When they saw the courage of Peter and John and realized that they were unschooled, ordinary men, they were astonished and they took note that these men had been with Jesus" (Acts 4:13).

How could God use you as a catalyst to move your church toward spiritual awakening and to be on mission with God? Check the ways you would be willing for God to use you.
- ☐ Be part of a round-the-clock prayer chain to pray for revival.
- ☐ With a prayer partner commit to pray for your church's renewal.
- ☐ Study revivals in God's Word and share the burden with others.
- ☐ Prayerwalk around your church, praying that revival will occur there.
- ☐ Other _____

He calls all His people, even those with great weaknesses, to be on mission with Him!

Two women's prayers were credited by many as the cause of the revival during D. L. Moody's crusades.[1] Every great revival has been preceded by obscure, praying people who have a heart for God and His mission. God may call you to be the person He uses to awaken His church to its mission.

3. God initiates a covenant of promise and obedience with His corporate people.

Read one of God's covenants with his people in the margin (2 Chron. 7:14). Note that the key words are *if* and *then*.

If God told the people in your church to stop everything and spend 10 days in prayer for revival, how would they respond? God promises you power if you wait on Him. One reason for powerlessness today is the fact that secular pursuits crowd out spiritual things. We spend so much time on secular matters that we don't have time to be truly on mission with God.

Jesus fed 5,000 people, 500 saw Him at one time after His resurrection, but only 120 took His promise seriously and waited and prayed in the upper room until the Holy Spirit came on them.

" 'If my people, who are called by my name, will humble themselves and pray and seek my face and turn from their wicked ways, then will I hear from heaven and will forgive their sin and will heal their land' " (2 Chron. 7:14).

Read Acts 1:8 in the margin. Answer these questions.

1. What did Jesus promise the Holy Spirit would give His apostles?

_____

2. What did Jesus promise they would be?

_____

" 'You will receive power when the Holy Spirit comes on you; and you will be my witnesses in Jerusalem, and in all Judea and Samaria, and to the ends of the earth' " (Acts 1:8).

3. Where did Jesus promise they would be witnesses?

_____

Jesus invites you to be a part of His empowered body to go on mission with Him. He promises to be with you to the end of the age. Revival will come to you personally and to your church when you become an Acts 1:8 church, abandon your personal agenda for kingdom purposes, and wait on God to fill you to overflowing with His Spirit.

Is your church on mission with God in ...
☐ Your Jerusalem?
☐ Your Samaria?
☐ Your Judea?
☐ The ends of the earth?

Are you a part of a prayer group in your church? ☐ Yes ☐ No

If not, why not? _____

4. God prepares His people for His mission.

God prepared His people at Pentecost through corporate prayer. Nothing makes you more transparent with the Lord than praying with others. One reason God had the 120 together in the upper room for 10 days before the Holy Spirit came was to unify them. He knew they needed to bond to prepare to handle the influx of 3,000 people who would soon come into the church. God knows that the sum of the body's combined efforts exceeds the total of all the individuals.

We can pray, "God, do again among Your people what You did in Acts." In the past two hundred years the church has performed missions by relying on institutional approaches brought from the sending countries. In this century we must use the same methods required in the first century if we want to see God do what He did in the first century. Those include—
• developing relationships with people;
• allowing God to work through us in ways we cannot imagine;
• depending on God instead of worldly power;
• letting God use us as catalysts in Church Planting Movements.

I hope that is your prayer for you and your church. You may say, "I or my church certainly couldn't be used to bring spiritual awakening and a Church Planting Movement." God has always chosen the people you would least expect to be catalysts for revival. When God speaks to you and your church, don't say no but "Yes, Lord, Your servants hear." God has a unique mission for every church. Discover His mission for your church. Then help your church get in position for God to use it.

When God speaks to you and your church, don't say no but "Yes, Lord, Your servants hear."

What God-sized mission has the Lord given your church to do?

_____

5. God sends His people where He can best work through them to accomplish His mission.

Sometimes God takes drastic steps to get His people to go where He tells them to go. About 10 years after Pentecost the disciples were still in Jerusalem. God used persecution to send His people on mission (see Acts 8:4 in the margin). The apostles stayed in Jerusalem (see Acts 8:1 in the margin), but the Lord worked so powerfully through Philip in Samaria that the church in Jerusalem sent Peter and John to help them!

In Acts the members of the body spread out, taking the gospel with them and declaring it with great boldness. In the first century a supportive synergy occurred in their working together to reach beyond their home church. As individuals and churches today, we can combine our gifts into the corporate people of God to maximize our potential to reach the whole world!

One of the greatest needs in America and throughout Christianity is a spiritual awakening that will lead to a Church Planting Movement among each of the world's unreached peoples! In Acts spiritual awakening occurred among ordinary people, resulting in a Church Planting Movement. God moved through Peter as a key leader to bring that about. Seek God so that He can use you to do what only He can do among the people to whom He sends you.

"Those who had been scattered preached the word wherever they went" (Acts 8:4).

"On that day a great persecution broke out against the church at Jerusalem, and all except the apostles were scattered throughout Judea and Samaria" (Acts 8:1).

6. God guides His corporate people on His mission.

Have you ever been in such a confusing situation that you needed God's instant guidance to discern exactly what was happening? That happened to Peter when He went to Samaria to help with the revival there. Simon the sorcerer, known there as the Great Power because of his magic, put Peter's reliance on God's guidance to the test.

Read Acts 8:9-24 in your Bible. Answer these questions.

1. Who thought Simon the sorcerer was the divine power? _____

2. Who believed, was baptized, and followed Philip everywhere? _____
   What four points did Peter assert about Simon when he tried to buy God's power?

   - " 'You thought _____.' "
   - " 'You have no _____.' "
   - " 'Your heart is _____.' "
   - " 'You are full of _____.' "

4. What did Peter tell Simon he must do to be restored?

   _____

5. What did Simon ask Peter to do to avoid God's judgment?

   _____

"Mark this: There will be terrible times in the last days. People will be lovers of themselves, lovers of money, boastful, proud, abusive, disobedient to their parents, ungrateful, unholy, without love, unforgiving, slanderous, without self-control, brutal, not lovers of the good, treacherous, rash, conceited, lovers of pleasure rather than lovers of God—having a form of godliness but denying its power. Have nothing to do with them"(2 Tim. 3:1-5).

"The man without the Spirit does not accept the things that come from the Spirit of God, for they are foolishness to him, and he cannot understand them, because they are spiritually discerned. The spiritual man makes judgments about all things, but he himself is not subject to any man's judgment"(1 Cor. 2:14-15).

Simon put on a good show before the apostles and all the people. He might have gone on fooling everyone if Peter had not relied on God for guidance. God has placed the church of Jesus in confusing and evil times. In 2 Timothy 3:1-5, in the margin, Paul spelled out what people would be like in the last days.

In this catalog of "terrible times," the last statement seems the most chilling. Spotting blatant misconduct is easy, but when people cloak it in a form of godliness, discerning and dealing with it is difficult. Christ's body needs to have such an intimate relationship with the Lord that it will immediately discern who and what is of God. Otherwise, great damage will be done to the cause of Christ.

The Holy Spirit's power is what makes the difference. In 1 Corinthians 2:14-15 (in the margin) Paul stated the situation plainly. If the Holy Spirit fills you at all times, you can discern God's guidance in every situation. You will know where He wants you to go, what He wants you to say, and what He wants you to do as you join Him on mission.

7. God uses His corporate people to fulfill His mission.

God mightily used Peter, first as he went throughout Judea and Samaria and later as he went to the seacoast towns. God used him to heal a paralytic and raise a woman from the dead! No doubt Peter remembered times when he had seen Jesus do the same thing. Peter must have felt that God had used him to do the very ultimate in His kingdom. Little did Peter know what God would have to do to get him ready for the rest of His mission.

A few miracles that brought God glory were not sufficient. God had planned for all peoples to glorify Him. He would use Peter as the pivotal point to set the church free to do what it was designed to do. Peter would be the rock that would serve as the launching pad for the church on mission. God still had to do in Peter's life what He planned to do in the church. He had to set him and the church on fire to go beyond all they had envisioned!

DAY 5

GOD FULFILLS HIS PURPOSE THROUGH HIS PEOPLE

Read Acts 10 in your Bible. Don't miss this pivotal point in God's eternal mission. Jot notes in the margin wherever you see God taking the initiative in this account.

1. God initiates conviction in the hearts of the lost.

No doubt Peter was doing a great job of leading the body of Christ. He had preached the gospel in Samaria and was now preaching in Judea. He had even raised a woman from the dead. However, he was not doing all God wanted him to do. Approximately 10 years had passed since Christ gave the Great Commission. At Pentecost people of many languages and nations had heard the "wonders of God" (Acts 2:11), but that did not seem to impress on the disciples the urgency of being Christ's witness everywhere. Peter and the church still concentrated on the Jews. Many sheep from other folds needed to hear the gospel.

List the percentage of praying, going, and giving that you think your church does in each of the four assignments.
_____ percent in Jerusalem—the place where you are located
_____ percent in Judea—the area surrounding you
_____ percent in Samaria—the area beyond your kind of people
_____ percent in the uttermost parts—the rest of the world

Only a few miles away in Joppa, Cornelius sought God, but he didn't know how to be saved. God initiated a vision in which Cornelius saw and heard an angel speak to him. Note that the angel didn't tell him how to be saved but directed him to send men to Joppa to inquire for Peter. God had determined that the salvation message will be told only by people who have been saved. That's why God uses saved sinners to tell the story—people who have been redeemed.

> God uses saved sinners to tell the story— people who have been redeemed.

Today God works among all peoples, causing many to seek Him. In a restricted country a man arrived at the house of a Christian representative from America. The Christian asked, "Can I help you?" He said, "I have had a vision for the past three years on the last night of the 40-day fast, Ramadan. As you know, we Muslims believe that God gives revelations on the last night of the fast just before the holy day, *Idul Fitri*. For the past three years on that night I have dreamed of Jesus coming to me and saying, 'Follow Me.' Last night I had that same dream again. This time He said, 'Follow Me' but added, 'Go to the house of the foreigner. He will tell how to follow Me.' Can you tell me how to follow Him?" God still takes the initiative among the thousands of Muslims who report seeing Jesus in dreams and hearing Him beckon them to follow Him.

I met a Hindu man in Myanmar (formerly Burma) who also dreamed of Jesus. Jesus told him to go to another village and talk to a friend of his, who would tell him about the Book. When he did, the friend said, "The man in your dream is Jesus. The book is the Bible. I am not a Christian myself, but I know one in another village. He has the Book. Go ask him." When the man arrived at the other village, the Christian explained how he could be saved. The Hindu man believed. In a few weeks he had led 26 persons to Christ. The Hindu village forced him to leave. He went to his wife's village, 20 kilometers away, and soon won 23 people there. I met them the week they were baptized in Yangoon.

God is at work all over the world convicting people that they need a Savior. But God's people do not witness to them. Some even have prejudices or beliefs that keep them from witnessing to others who differ from them. Peter couldn't imagine Gentiles (another word for *all peoples*) following Christ, although throughout Scripture God revealed that He was concerned for all people.

2. God interrupts *His people to involve them in His mission.*

God came to Cornelius in a vision, but He had to put Peter in a trance before Peter could hear Him. The Lord started the encounter with Cornelius before He shocked Peter into seeing what He was doing. The key component in both cases was prayer. God was at work in both places at the same time to bring about a breakthrough that Peter could never have imagined. Even if he could have imagined it, he wouldn't. He was too prejudiced to hear God on this issue!

The average Christian narrowly views life in a way that does not extend beyond his or her own cultural context. Strangers and people of different races are overlooked. God wants you to raise your sights to glimpse His global vision.

This week keep a list of every person with whom you have contact who differs from you culturally. In the margin make notes on your spontaneous response to them. Be prepared to talk about your experiences in the group setting this week.

God interrupted Peter to teach him God's heart for all peoples.

In the midst of all Peter's good works God interrupted him to teach him God's heart for all peoples. While Peter prayed on the rooftop, he fell into a trance. He saw something that looked like a sheet coming from heaven with all kinds of animals, reptiles, and birds that were unclean, according to Old Testament law and Jewish tradition. He heard God say, "Get up, Peter. Kill and eat."

Peter couldn't believe his ears. He could have said, "Yes, Lord, yes!" Instead, he said, "Surely not, Lord! I have never eaten anything impure or unclean." He couldn't imagine God's commanding him to do this. Three times the Lord insisted, "Get up, Peter. Kill and eat." The Lord continued to drop the sheet full of unclean animals in front of him. This experience was totally opposite to anything Peter had ever seen or believed. Talk about tradition getting in the way! Peter didn't just have tradition; he had the whole Old Testament to back him up. Understandably, Peter was very confused. His theology did not match what God was saying. God will interrupt you to get you to follow His commands.

Is God interrupting you in the middle of your life and work by telling you to do something else? Check any of the statements in which God seems to be saying what sound like interruptions to you.
☐ Meet Me every morning for worship and fellowship.
☐ Witness to your neighbor or fellow worker
☐ Be more enthusiastic in your worship of Me.
☐ Get out of your comfort zone to do what I am commanding you.
☐ Look for opportunities to witness to people different from you.
☐ Participate in a volunteer mission trip.
☐ Be a short-term missionary for a couple of years.
☐ Leave your job and serve Me among unreached peoples.

You can't say no if He is your Lord. He isn't your Lord if you don't follow Him.

You may say, "I'm doing a lot of good. God uses me where I am. That's what Peter—the recognized Christian leader of his day—thought! When God interrupts you, don't reply as Peter did, "No, Lord." You can't say no if He is your Lord. He isn't your Lord if you don't follow Him.

3. God instructs *the committed on the way.*

While Peter was still trying to understand the meaning of abandoning his traditions, the Holy Spirit perfectly timed His further instructions: "Simon, three men are looking for you. So get up and go downstairs. Do not hesitate to go with them, for I have sent them." Peter surely would have hesitated to go with them if the Spirit had not been so specific! How did God lead Peter to obey in the face of all his tradition? The Holy Spirit first spoke through prayer, then through the living Word of God, and finally through circumstances. Before the incident was over, the Spirit led Peter and the church to declare the mystery of God—hidden for ages—that all peoples are to worship and serve Him.

While Peter pondered these strange things, God engineered the next step in the saga. The three emissaries of Cornelius showed up at the exact time Peter was trying to understand what God was saying. He still didn't know what God was up to, but God clearly instructed him by saying, in effect, "Simon, three men are at the gate. Go with them, nothing doubting, for I have sent them." Peter immediately responded, inviting the men to stay overnight. However, he took his time getting from Joppa to Caesarea. In fact, he took three times as long to make the trip as the men had taken to reach him.

Although Peter did not know what God was leading him to do, he followed. You too may have sensed God speaking to you. He may have instructed you on the first step you are to take. Do you press on with what you know, or do you wait for more? If you step in the direction He gives you, He will guide you further. A flashlight shines perhaps 50 feet or 50 yards, depending on the beam's intensity. It won't shine any farther until you take a step toward the light. For every step you take toward the light, the farther the light shines.

> You too may have sensed God speaking to you.

> For every step you take toward the light, the farther the light shines.

Describe the light you believe God has given you about being on mission with Him.

_____

_____

God instructed Peter on the way when Peter got out of the way, but this was not easy. At Cornelius's house he was offensive at first. He said, " 'You are well aware that it is against our law for a Jew to associate with a Gentile or visit him'" (Acts 10:28). Cornelius, however, graciously replied, " 'It was good of you to come' " (Acts 10:33).

> God instructed Peter on the way when Peter got out of the way.

Peter continued, " 'But God has shown me that I should not call any man impure or unclean. [At least he had correctly interpreted the vision.] So when I was sent for, I came without raising any objection' " (Acts 10:28-29). Half true! When the men arrived, he didn't object to them, but he had objected plenty to God. Peter began to understand the vision: " 'I now realize how true it is that God does not show favoritism but accepts men from every nation who fear him and do what is right' " (Acts 10:34-35). God instructs you along the way, as He did Peter.

4. *God* intervenes *to complete His plan as you obey Him.*

Peter may not have been happy with his assignment at first, but God's heart must have thrilled to see His kingdom established in the hearts of the Gentiles. God's grand design was coming to fruition. In fact, God couldn't wait for Peter to finish his sermon. He interrupted him right in the middle of it! "While Peter was still speaking these words, the Holy Spirit came on all who heard the message. The circumcised believers who had come with Peter were astonished that the gift of the Holy Spirit had been poured out even on the Gentiles. For they heard them speaking in tongues and praising God" (Acts 10:44-46).

Perhaps you're like Peter, wondering what God is doing with you and saying to you. But if you know and hear the voice of God, respond to Him. If the Lord says things that don't make sense to you, stay before Him. Wait on Him. Listen to what He says. When you follow Him, God will bless you and will bless others through you.

> If you know and hear the voice of God, respond to Him.

Because Peter obeyed and delivered the message God desired, the Holy Spirit came on all who heard the message. Everyone believed and was baptized in the Holy Spirit and in water. Almost one-third of the world's people still wait to hear the gospel. Millions of them would believe if the gospel were just explained to them. Another third have heard the gospel but have not understood it, so they have not believed. Almost another third have the truth but have not shared it. People everywhere wait for you to share the message with them so that God may be glorified among all peoples!

What kind of people would you feel uncomfortable around if God were to direct you to share the gospel with them?

_____

Check steps you can take to reach out to these people.
- ☐ Teaching English as a second language.
- ☐ Minister to new immigrants.
- ☐ Teaching Bible classes to underprivileged children.
- ☐ Other _____
- ☐ Participate in prison ministry.
- ☐ Work in a homeless shelter.
- ☐ Study Bible teachings on God's love for all people.

5. God intends *to be glorified among all peoples.*

Have you ever done what you believed God had told you to do and gotten into trouble for doing it? Peter was usually in trouble, so it probably didn't surprise him that he was criticized for preaching the gospel to the Gentiles! Some of the first church's leaders were absolutely convinced that Peter didn't behave acceptably. Things haven't changed much, have they?

Read Acts 11:1-18 in your Bible. Answer the questions below.

1. Who heard that the Gentiles had received God's word? _____

2. Who criticized Peter for visiting and eating with them? _____

3. What words of Jesus did Peter remember? _____

4. What did Peter's critics do in the end? _____

Peter was wise to take six circumcised Jewish believers with him when he went to Cornelius's house. When he returned to Jerusalem, he took with him all six to establish the truth of his testimony. He also answered wisely, because he told his critics exactly what happened. He gave a report to this effect: "I didn't finish my sermon. I didn't give an invitation. I was just getting started preaching." (Read Acts 10:34-43 in your Bible.) "When I got to the place where all the prophets bear witness that this Jesus is the Son of God and that through His name, forgiveness of sin is given—wow! They believed, just like that! God interrupted my sermon to send the baptism of the Holy Spirit on them just as He had on us. Who was I to oppose God?" Pretty good answer, don't you think? He totally depended on God to give him the right words in this delicate situation. Do you think that group of circumcised Jewish believers would accept or reject their leader's explanation? ☐ Accept ☐ Reject

Look back at Acts 11:6-18, which you just read. In each blank write the number of the verse that corresponds to the way God speaks to us.
_____ 1. Word   _____ 3. circumstances
_____ 2. prayer   _____ 4. church

The good news is "When they heard this, they had no further objections and praised God, saying, 'So then, God has granted even the Gentiles repentance unto life' " (Acts 11:18). You can almost hear the incredulity in their voices! Their task had been enlarged; they had no choice but to go to the ends of the earth to reach all the Gentiles! God knew this from the very beginning—where and how He would use Peter and what He would do through him. They knew the Great Commission, but it took an experience with God to motivate them to fulfill it. God worked through Peter as a catalyst to steer the corporate body in the right direction to reach the unreached so that God would be glorified among all peoples!

God has a plan for your life as He did for Peter's life. Peter's kind of obedience is necessary to hear God, to know what He wants, to be available to be used by God to do what He wants you to do. Only through God's people will the unreached be reached. Nothing else satisfies God or brings Him the glory He deserves! God makes sure it happens. What part does God want you to play in His eternal plan?

Check each statement that applies to you.
☐ God is INITIATING activities in my life and the life of my church.
☐ God is INTERRUPTING me and my church to involve us in His mission.
☐ God is INSTRUCTING us as we join Him on mission.
☐ God is INTERVENING to show His power in our ministries.
☐ God INTENDS to use us to help all peoples glorify Him.

Pray that you will experience God's purpose and glory as Peter did when he accompanied God on mission.

> They knew the Great Commission, but it took an experience with God to motivate them to fulfill it.

> God worked through Peter as a catalyst to steer the corporate body to reach the unreached.

> What part does God want you to play in His eternal plan?

---

1 Arthur Percy Fitt, *Moody Still Lives: Word Pictures of D. L. Moody* (New York: Fleming H. Revell Co., 1936), 28–29.

PAUL

ON MISSION WITH GOD: A GOSPEL FOR ALL PEOPLES

Heart Focus

"God, who said, 'Let light shine out of the darkness,' made his light shine in our hearts to give us the light of the knowledge of the glory of God in the face of Christ. But we have this treasure in jars of clay to show that this all-surpassing power is from God and not from us" (2 Cor. 4:6-7).

This Week's Lessons

Day 1: Experiencing God on a Wrong-Way Street
Day 2: The Legacy of Living on Mission with God
Day 3: The Reward of a Life in Step with God
Day 4: God's People Joining Him on Mission
Day 5: All Peoples Glorifying God

This Week's Learning Focus

You will be able to explain the way God revealed through Paul the mystery of the ages—that He includes all peoples in His redemption and sends missionaries to all nations, tribes, tongues, and peoples.

DAY 1

EXPERIENCING GOD ON A WRONG-WAY STREET

I talked with some missionaries in a resistant African country who began studying *Experiencing God* together. They wanted to hear what God was saying and to see what He was doing in their area. They went on a prayer retreat in a government park and asked God to speak to them about where He was working. Early one morning one of the single women exercised by walking down the road near the park. A young man walking up the road stopped her and asked why she was in that part of Africa. She told him her group were Christians and were there praying. The Muslim young man was surprised, thinking Christians do not pray much. As he asked more questions, the woman realized that he was seeking God. She took him back to camp, where a friend who knew his heart language, Zarma, shared Christ with him. He readily trusted Christ and asked the missionaries to go to his village in the bush and tell his family.

The woman who led the young man to Christ, along with a missionary couple, went with him 17 kilometers into the bush, wondering whether their Land Rover would be hijacked in the process! They told the village chief that at the young man's request they had come to tell his family about Jesus. The chief asked, "Why should they hear it and not all the rest of us?" He invited the whole village to come together. One missionary preached while his colleague translated. He told about the first African who came to know Christ—the Ethiopian eunuch. In the middle of the gospel story the Muslim call to prayer sounded. Some got up and washed, said prayers, and returned for the rest of the story. At the end the missionary issued an invitation.

An elderly man came forward and drew two lines in the sand. He said, "There must be two ways to God." The preacher said the one verse he had memorized in Zarma: "Jesus answered, 'I am the way and the truth and the life. No man comes to the Father except through me' " (John 14:6). With that the old man said, "I thought so. Jesus' way must be the way. How do we do it?" It took about 20 or 30 minutes to teach them how to pray. Then 14 men stood up, shoulder to shoulder, and trusted Christ.

Later, when the missionaries went back to check on them, they said, "We've already been over to the next village and told them, and another person believed. So we discipled and baptized him. Is that OK?" From the simple request that God reveal where He was working has sprung an incredible harvest of souls in a restricted country. That harvest continues today!

Before he met Jesus, Paul was not a likable fellow. His major weakness was his confidence in what he could do. Incredibly zealous, he persecuted the church of God. The Sanhedrin likely said, "Go to it, Paul. We gave you the best education we could give you under Gamaliel. Go stop those Christians!" As powerful leaders often do, they got him to do their dirty work. Like zealous young people in every age, Paul did. But while he was headed the wrong way, Paul was about to experience God!

1. *God is at work around you even when you work against Him.*

God was at work all around Saul of Tarsus, but Saul completely missed Him. He was so focused on what he would do for God that he missed what God was doing. He didn't see that God was using everything that happened to the young churches to accomplish His purpose. Somehow God began to penetrate his heart. It may have started when Gamaliel gave to the Sanhedrin the advice in the margin (Acts 5:38-39). Could that have planted a seed in Paul's heart?

The experience that most piqued Paul's conscience was the stoning of Stephen. As Saul raged toward Damascus, he couldn't forget how Stephen died while Saul held the clothes of his murderers. Perhaps Saul could still hear Stephen saying, " 'Lord, do not hold this sin against them' " (Acts 7:60). Jesus appeared to Saul in a blinding light and said, " 'Saul, Saul, why do you persecute me? It is hard for you to kick against the goads' "(Acts 26:14). Goads were sharpened sticks protruding from a cart to keep the oxen from kicking. Saul kicked one too many times. Persecution and martyrdom are fertilizer for the church. Most Church Planting Movements don't occur without suffering.

Godly men buried Stephen, and the apostles stayed in Jerusalem. However, because of the persecution that arose, the disciples were scattered and went everywhere preaching. Saul went after them, wreaking havoc among God's people. His zeal drove him to imprison men and women. But God did not permit Saul to pursue "righteousness" in his own rebellious fashion. He brought Paul to a screeching halt! The Lord met him face-to-face on the road to Damascus. This unexpected event—a life-changing encounter with the risen Lord—changed Saul forever.

He was so focused on what he would do for God that he missed what God was doing.

" 'In the present case I advise you: Leave these men alone! Let them go! For if their purpose or activity is of human origin, it will fail. But if it is from God, you will only find yourselves fighting against God' " (Acts 5:38-39).

Most Church Planting Movements don't occur without suffering.

In every movement of God are people who fought God and Christianity with all their might, only to be conquered by Christ and become His zealous disciples. Even when you work against God, God works all around you. When you see someone opposing God, recall that this rebellious one may be fighting the reality of God's working in his or her heart. Don't run from that person. Like Stephen, stand your ground; witness for Christ.

2. God seeks a personal love relationship with you regardless.

Three accounts of Paul's personal encounter with God appear in Scripture—in Acts 9; 22; and 26. In the last two Paul gives his testimony. Each account has distinctive elements. In Acts 9 Jesus appears in a great light to Saul and says, " 'Saul, Saul, why do you persecute me?' " (v. 4). Not only was God at work around him, but He was also showing His love through Jesus. God was pursuing a love relationship with Saul when Jesus came face-to-face with him.

God was clearly pursuing a love relationship with Saul when Jesus came face-to-face with him.

The amazing transformation in Saul was almost instantaneous. From one giving authoritative orders for the imprisonment of others, He became a submissive, obedient prisoner of Christ. As the light flashed around him and the voice sounded in his ears, he called Jesus Lord and asked to know more about Him. He took the energy he had used to murder disciples of the Way and turned it to prayer, fasting, and waiting on God. God worked in the lives of both Saul and Ananias to bring about healing and restoration in this new brother. Within three days Saul's sight was restored, he was filled with the Holy Spirit, he was baptized, and he proved to the Jews that Jesus was the Messiah.

Perhaps your encounter with the living Lord was not as dramatic as Saul's, but God still pursued you as relentlessly as He did Saul to draw you into a loving relationship with Himself. He now pursues you to invite you to join His mission of bringing Christ to the unreached people groups of your day!

Write several ways God has revealed His love for you as He has pursued you.

_____

_____

What was your first impulse after Christ saved you?

_____

_____

For most of us, our first impulse is to tell someone else about our experience. In the Acts 22:14 testimony Saul repeated Ananias's words as he told the three reasons God chose him: "to know his will," "to see the Righteous One," and "to hear words from his mouth." All involve intimate relationships. God said, "I want an intimate relationship with you. Then you will be a witness of Me to all men of what you have seen and heard." The Lord desires the same of you!

3. God's revelation is His invitation to go with Him.

Through the obedient Ananias, Saul immediately knew his mandate to carry the gospel to the unreached people of his day. The Lord made His purpose in saving Saul crystal clear. Read about it in Acts 9:15, in the margin.

This revelation was Saul's invitation to be on mission with God—to take the gospel to the Gentiles—all unreached peoples. What has God revealed to you that introduces His invitation to join Him?

Write God's invitations for your life as you understand them.

_____

_____

How have you responded to God's revelations during the past month? Put a check mark beside the statements that illustrate your thinking.
- ☐ I keep seeing interesting Scripture verses that seem to relate to me.
- ☐ The same thought comes to me again and again when I pray.
- ☐ Different circumstances confirm the same thing I have thought about.
- ☐ Recently, several persons have confirmed a gift, ability, or calling in me.
- ☐ God, I recognize that You are speaking to me. I accept Your invitation. Show me what to do next.

Are you willing to embrace wholeheartedly God's will for your life, whatever it may be? ☐ Yes ☐ No If not, state what keeps you from doing so.

_____

Have you recognized the reason for which you have been saved—to be an instrument of God to reach the peoples who do not know Him? Saul wholeheartedly embraced God's will for his life. He immediately began persuading the Jews that Christ is the Messiah.

Even though the people of Saul's day did not understand the purpose for which the Lord chose him, Saul instantly set out to pursue God's goal for him. During his first attempts to preach in both Damascus and Jerusalem, the Jews tried to kill him, not once but twice! Saul needed the Holy Spirit's guidance to help him daily through the difficult transition from wicked oppressor to outstanding witness to the world.

4. God speaks by the Holy Spirit through the Bible, prayer, circumstances, and the church to reveal Himself, His purposes, and His ways.

Saul's reception of Christ as Messiah was not particularly pleasant to the Jews in Damascus and Jerusalem, who had viewed his former activities quite favorably. Now Saul wanted to be sure how the Lord wanted him to proceed at every turn to accomplish God's purpose. At every juncture in his life it was clear that Paul

"The Lord said to Ananias, 'Go! This man is my chosen instrument to carry my name before the Gentiles and their kings and before the people of Israel. I will show him how much he must suffer for my name'" (Acts 9:15).

All those who heard him were astonished and asked, 'Isn't he the man who raised havoc in Jerusalem among those who call on this name? And hasn't he come here to take them as prisoners to the chief priests?' Yet Saul grew more and more powerful and baffled the Jews living in Damascus by proving that Jesus is the Christ. After many days had gone by the Jews conspired to kill him, but Saul learned of their plan. Day and night they kept close watch on the city gates in order to kill him. But his followers took him by night and lowered him in a basket through an opening in the wall. When he came to Jerusalem, he tried to join the disciples, but they were all afraid of him, not believing that he really was a disciple. But Barnabas took him and brought him to the apostles. He told them how Saul on his journey had seen the Lord and that the Lord had spoken to him, and how in Damascus he had preached fearlessly in the name of Jesus. He talked and debated with the Grecian Jews, but they tried to kill him. When the brothers learned of this, they took him down to Caesarea and sent him off to Tarsus" (Acts 9:21-27,29-30).

had a personal relationship with God and that God spoke to him. This young Hebrew certainly knew the Scriptures, as his many epistles clearly show. From the outset of his new life Saul greatly depended on the Holy Spirit. He was a person of prayer who allowed the Lord to guide him through circumstances and the counsel of other members of the body of Christ.

God was at work through His Holy Spirit protecting Saul. When the Jews conspired to kill him, the Lord made sure Saul knew about it. The disciples in Damascus were tuned in to God's guidance system and at night quietly lowered Saul in a basket through a wall opening. The Lord also worked through Barnabas to personally introduce Saul to the fearful apostolic band, who could hardly believe the Lord had changed Saul's heart. When the second attempt was made on his life in Jerusalem, the brothers escorted Saul to Caesarea and sent him back home to Tarsus. Thirteen years later Barnabas brought him back to Antioch to help with the growing church there (see Acts 11:25).

5. God's invitation for you to work with Him always leads you to a crisis of belief that requires faith and action.

Saul's first crisis of belief was during his conversion experience. During the three days he was blind in Damascus, he didn't eat. This crisis of belief required faith and action. Everything he thought he knew, he didn't know anymore. However, he knew one new fact—that he had met Jesus. Ananias placed his hands on Saul, and his eyes were healed. Then Saul got up and was baptized. In this crisis Jesus directed Saul through someone he did not know. When Saul obeyed, God brought him right into the middle of His mission! However, those early days as a Christian were not the end of Saul's need to believe God.

Read Acts 9:21-27,29-30 in the margin. Write numbers beside the four times in the passage Saul's aligning with God's will caused a crisis of belief.

You might think it was too much to be rejected four times as a new Christian, but Jesus had warned Saul that he would suffer much for Him in preaching the gospel to the Gentiles. Read Philippians 1:29, in the margin on page 151, to learn what Paul said about this.

Describe two major adjustments you made since you became a Christian and ways you exercised your faith and took action.

	Challenge	Faith Required	Action Taken
1.	_____	_____	_____
	_____	_____	_____
2.	_____	_____	_____
	_____	_____	_____

6. You must make major adjustments in your life to join God in what He is doing.

In your Bible read the other account of Saul's testimony (see Acts 26:14-18). The Lord showed Saul that it was a God-sized task to which He had called him. If he was to know the Lord's power resting on him, the old, self-sufficient Saul needed to experience complete dependence on God. Nothing less would do on the mission God had for him!

7. You come to know God by experience as you obey Him and He accomplishes His work through you.

The secret of Paul's success in facing suffering was his intimate relationship with the living Christ. Look in the margin to see what Philippians 3:10 (from *The Amplified Bible*) says about this.

Read Philippians 3:10 several times. Take a few minutes to meditate on it. Write what God says to you during your reading and meditation.

The more Paul obeyed, the more he experienced Christ. God developed this budding apostle from glory to glory through experience. In the next two days you will look at ways God developed and used Paul.

"It has been granted to you on behalf of Christ not only to believe on him, but also to suffer for him" (Phil. 1:29).

"[My determined purpose is] that I may know Him—that I may progressively become more deeply and intimately acquainted with Him, perceiving and recognizing and understanding [the wonders of His Person] more strongly and more clearly. And that I may in that same way come to know the power outflowing from His resurrection [which it exerts over believers]; and that I may so share His sufferings as to be continually transformed [in spirit into His likeness even] to His death" (Phil. 3:10, AMP).

≈≈≈ DAY 2 ≈≈≈

THE LEGACY OF LIVING ON MISSION WITH GOD

1. God chooses you to be on mission with Him to reconcile a lost world to Himself.

The word for *chose* that Paul uses in Ephesians 1:4, "He chose us in him before the creation of the world to be holy and blameless in his sight," pictures the idea that God picked you out. As I mentioned in a previous week, it is as if God looked at a photograph and drew a circle around you. The same word is translated "chosen" in Acts 9:15, when God told Paul He was chosen.

Read Acts 9:15 in the margin. Ask God to reveal to you the reasons for which you were chosen.

At the outset of his Christian life Paul was deeply impressed by God's assurance through Ananias that God had chosen him. Nothing could have been clearer

"The Lord said to Ananias, 'Go! This man is my chosen instrument to carry my name before the Gentiles and their kings and before the people of Israel. I will show him how much he must suffer for my name' " (Acts 9:15).

God does not usually show a child of His all that is in store in the future.

than Paul's mandate from God. Yet Paul must have wondered, as you and I do, how God would work out the details. God does not usually show a child of His all that is in store in the future. Paul received a global glimpse of the reason God chose him, but he had to depend completely on the Holy Spirit for the day-to-day operation of His plan. More details of God's initial encounter with Paul appear in his later testimony before a Jewish crowd in Jerusalem.

Read Acts 22:6-21 in your Bible. Check the facts that directly relate to his being chosen.
❑ 1. Paul's friends saw the light but didn't understand the Lord's voice.
❑ 2. In Damascus Paul would be told all he had been assigned to do.
❑ 3. Paul was chosen to know God's will and to hear the Righteous One.
❑ 4. Paul was to be the Lord's witness to all people.
❑ 5. As Paul prayed in the temple, he fell into a trance and heard the Lord telling him to leave Jerusalem immediately.
❑ 6. The Lord told Paul He was sending him far away to the Gentiles.

The idea that Paul was chosen was fixed in his mind by numbers *2, 3, 4,* and *6.* Although God told him that he was chosen for His purpose, He did not tell him everything at once. God desires to build your trust in Him every step of the way. How wise the Lord is in not revealing all the future to you. God has chosen you for God-sized tasks that you can accomplish only if you seek first His kingdom and righteousness!

2. God calls you to Himself to go on mission with Him.

Christians often look at their experiences before they meet Christ to discern what God calls them to do. They may take personality tests to discover their abilities. But God's call is often different from what people would think. When He calls you, He gives you His Spirit, who distributes to you the spiritual gifts He wants you to have for your task.

With Paul's training in Scripture and his experience in the law, you might have expected God to call him to witness to the Scribes, the Pharisees, and the Sanhedrin in Jerusalem. However, God sent him to the Gentiles, who didn't even know God. God determines why He called you and what He wants you to do.

When an accountant is saved, church members want to make him or her the church treasurer. Of course, someone can use that skill for the kingdom, but it is not a sure-fire way to know what you are called to do. Others may tell you, "You are a good speaker. You are called to preach" or "You are a schoolteacher, so teach Sunday School." People often measure your abilities by what they can see physically.

Your SHAPE
S *piritual gifts*
H *eart or passion*
A *bilities*
P *ersonality (type)*
E *xperience*

In his book *The Purpose-Driven Church* Rick Warren uses the acrostic SHAPE to help Christians get a balanced understanding of God's call. See in the margin the words in SHAPE. Apply them to your life. When you look at all the aspects of your SHAPE, you get a balanced view of calling.[1] God is sovereign; He will ultimately reveal to you what He has in mind. God made you unique in order to fulfill His mission through you. Ask Him to show you what He has called you to do.

Describe your understanding at this point in your life of what God has called you to be and do on mission with Him.

_____

_____

Paul spent 3 years in Arabia and 10 in his hometown learning what God wanted him to do. Finally, Barnabas went to Tarsus and invited Paul to Antioch to help him in the new Gentile church there. After Paul's year-long discipling experience with the Christians in Antioch (see Acts 11:26), famine struck Judea. He and Barnabas went to the elders in Jerusalem with a gift from the Antioch church (see Acts 11:30). When they had proved themselves obedient, they returned to Antioch and continued faithful in worship and fasting before the Lord. While they were engaged in this activity with the elders of the church, the Holy Spirit spoke, giving the next steps in God's purpose for them: " 'Set apart for me Barnabas and Saul for the work to which I have called them' " (Acts 13:2). Thus began the first of three missionary journeys that took Paul throughout the Roman world of his day. God calls you to be faithful in a little so that He may give you much to do for His glory.

> God calls you to be faithful in a little, so that He may give you much to do for His glory.

God's calling continues throughout your lifetime as you move on in mission with Him. The Lord later called Paul to minister to the Macedonians after he had preached in many cities of Asia (see Acts 16:10). In several of his epistles Paul greets the churches in various cities as "called by God." In Romans he calls himself "a servant of Christ Jesus, called to be an apostle and set apart for the gospel of God" (Rom. 1:1). In 1 Corinthians he refers to himself as "called to be an apostle of Christ Jesus by the will of God" (1 Cor. 1:1).

The experience of being called can be an integral part of the self-concept of every child of God. Avoid thinking of it as a selfish idea for which you pat yourself on the back. Your calling is based on God's grace, not on your ability. Keep watching to see what God wants to do through your life. Like Paul, you have been called to be on mission with Him!

> Your calling is based on God's grace, not on your ability.

Be faithful in learning this week's memory verse. Study it carefully, absorbing its truth. Be prepared to repeat it in your group.

3. God initiates a covenant of promise and obedience with you.

As you have seen throughout the Bible, God makes a covenant with those He calls. He told Paul, " 'I will rescue you from your own people and from the Gentiles' " (Acts 26:17). That's a promise. Paul had a lot of opportunities to prove that one! In dangerous situations in Ephesus and Corinth and suffering shipwreck on the way to Rome, Paul experienced God's glory in seeing His promise fulfilled. God was promising Paul, "You're My servant, you're My witness, and I'm making a covenant with you. As you follow Me, I will rescue you." God's covenant is a promise that always demands obedience.

> God's covenant is a promise that always demands obedience.

Like Abraham, Paul considered himself to be a blessed individual in a covenant relationship with God. Indeed, the great apostle of the New Covenant had a clear grasp of the covenant God made with the great patriarch under the

Old Covenant. He was fascinated by the blessings that would flow to the Gentiles through God's promises to Abraham 430 years before the law was ever given.

> **In your Bible read Galatians 3:6-18. Underscore phrases referring to "Abraham," "Gentiles," "blessed" or "blessing," and "covenant" or "promise."**

As you have already seen, Paul's obedience in his covenant connection with God brought him many hardships. However, he would be the first to admit that he was blessed above measure in his intimate relationship with the risen Christ. You see no hint that the great apostle was selfish with anything God had given him. Rather, he was ready to expend all his energy in blessing all peoples.

Paul fully knew that during his entire lifetime He was to be on mission with God for that purpose! Paul was prepared to be as flexible as God wanted him to be in order to win people to Jesus Christ. You and I are blessed to have his example to help keep our kingdom priorities straight!

> **Describe your most recent witnessing opportunity as you sought to fulfill your covenant responsibility to share the gospel with someone. Explain how God fulfilled His promise to be with you.**

DAY 3

THE REWARD OF A LIFE IN STEP WITH GOD

4. God prepares you for His mission.

God fulfills His covenant to you by preparing you for the task He has assigned you. The Lord knew He would make Paul a witness and a servant to all peoples. Look at all that happened to bring that about. When Paul was a young man, God sent him to school and let the Sanhedrin pay for it! Paul learned the Old Testament Scriptures. He got credentials that allowed him to step into any synagogue and people would say, "Speak to us, Paul." In Galatians he reported that he spent 3 years in Arabia. He recorded that he was not taught by any man (see Gal. 1:16). God taught Paul, reforming his whole heart and mind. He prepared Paul to be that witness.

Often God's choicest fruit ripens best in shade.

We don't know a lot about Paul's early ministry in the area of Galatia, but he served obscurely for 10 years. Often God's choicest fruit ripens best in shade. Ask yourself the question "Am I willing to let God shape me and use me?"

Then one day Barnabas traveled the two hundred kilometers to Tarsus to find Paul and bring him back to Antioch. For a whole year, as they taught the church there, Barnabas discipled Paul, teaching him all about what had really happened in the first church and how things were to be done. Fourteen years of preparation occurred before Paul became prominent in ministry, and many experiences after that prepared him for the rest of his life. The bigger the job, the greater the preparation.

Paul survived many crises as he sought to put his faith into action. Throughout his lifetime he responded positively to many negative situations that faced him. Notice in Acts 14:5-7,19-22 that Paul and Barnabas did not retreat from Iconium when unbelieving Jews stirred up Gentiles by poisoning their minds against the two apostles. Instead, they spent considerable time there, preaching boldly as the Lord enabled them to perform miraculous signs and wonders. When both Jews and Gentiles plotted to mistreat and stone them, they didn't head home. Instead, they went to the nearby cities of Lystra and Derbe and surrounding area to share the good news.

A crisis occurred and Paul hit bottom when Jews from Antioch and Iconium arrived and persuaded the people of Lystra to stone him and drag his seemingly dead body outside the city. Paul showed himself to be indisputably a man of faith and action when he got up from that situation and went back into the same city and encouraged the disciples there! Instead of taking time off to recover, he departed the next day for Derbe. There he and Barnabas again preached the good news and won many to Christ.

Modern Christians often forget that suffering accompanies service. Perhaps you have answered God's invitation to go on mission with Him, only to be met by discouragement and difficulties along the way. Be like Paul as you determine to endure and even embrace unfolding events.

Learn the resources God gives you and see the results when you let God prepare you. Read Romans 5:1-5 in the margin. Match the following.

____ 1. We have been justified.	a. By the Holy Spirit
____ 2. We have peace with God.	b. Through faith
____ 3. We have gained access to grace.	c. Through our Lord Jesus Christ
____ 4. God has poured His love into our hearts.	d. By faith

From the same passage fill in the blanks:

Suffering produces _____.
Character produces _____.
Perseverance produces _____.
Hope does not _____.

As Paul obeyed God, Christ's character was formed in him through the sufferings he endured. The perseverance he learned led to this Christlikeness. Paul was ever hopeful and never disappointed, because he expected to suffer in this life, knowing that he was sharing in His Lord's sufferings. Indeed, Paul learned to glory in his sufferings. The measure of the success you exhibit under similar circumstances can come from the same limitless Source!

"Since we have been justified through faith, we have peace with God through our Lord Jesus Christ, through whom we have gained access by faith into this grace in which we now stand. And we rejoice in the hope of the glory of God. Not only so, but we also rejoice in our sufferings, because we know that suffering produces perseverance; perseverance, character; and character, hope. And hope does not disappoint us, because God has poured out his love into our hearts by the Holy Spirit, whom he has given us" (Rom. 5:1-5).

"In a large house there are articles not only of gold and silver, but also of wood and clay; some are for noble purposes and some for ignoble. If a man cleanses himself from the latter, he will be an instrument for noble purposes, made holy, useful to the Master and prepared to do any good work" (2 Tim. 2:20-21).

"I can almost hear your retort: 'If this is so, and God's will is irresistible, why does God blame men for what they do?' But the question really is this: 'Who are you, a man, to make any such reply to God?' When a craftsman makes anything he doesn't expect it to turn round and say, 'Why did you make me like this?' The potter, for instance, is always assumed to have complete control over the clay, making with one part of the lump a lovely vase, and with another a pipe for sewage. Can we not assume that God has the same control over human clay?" (Rom. 9:19-21, Phillips).

When you think life is the most difficult, God is merely getting you ready for a bigger job—to do something with you that you have not anticipated but that He has called you to do. Using a simple analogy (read 2 Tim. 2:20-21 in the margin), Paul wrote to young Timothy about being prepared for God's mission. As God prepared Paul and Timothy, He has been preparing you from your earliest days to be an effective witness in His kingdom. Trials and tribulations toughen you spiritually so that you will persevere under difficult circumstances!

With which article(s)—gold, silver, wood, or clay—do you identify

in this Scripture? _____ Why? _____

_____

Are you cleansed from ignoble (degraded) purposes? ❑ Yes ❑ No
Are you holy and prepared to do any good work?   ❑ Yes ❑ No

If you thought of yourself as clay, read Romans 9:19-21 in the Phillips translation in the margin.

Which would you rather be—a Chinese Ming vase or a sewer pipe? Think how a sewer pipe would look with flowers in it atop a baby grand piano or how a plumber would struggle if he or she only had vases when sewer pipes are needed. Both items are exactly suited for their use. God will use you best if you are dedicated to fulfilling His purpose for you. Pause and ask the Lord to cleanse and make you holy so that you will be useful to the Master, prepared to do any good work to which He calls you!

5. God sends you to the place where He can best work through you to accomplish His mission.

From the beginning of his relationship with the risen Christ, Paul knew to whom he was being sent—the unreached, outcast peoples of his day. During your lifetime you have the same privilege Paul had—reaching those who have never even heard the name of Jesus.

Today, some 1.7 billion people still do not have access to the gospel. To put that in perspective, if you could tell one person a second, it would take 54 years to share the gospel with them! In addition, another 1.4 billion are unreached by a gospel to which they may have technically had access but have not understood. Another 1.5 billion do not understand the gospel, although it has reached their countries and to some degree penetrated their cultures. That means that today at least 4.6 billion people constitute the unfinished task!

How can you tackle such a gigantic job? Realize that God wants to use everyone on mission. You may be exactly where He can best work through you to accomplish His mission. These unreached people of the world may show up in your life as taxi drivers, supermarket clerks, or your next-door neighbors. Or God may have another destination. You may not have had a dramatic, road-to-Damascus experience as Paul did, but the same Lord desires to reach everyone in the world with the good news of the gospel. As you pray, has God directed your thoughts to a certain people or a certain part of the world? It may be the place He wants to send you to be His instrument, as Paul was during his lifetime.

Read this list of ways people go on mission. Circle the numbers of any you think God might have you do for unreached peoples.
1. Volunteering from one to three weeks in a role such as a prayerwalker among a restricted-access people
2. Teaching English as a second language to unreached people
3. Leading Vacation Bible School in the inner city
4. Serving as a semester missionary overseas or as a Journeyman for two years after college
5. Serving as an International Service Corps missionary from four months to three years, using your skills to aid a missions cause
6. Serving as a career missionary in one of the occupations missionaries fill
7. Witnessing to persons of another race as you encounter them

6. *God guides you on His mission.*

In the Scriptures recounting Paul's life are many instances of God's guidance through the Holy Spirit. One, in Acts 16:1-10, is particularly outstanding. Many elements were involved in the Lord's leading Paul in this instance. The Holy Spirit both prevented Paul from going and permitted him to go in certain directions. So he continued in the previous direction God had given him. When he got to the end of the land and waited by the Aegean Sea, Paul received a vision. From the events he and the party with him concluded that God was calling them to another continent to preach—Europe instead of Asia. When they worked their way from Troas to Samothrace to Neapolis and finally to Philippi, they found a woman (not the man he had seen in the vision) whose heart the Lord opened to respond to Paul's message! God led him to the keeper of the prison (the man of Macedonia?), who asked, " 'What shall I do to be saved?' " (Acts 16:30). The way God guides is never stereotyped or boring. If Paul had allowed gender or Jewish prejudice to prevent him from preaching to Lydia, he would have missed God's will in this moment.

> The Holy Spirit both prevented Paul from going and permitted him to go in certain directions.

Perhaps you have felt confused or believed you did not have all the information you needed to follow the Lord. God guarantees you as much guidance as you need. As you follow the light He gives you, He provides more light. Do not allow personal prejudice to prevent you from doing the Lord's will. The path before you will unfold as you respond to do His work the way He chooses!

> The way God guides is never stereotyped or boring.

Can you recall an incident when God gave you partial instruction about a situation, followed by more information as you obeyed Him? Jot down notes of what happened.

_____

_____

_____

God used many means to speak to Paul. Write N before natural ways and S before supernatural ways God spoke to him.

_____ the Scriptures   _____ prayer
_____ circumstances   _____ the church
_____ directly   _____ trance
_____ vision   _____ an angel

"*The Lord will rescue me from every evil attack and will bring me safely to his heavenly kingdom. To him be glory for ever and ever. Amen*" (2 Tim. 4:18).

"*Five times I received from the Jews the forty lashes minus one. Three times I was beaten with rods, once I was stoned, three times I was shipwrecked, I spent a night and a day in the open sea. I have been constantly on the move. I have been in danger from rivers, in danger from bandits, in danger from my own countrymen, in danger from Gentiles; in danger in the city, in danger in the country, in danger at sea; and in danger from false brothers. I have labored and toiled and have often gone without sleep; I have known hunger and thirst and have often gone without food; I have been cold and naked*" (2 Cor. 11:24-27).

"*I consider that our present sufferings are not worth comparing with the glory that will be revealed in us*" (Rom. 8:18).

God supernaturally spoke to Paul through visions or a trance. God also spoke directly to him and through an angel. He spoke through Ananias as a representative of the church. He used Barnabas and the apostles to convince him to leave Jerusalem. God used circumstances, such as the Jews in Damascus and Jerusalem wanting to kill Saul, to convince him to leave. God spoke to Saul in prayer and while he was fasting.

Paul lived a life so open to the Holy Spirit that he experienced continual guidance for His mission. You have already seen how the Lord guided him to Europe when he was preaching on the continent of Asia. Although you find instances in which he seemed to take matters into his own hands, God still worked all things together for good, because Paul loved Him and was called according to His purpose (see Rom. 8:28). Take heart—even though the great apostle was not perfect, he repented when he knew he had been headstrong.

Even at the end of his life Paul had little doubt that God had guided him throughout his life and ministry. He was content to say the words of 2 Timothy 4:18, in the margin. Be assured that the same Lord will be equally strong on your behalf as you obediently go on mission with Him!

7. God uses you to bring glory to His name.

The apostle to the Gentiles played a major part in God's mission to peoples the Jews had failed to bless. God also used Paul to write almost half of the New Testament. Do you see how much glory God can get through one person's life? God would have found someone else through whom He could work, but Paul would have missed his reward for being a faithful servant.

Read 2 Corinthians 11:24-27 in the margin. Complete the following exercise.

Draw a line between the hazard and the number of times Paul endured it.

39 lashes	three
beating with rods	five
stoning	three
shipwrecked	one

In all of this Paul followed in the footsteps of his Lord. In the midst of difficulties he uttered the words found in Romans 8:18, in the margin. By setting such an example, he could urge young Timothy, "Endure hardship with us like a good soldier of Christ Jesus" (2 Tim. 2:3). May the same be true of you and me as we leave large footprints for others!

You may think you could not accomplish anything that compares to what this apostle did during his life. Your weaknesses may overwhelm you at times and make you feel unworthy to join God on His mission. Realize that Paul considered himself totally unworthy because he persecuted the church (see 1 Tim. 1:15). Gradually, he learned to glory in his weaknesses, allowing God's strength to work through him (see 2 Cor. 13:9).

Toward the end of his productive life Paul could make the statement in 2 Timothy 4:17, in the margin. The aging apostle could look back on a faithful ministry in which He allowed God to substitute His power for Paul's weakness. He could rejoice that the Lord worked through him to fully proclaim the gospel so that all the Gentiles could hear it.

God will do His work with or without you. Wouldn't you rather He do it with you and through you? One way or the other, God will bring representatives from every people to worship Him and glorify Him. You are privileged to be chosen, called, promised, prepared, sent, guided, and used to bring peoples to glorify Him for all eternity!

"The Lord stood at my side and gave me strength, so that through me the message might be fully proclaimed and all the Gentiles might hear it. And I was delivered from the lion's mouth" (2 Tim. 4:17).

DAY 4

GOD'S PEOPLE JOINING HIM ON MISSION

Although Paul worked tirelessly himself, he strongly believed in discipling and mentoring others to proclaim God to all peoples. He rarely went on a missionary journey alone but took with him at least one other person and often several. Paul deeply sensed the corporate nature of the church as Christ's body. Read the four passages listed at right. He taught the importance of team and body ministry and appointed elders in every church to equip the body to minister.

Paul was the chief proponent of a Church Planting Movement in his day. A Church Planting Movement (CPM) is the rapid multiplication of indigenous churches among a people or population segment that enables them to spread the gospel among their people and to other peoples of the world. Paul certainly modeled that concept as he sought to follow God's plan in reaching the world with the gospel of Christ. God wants to start a CPM in every people group. This biblical concept is God's way to bring glory to Himself by bringing thousands into the kingdom and instituting a way for the church to continue multiplying. We must initiate and facilitate CPMs today because they are biblical and represent the only way to reach the billions of people in the 13,000 people groups in the world. Only God can begin and sustain a CPM, but He uses human catalysts to do so.

God initiated a CPM while I was serving in Indonesia. The Communists attempted a coup. Approximately 500,000 people were killed within the next three months. But in the aftermath people started seeking the Lord. Most of the churches working with the Javanese doubled, at least.[2] In just over five years more than two million people were baptized into Indonesian churches. A Church Planting Movement began in a country where 85 percent of the people claimed to be Muslims! God can start CPMs anywhere. I have seen CPMs among peoples with animist, Hindu, Muslim, and Buddhist backgrounds.

"Just as each of us has one body with many members, and these members do not all have the same function, so in Christ we who are many form one body, and each member belongs to all the others" (Rom. 12:4).

"Do you not know that your body is a temple of the Holy Spirit, who is in you, whom you have received from God? You are not your own; you were bought at a price. Therefore honor God with your body" (1 Cor. 6:19).

"The body is a unit, though it is made up of many parts; and though all its parts are many, they form one body. So it is with Christ" (1 Cor. 12:12).

"For we are members of his body" (Eph 5:30).

God used Paul to teach the church how to start and nurture CPMs among all peoples that will continue to reach out until all peoples are reached. The best example of such a movement occurred in Jerusalem after Pentecost, where the believers may have numbered 100,000. But to see a CPM begin without the one-of-a-kind Pentecost conditions, look at Paul's experience in Ephesus. Remember that God had prevented Paul from going to Ephesus and Asia earlier—the timing wasn't right (see Acts 16:6-10). At the right time God led Paul back to Ephesus because He was ready to do something in Paul's life and in Ephesus that would model for us a CPM among the unreached that would spread throughout Asia. Paul's greatest impact on the corporate body of Christ was in the midst of starting CPMs.

For an overview of the biblical CPM that you will study today, stop and read Acts 19—20 in your Bible.

"This went on for two years, so that all the Jews and Greeks who lived in the province of Asia heard the word of the Lord" (Acts 19:10).

After Paul told people about Jesus and they believed in Him, he baptized them in Jesus' name. Then he prayed for them to be filled with the Holy Spirit. Paul spent three months teaching in the synagogue before he was ejected. Paul took his disciples with him and daily had discussions in the lecture hall of Tyrannus. In the margin read Acts 19:10, an amazing verse.

Did Paul preach to all of them? No. He stayed in the school of Tyrannus! He discipled the disciples to go make disciples and begin congregations of believers. He was a CPM missionary.

" 'Everyone who calls on the name of the Lord will be saved.' How, then, can they call on the one they have not believed in? And how can they believe in the one of whom they have not heard? And how can they hear without someone preaching to them? And how can they preach unless they are sent? As it is written, 'How beautiful are the feet of those who bring good news!' " (Rom. 10:13-15).

A. In a Church Planting Movement someone must go where the people live, because the gospel will never get there unless an outsider takes it to them (see Acts 19:10). Pastor Michael Wright of Calvary Baptist Church in Tyler, Texas, challenged his people to adopt an unreached people group. They had never personalized missions in this way but began to pray in earnest. The congregation was electrified when Pastor Wright told the church that a couple from another church was considering going as missionaries to their adopted people. To support the couple in prayer, the church sent a group to the church that was commissioning the couple before they left for India. This praying church understood that someone from outside must first go to the people.

Read Romans 10:13-15 in the margin. Supply the missing words.

They cannot _____ on one they have not believed in.
They cannot _____ in one of whom they have not heard.
They cannot _____ without someone preaching to them.
They cannot _____ unless they are sent.

B. In a Church Planting Movement someone needs to research the situation to learn what God has done and is doing (see Acts 19:1-4). God prepared the way in Ephesus when some of John's disciples made converts. God used John to prepare for Jesus in Palestine; He used John's disciples to pave the way for the gospel in Ephesus.

A strategy coordinator began to focus on an unreached people group composed of 90 million people in North India. He discovered that the 28 Swedish Baptist churches started by a Swedish missionary organization in William

Carey's era had not started a church in more than 25 years. The coordinator first advocated that they leave their protective shell—caused by persecution—and reach out. He did not stop there. He mobilized other Great Commission Christians (from other mission groups and denominations) to begin evangelizing. Unfortunately, some Christians used methods from South India that were highly offensive methods with this unreached people. Six evangelists were martyred before the Christians discovered how to evangelize among this people. As the strategy coordinator agonized over these events, God showed him that Jesus had told His disciples to find the man "of peace" in the villages where He sent them and to stay with him (see Luke 10:5-7). Once they began following this biblical pattern among this people group, they began to see great results. In just 10 years the number of churches has grown from 28 to 4,3000 and 260,000 believers!

C. In a Church Planting Movement someone must communicate the gospel (see Acts 19:4-5). Paul immediately made the connection between the preaching of John on repentance and the gospel of salvation by faith. In this case Paul already knew the language of the people—Greek. Among new people groups worship is typically in the heart language of the people. Although God's Word may be available in a language they can understand, it needs to be communicated in the heart language of the people—the one they love, cry, and get angry in. Missionaries must keep their prayers, songs, sermon illustrations, and applications in this language so that worship is accessible to all and easily reproduced.

D. In a Church Planting Movement someone must move out of the group of believers using the bridges of God to people who need the messages (see Acts 19:8-10). Paul began in the local synagogue. He felt obliged to preach the gospel first to the Jews. If they rejected it, he moved to the Gentiles. When most Ephesian Jews rejected the message, Paul focused on the unreached Gentiles.[2]

E. In a Church Planting Movement someone must find a neutral place to freely share the gospel and teach the disciples (see Acts 19:9). Tyrannus was probably a Greek philosopher who rented his hall to Paul. Public life in the Ionian cities regularly ended at the fifth hour (11:00 a.m.); thus, the hall would be free for Paul to use the rest of the day.

> **Read the following case study of a CPM among the Kui people of Orissa, India. Underline ways the missionaries approached the non-Christian Kui people on neutral ground.**

A CPM began among the Kui people of Orissa, India, in the 1990s. International Mission Board missionaries had begun short-term training for leaders in 1986. From that a remarkable awakening and CPM exploded. In 1993 a lone agricultural missionary went in on a tourist visa and lived there for about two years. He began agricultural methods to save and use the depleted land. Impressed, the government appropriated $2 million to make one method available all over the area.

While this was occurring agriculturally, the missionary decided to broadcast a 15-minute radio program in the Kui language twice weekly—something that had never occurred before. The first seven or eight minutes focused on agriculture or public health. The second half recounted Bible narratives. From this sprang the idea of listener groups, for which 175 Indian believers were trained as leaders. They went to villages where no believers existed and gathered people to listen to the radio program and then discuss implications both for farming and for faith. Listener groups began developing into churches. More listener group leaders were trained and entered other villages. In seven years the number of churches increased from two hundred to approximately nine hundred.

Today the Kui worship style and music are totally indigenous. This has contributed to the spread of the gospel in the surrounding Khond Hills. The curriculum includes chronological Bible storying, or simple Bible content. As pastors are trained, they study public health, the Bible, and more storying as well as agriculture so that they can help support themselves. In 1998 men came from a remote area of the Khond Hills with a petition from 3,500 heads of households saying they wanted to become Christians. To date approximately 100,000 people, one-tenth of the Kui, have become Christians.

" 'You know that I have not hesitated to preach anything that would be helpful to you but have taught you publicly and from house to house' " (Acts 20:20).

F. In a Church Planting Movement someone must make disciples (see Acts 19:9-10; 20:17-25; 2 Tim. 2:2). A CPM exists only when disciples are multiplied. Read Acts 20:20, in the margin, to see what Paul reminded the elders at Ephesus. He did the two things a missionary must do—preach and teach—where a missionary must do them—publicly and from house to house. Paul lived out the vision among them, taught them to shepherd, and built them up with the word of God's grace.

Spiritual reproduction is a must in a CPM. The idea is that believers reproduce mature believers by discipling others, who in turn disciple others. The result is multiple generations of disciples who continually multiply the number of mature believers throughout the world.

G. In a Church Planting Movement someone must pray and expect God to do a supernatural work before those who oppose the gospel (see Acts 19:11-17). This can occur only through prayer. Paul prayed much and enlisted people to pray for him. No CPM ever began without prayer.

Read Acts 19:11-20 in your Bible. Below list three supernatural events.

1. _____

2. _____

3. _____

Supernatural power was necessary for the people to be healed, for the evil spirits to be cast out, and for the people to burn their sorcery paraphernalia, which was worth the daily wage of a laborer for 208 years!

H. In a Church Planting Movement someone must equip multiplying leaders to lead the congregations (see Acts 19—20). We don't know how many churches began, but for everyone in Asia to hear the Word of the Lord, it must have been many. We do know that the seven churches Christ addressed in

Revelation 2—3 were part of the churches of Asia. When Paul came back, he called all the elders (what we call pastors today) to meet him in Miletus. In Acts 20 Paul described the way he equipped them to be multiplying leaders. Later, Paul wrote Ephesians to train the whole church and leaders in particular.

I. In a Church Planting Movement someone must equip disciples and leaders to multiply themselves and to multiply churches (see Acts 19:10; 20:17,32). If the missionary does it right, the churches will be indigenous and will start other churches on their own. Aquila and Priscilla, Paul's companions, helped start a church in their home and ultimately helped lead to phenomenal growth of the churches in Asia. Theirs was truly a first-century Church Planting Movement. Their church had no buildings but met all over town for worship and fellowship. As soon as disciples were equipped, they began new churches. They planned to move to Rome to start a church in their home as a beachhead for evangelizing the whole Roman Empire.

J. In a Church Planting Movement the leaders move on and let the indigenous leaders lead the work—although the leaders retain a fraternal relationship with them, as Paul did (see Acts 20:32-38). God enacted His plan to start a CPM in Asia by using Paul to disciple the disciples. He equipped them and trained them for that purpose. Acts 20:20 gives Paul's 20/20 vision for the church. He preached and taught among them both publicly and privately and then told them good-bye. That's a missionary's job—to be the catalyst for a CPM—to train, model, and equip people who can carry out the Great Commission and then to back off. When you do that, God sets in motion through you something that can impact a whole people.

Just as the Lord chose Paul to be on mission with Him, He chose others to come alongside and help. Paul believed in team ministry as he planted churches. Today the Lord puts His people together in families called churches, where you are surrounded by fellow laborers. Beyond that, churches organize themselves into denominations with missions agencies. Churches also work with parachurch organizations, which focus on specific parts of the mission, such as Bible translation, *Jesus*-film distribution, communications, literature, and service groups. God has not called you to take on this God-sized task alone. As He did for Paul, He provides many co-laborers in His harvest field.

> Today the Lord puts His people together in families called churches, where you are surrounded by fellow laborers.

1. **Name several Christians on mission with God with whom the Lord has linked your life.** _____

2. **Has anyone discipled you?** ☐ Yes ☐ No **Do you have someone who has or is mentoring you?** ☐ Yes ☐ No **Do you have an accountability relationship with another Christian?** ☐ Yes ☐ No **If not, write the name(s) of someone you would like to have a discipling, mentoring, or accountability relationship with (perhaps consider someone in your *On Mission with God* group).**

3. **Set a time or plan to talk to the person(s) about beginning a relationship to prepare you to carry out the mission God has chosen for you.**

Date: _____

Time: _____

Place/situation: _____

✸ DAY 5 ✸

ALL PEOPLES GLORIFYING GOD

God's mission becomes crystal clear in His breathtaking revelation to Paul that all peoples will glorify God. God had to reveal it to Paul because the Jews had missed what God, throughout Scripture, had said about including all peoples. From today's perspective you wonder how the Jews could have missed it. But you could also ask how the church today misses the heart of God for all peoples and focuses more on its own kind.

Paul's clearest expression of God's heart and therefore his heart for all peoples is Romans 15. Read this chapter to discern Paul's heart for unreached peoples. Write what you think Paul's life message is.

_____

_____

_____

Paul's life message is all peoples glorifying God—a message that has become his eternal legacy to the body of Christ. God chose Paul to fulfill his divine destiny as the Apostle to the Gentiles. Paul described himself as someone born out of due time (see 1 Cor. 15:8), because he didn't get to accompany Jesus on earth as the other apostles did. But in God's plan Paul was born right on time! He was to be the transitional leader from the apostles who had lived with Jesus and had seen His glory to the rest of us who experience His glory by faith without sight. You too have been born at the right time in history for God to fulfill His eternal purpose through you.

Because Paul obeyed, God could accomplish His eternal purpose through Paul's life. Because Paul had a passion for eternal results, he allowed nothing to stand in the way of doing God's will. Often people make excuses or complain about circumstances. Not Paul! Paul knew that God loved him and had a plan for his life. He responded positively in all circumstances. In the margin read what he told the Thessalonians.

"Be joyful always; pray continually; give thanks in all circumstances, for this is God's will for you in Christ Jesus" (2 Thess. 5:16-18).

God doesn't just work in spite of circumstances. He works through them. When you face an obstacle, "give thanks in all circumstances, for this is God's will for you in Christ Jesus," as Paul advised in 1 Thessalonians 5:18. God's Spirit will help you interpret circumstances and work through them to fulfill His purpose. When you conclude something about a circumstance, ask God for confirmation through His Word, prayer, other Christians, and the Holy Spirit's guidance. Don't let negative situations stop you from doing God's will.

So now to the heart of the matter—what is God's mission? You've studied this question for seven weeks. In the margin read the verses from Romans 15. Underline Paul's five uses of the phrase "so that" or "in order that." These phrases are signposts pointing to God's purpose or mission.

What is your conclusion about the purpose or mission of God? Write it below.

_____

_____

Paul's life message is for all the peoples of the world to glorify God. To sharpen your understanding, write in your own words a personal statement of what the mission of God is to be in your life.

_____

_____

I believe that God wants to start and duplicate Acts among every people in this world. God is moving in this generation in a special way to get you to join Him on mission so that all peoples of the world will glorify Him.

Should conducting missions be the ultimate goal of the church?
☐ Yes ☐ No Why or why not?

_____

_____

The heart of God is that all nations glorify Him. You may ask, "Is God so egotistical that He wants everybody to glorify Him?" Of course not, because He is God. It's egotistical for anyone else to want to be glorified, but He is God! You may ask, "Is God selfish in calling attention to Himself and in wanting to be glorified by all peoples?" Whom do you think God would recommend to be glorified besides Himself? Because He is the one true God, no one or no thing should be glorified more than God is! He wants all peoples to come to the realization of who He is, repent of their sins, and worship Him.

Paul made his case in Romans 15 by showing four reasons the mission of all peoples is to glorify God.

"May the God who gives endurance and encouragement give you a spirit of unity among yourselves as you follow Christ Jesus. Accept one another, then, just as Christ accepted you, in order to bring praise to God. For I tell you that Christ has become a servant of the Jews on behalf of God's truth, to confirm the promises made to the patriarchs so that the Gentiles may glorify God for his mercy, as it is written. May the God of hope fill you with all joy and peace as you trust in him, so that you may overflow with hope by the power of the Holy Spirit. To be a minister of Christ Jesus to the Gentiles with the priestly duty of proclaiming the gospel of God, so that the Gentiles might become an offering acceptable to God, sanctified by the Holy Spirit. It has always been my ambition to preach the gospel where Christ was not known, so that I would not be building on someone else's foundation" (Rom. 15:5,7-9,13,16,20).

"May the God who gives endurance and encouragement give you a spirit of unity among yourselves as you follow Christ Jesus, so that with one heart and mouth you may glorify the God and Father of our Lord Jesus Christ. Accept one another, then, just as Christ accepted you, in order to bring praise to God" (Rom. 15:5-7).

" 'My prayer is not for them alone. I pray also for those who will believe in me through their message, that all of them may be one, Father, just as you are in me and I am in you. May they also be in us so that the world may believe that you have sent me. I have given them the glory that you gave me, that they may be one as we are one. I in them and you in me. May they be brought to complete unity to let the world know that you sent me and have loved them even as you have loved me' " (John 17:20-24).

"I have written you quite boldly on some points, as if to remind you of them again, because of the grace God gave me to be a minister of Christ Jesus to the Gentiles with the priestly duty of proclaiming the gospel of God, so that the Gentiles might become an offering acceptable to God, sanctified by the Holy Spirit.

1. Christ suffered so that all peoples would glorify God.

Read Romans 15:8-9 in your Bible. Christ stated that He did things so that the Scriptures might be fulfilled. He fulfilled more than 365 prophecies made about Him. Paul stated that Jesus' suffering was to confirm promises made to the patriarchs so that the Gentiles can also know God.

2. The message of the entire Scriptures is that all peoples glorify God.

Read Romans 15:4,8 in your Bible. Write T for (true) or F for (false) beside each statement.
___ 1. The whole Bible was written to teach us. Therefore, we should follow the example of the godly men we have been studying.
___ 2. Paul based his teachings on Scripture.
___ 3. If we believe the Scriptures are true, we will be encouraged.
___ 4. The Scriptures encourage us to have hope.
___ 5. Jesus served the Jews because they were the only chosen people.
___ 6. Jesus fulfilled the promises made to the patriarchs by making a way for all peoples to glorify God.

Paul pressed home the point that God gave him to be the minister of Christ Jesus to the Gentiles, which can be translated "all peoples." He was called to offer up the offering of unreached people groups to God and urged the Romans to join him in that sacred task. If you believe the Scriptures, you, like Paul, will show it by your actions. All statements in the exercise, except number 5, are true.

3. God's desire for the unity of God's people is that He will be glorified among all peoples.

In the margin read Romans 15:5-7 and John 17:20-24, Jesus' prayer the night before He was crucified. Notice that all the desires of God's heart for the world hinge on what He wants for His people. Obviously, God's desire for unity among Christians is so that all the world will know Him.

How do we work together when we believe many different things and do things in different ways as churches, individuals, and organizations? That brings us back to the Scripture you just read, Romans 15:5-7. Today this Scripture is being fulfilled. But we have a long way to go for all of us to accept one another as Christ has accepted us. Only God can give us the spirit of unity so that we all can participate in His mission—so that with one heart and mouth we can glorify the God and Father of our Lord Jesus Christ. Today calls for a practical unity focused on the mission—that all peoples will glorify God. We will not come together based on doctrinal distinctives or organizational models. We will come together to affirm what is on God's heart—the nations.

Being on mission with God can do what all the councils, all the ecumenists, and all the religious authorities that have ever tried to force unity could not do. The 21st century could be the time when Jesus' prayer is answered and Christians link arms as we march on mission with God to the last peoples on earth who do not know Him, so that they can glorify Him and worship Him with us.

Describe your personal commitment to the unity of all true believers so that all peoples will glorify God together.

_____

4. The reason God calls missionaries is so that all peoples will glorify Him.

Read Romans 15:15-24 in the margins on page 166-167.

In verse 16 Paul went back to his missionary call. He reminded them of what he had already mentioned—that God gave him grace to be a minister of Christ Jesus to the Gentiles. He then used the analogy of a priest who had a duty to present an offering to God. His offering was the Gentiles accepted by God and sanctified by the Holy Spirit. In verse 20 he stated his holy ambition to be a missionary pioneer who goes where no one else has ever gone with the gospel so that

"those who were not told about him will see,
    and those who have not heard will understand" (Rom. 15:21).

The statement in verse 23 is surprising because Paul said there was no more place for him to preach since he had fully proclaimed the gospel of Christ from Jerusalem all the way around to Illyricum. Does that mean that all those people had heard or understood the gospel? I don't think so. He meant that the gospel had been made accessible to them and that he had planted enough new churches that they would carry on the rest of the work of evangelization in those areas. He was still looking for the pioneer field, so he set his sights on Spain. That is the essence of the missionary call—to proclaim Christ where peoples have never heard or understood.

We have established that all Christians are to be on mission with God. We have said that they can be on mission in thousands of ways as God leads. However, a specific missionary call is for a portion of God's people who are called to take the gospel across cultural and geographical lines. How would you know whether you were called to be a missionary?

You know you are called if God speaks to you about being a missionary in one or more of the key ways He speaks. God sometimes speaks in very dramatic events, as He did with Paul. But we have no such accounts of Silas, Timothy, or Titus being called. God sometimes also uses a process over time to slowly bring you to the realization that He is calling. You need to know you are called before you give your life to live among another people as a missionary.

Place an X on each continuum to indicate the degree to which your experience corresponds to my description.

1. You know you are called if God speaks to you through Scripture by continually impressing a passage or passages on your heart about being a missionary. Sometimes your call occurs in your quiet reading of Scripture, a preacher's enthusiastic challenge, or a missionary's exciting testimony.

Seldom   Sometimes   Often

Therefore I glory in Christ Jesus in my service to God. I will not venture to speak of anything except what Christ has accomplished through me in leading the Gentiles to obey God by what I have said and done—by the power of signs and miracles, through the power of the Spirit. So from Jerusalem all the way around to Illyricum, I have fully proclaimed the gospel of Christ. It has always been my ambition to preach the gospel where Christ was not known, so that I would not be building on someone else's foundation. Rather, as it is written:
*'Those who were not told about him will see,
    and those who have not heard will understand.'*
This is why I have often been hindered from coming to you.

But now that there is no more place for me to work in these regions, and since I have been longing for many years to see you, I plan to do so when I go to Spain. I hope to visit you while passing through and to have you assist me on my journey there, after I have enjoyed your company for a while" (Rom. 15:15-24).

2. You know you are called if, when you pray, God repeatedly speaks to you about being a missionary. You may be surprised by how often God brings the subject to your mind when you pray. You may want to go to another country on a prayerwalk, where you can pray "on site with insight."

Seldom   Sometimes   Often

3. You know you are called if God repeatedly speaks to you through circumstances. Circumstances alone are insufficient, but they awaken you or confirm that you are called. Often people who go on short-term mission trips have a missions call confirmed or realize they are not called to that kind of ministry. God uses all kinds of circumstances to call you to missions.

Seldom   Sometimes   Often

4. You know you are called if God repeatedly speaks to you through His body, the church. When you ask godly leaders what they think about the possibility of your being a missionary, they often endorse the idea. At other times someone may mention the possibility to you. As you follow God's leadership, you need God's people to affirm you in many ways. Mission boards have consultants who can discuss the requirements with you, such as references, medical exams, and gifts needed for certain assignments. Sometimes one mission board will not accept you, but another one will. If you feel called, pursue all avenues God opens to you.

Seldom   Sometimes   Often

Look at your answers again. What do they reveal that God is saying to you about being a missionary?

_____

_____

If you marked *often*, you can be assured that God has called you to be a missionary. If you sometimes have these experiences, keep seeking God's will. If God seldom speaks, continue to find ways to support God's purpose so that all peoples will experience His glory.

---

[1] Rick Warren, *The Purpose-Driven Church* (Grand Rapids, MI: Zondervan, 1995), 370.

[2] See my book *Indonesian Revival: Why Two Million Came to Christ* (Hattiesburg, MS: William Carey Library Publishers, 1978).

[3] Donald Anderson McGavran, *The Bridges of God: A Study in the Strategy of Missions* (New York: Friendship Press, 1955), 12. In this book McGavran shows how God develops "bridges" (or openings) over which the gospel may travel from one people group to another.

JOHN

ON MISSION WITH GOD: EXPERIENCING ALL PEOPLES WORSHIPING GOD

This Week's Lessons

Day 1: Experiencing God Personally
Day 2: The Encounter of a Lifetime
Day 3: Prepared to Experience God's Glory
Day 4: When Jesus Appears
Day 5: Glory to God

This Week's Learning Focus

You will be able to describe how God will establish His kingdom and how representatives of all peoples will worship and glorify Him forever in heaven.

DAY 1

EXPERIENCING GOD PERSONALLY

One Saturday morning when I was 21 I found a babbling brook in the San Bois Mountains of southeastern Oklahoma. I sat on a rock and with my trusty *Nave's Topical Bible* read all the Scriptures in the Bible about God's glory. It blew my mind.

With Moses I saw the glory of God on the burning bush, in the pillar of fire, in dark clouds on the top of Mt. Sinai, covering the tabernacle and finally the "backside of God" when Moses asked to see God's glory. I gloried when God showed His power in the storied plagues and the miraculous opening of the Red Sea so His children could leave slavery in Egypt and worship God freely.

In the second hour, I visited Solomon's temple through the mirror of Scripture when God's glory came down on the temple and all the priests rushed outside because God's glory was so overwhelming. With Isaiah I looked into heaven at God on His glorious throne and heard the Seraphims crying, "Holy, Holy, Holy, Lord God Almighty." On and on I read and pictured what was happening to these men as they experienced God's glory.

Somewhere during the third hour I beheld God's glory in Jesus on the Mount of Transfiguration and in His resurrection body outside the garden tomb. All morning long I felt the mounting crescendo of His glory rising within me until it exploded in Revelation 5 with peoples of every tribe and language and people and nation singing in a mighty chorus:

Heart Focus

*"I looked and there before me was a great multitude that no one could count, from every nation, tribe, people and language, standing before the throne and in front of the Lamb. They were wearing white robes and were holding palm branches in their hands. ... All the angels were standing around the throne and around the elders and the four living creatures. They fell down on their faces before the throne and worshiped God, saying:
'Amen!
Praise and glory
and wisdom and thanks
and honor
and power and strength
be to our God for ever
and ever.
Amen!' " (Rev. 7:9-12).*

"The Lamb is worthy—the Lamb who was killed.
He is worthy to receive power and riches
and wisdom and strength
and honor and glory and blessing.
And then I heard every creature in heaven and on earth
and under the earth and in the sea.
They also sang:
'Blessing and honor and glory and power
belong to the one sitting on the throne
and to the Lamb forever and ever. And the four living beings said, "Amen!"
And the twenty-four elders fell down and worshiped God and the Lamb.'"
(author's paraphrase)

I could sit still no longer. I leaped to my feet shouting "Glory, glory, glory!" I had not seen God's glory with my physical eyes like the men of the Bible, but I experienced God's glory. I had been introduced to the purpose of God's mission —that He would be worshiped and glorified by all peoples.

That experience helped me begin to see my life from God's perspective. We are looking from the inside out, and He is looking at us from the outside in. He sees our lives in full perspective, from beginning to end. And He sees how our lives fit together in His greater plan and purpose. It has helped me throughout the course of my life to try to see my life as God sees me.

Do you remember the first time you wondered what the world was all about and why you had been born into it? As his Gospel and epistles show, John, "the one Jesus loved" (John 20:2), was a deep thinker who pondered the major issues of life. As a young Jewish boy, he was probably always asking about the meaning behind the Old Testament heroes' lives. He was probably fascinated by the way God worked through them and wondered whether he would grow up to be like them. One day he heard about John the Baptist, who sounded just like the prophet Elijah. He was sure God was working after he saw John in action and heard him preach about repentance!

1. God is always at work around you.

John was the son of fairly wealthy parents, who owned a Lake Galilee fishing business big enough to require hired help as well as their sons' labor. John was probably the younger brother of James. John's ambitious mother followed Jesus and helped provide for His needs. Her son John was probably very much like her—determined and rather ambitious!

John knew and was possibly a relative of the high priest. Responding to Jesus' last request of His friend, John took Jesus' mother, Mary, into his own home to care for her, so he owned a home large enough for guests.

The Scriptures in the margin reveal the weakness of John and his brother James. Below check weaknesses you see in John and James.
☐ Fiery temper
☐ Vindictiveness toward those who rejected them
☐ Presumption that they had power to call down fire from heaven
☐ Ambition
☐ Possessiveness

"The mother of Zebedee's sons came to Jesus with her sons and, kneeling down, asked a favor of him. 'What is it you want?'" he asked. She said, 'Grant that one of these two sons of mine may sit at your right and the other at your left in your kingdom.' 'You don't know what you are asking,' Jesus said to them. 'Can you drink the cup I am going to drink?' 'We can,' they answered" (Matt. 20:20-21).

"James son of Zebedee and his brother John (to them he gave the name Boanerges, which means Sons of Thunder)" (Mark 3:17).

"He sent messengers on ahead, who went into a Samaritan village to get things ready for him; but the people there did not welcome him, because he was heading for Jerusalem. When the disciples James and John saw this, they asked, 'Lord, do you want us to call fire down from heaven to destroy them?'" (Luke 9:52-54).

All of these were weaknesses of John and James. Their mother shared their ambition! In the list, circle weaknesses you see in yourself.

God knows your weaknesses and chose you anyway. He not only wants to work around you, but He also wants to work in you. Each of the seven greatest characters in the Bible, except Jesus, had defects. The fact that Jesus had no weakness makes His love for you even greater! Jesus expressed God's love even for the Sons of Thunder! John was not a tenderhearted, loving individual, but God was at work in and around him.

2. *God pursues a continuing real and personal love relationship with you.*

God pursued John from the start. He caused John to grow so fascinated with John the Baptist's preaching that he became his disciple.

John's interest in seeing God at work culminated in a dynamic encounter with the Son of God! John the Baptist's disciples heard him say, " 'Look, the Lamb of God, who takes away the sin of the world' " (John 1:29). They experienced God's glory as they watched him baptize Jesus in the river Jordan. They saw the dove descend and heard God's voice say, " 'This is my Son, whom I love; with him I am well pleased' " (Matt. 3:17). An incredible encounter occurred when Jesus established a personal relationship with John and Andrew.

God's first step with you is to establish a personal relationship. Of all the disciples John felt he had the closest relationship with Jesus, calling himself the disciple Jesus loved (see John 20:2).

Stop and think about Jesus' love for you. Ask Him how He wants to relate to you. After praying, write what He said.

_____

_____

_____

That day John had an opportunity to begin to know Jesus personally and to ask Jesus questions about Himself and God's purpose in sending Him. John may have been amazed at the preaching of John the Baptist, but He had to be even more astounded at the teaching of the Messiah of God!

3. *God invites you to become involved with Him in His work one revelation at a time.*

Soon Jesus took the second step in this personal relationship with John. This time He came seeking John. The Lord didn't call John and the other disciples to merely spend time with Him. His Heavenly Father had always been working, and Jesus had just joined Him in His earthly ministry. John records Jesus' words " 'My Father is always at his work to this very day, and I, too, am working' " (John 5:17). John experienced the second step of a long journey when Jesus joined His Father at work.

Jesus recruited fishermen James and John to become fishers of men. He was not just giving them a fish; He would teach them how to fish!

Put a check mark beside the highest level of the love relationship you have experienced with Jesus.
- ❏ A desire to have a personal relationship with Him and experience His salvation
- ❏ A desire to develop a mature relationship with Him
- ❏ A desire to minister with Him
- ❏ A desire to be on mission with God
- ❏ A desire to experience God's glory as He accomplishes His mission through you

4. God speaks to you to reveal Himself, His purposes, and His ways.

John and the other disciples had the rare privilege of hearing God speak through the lips of His Son. John also heard the voice of God speak at Jesus' baptism and on the Mount of Transfiguration. He heard God speak through the Old Testament Scriptures, particularly after hearing Christ teach about fulfilling them. He heard God speak to him in prayer, particularly while he was exiled on the Isle of Patmos.

Throughout his life John experienced circumstances that echoed the voice of God. The Lord rebuked him for being too zealous and having the wrong motive in mind when John wanted to call down fire on the Samaritan town that rejected Christ. Another time He rebuked James, John, and their mother. The reason God speaks to you is to reveal Himself, His purposes, and His ways.

Write one way God has revealed Himself, His purposes, and His ways during your study of *On Mission with God*.

1. Himself _____

   _____

2. His purposes _____

   _____

3. His ways _____

   _____

5. God's invitation for you to work with Him leads you on the bumpy road of a crisis of belief.

Have you experienced an invitation from God that required you to believe Him and act quickly? John had that happen when Christ first summoned him to follow Him. The Gospel of Mark adds a fascinating detail about that call.

Read Mark 1:16-20 in the margin. Fill in the blanks.
- Peter and Andrew: "___ _____ they left their nets and followed him."

- James and John: "_____ _____ he called them, and they left their father Zebedee in the boat with the hired men and followed him."

Peter and Andrew followed Jesus "at once." "Without delay" Jesus called John and his brother, as if to set the example of how they were to respond to Him. The four fishermen were quick to respond. Soon Jesus had them right in the thick of His ministry in Capernaum.

Has God invited you to join Him in His work? ☐ Yes ☐ No
Check any of these that delay you in following Him on His mission.
☐ Your job   ☐ Your lack of intimacy with God
☐ Your financial situation   ☐ Your parents' concerns
☐ Your family obligations   ☐ Other _____
☐ Your friends' opinions

Although God relates to you personally, He has far more in mind than your personal experience. Before you move on, meditate on this statement by missiologist Jeff Lewis. Ask God what He has in mind for your life when He encounters you personally: "Jesus is not our personal Savior. We live in a culture where personal means mine. You don't get a personal-pan pizza to share it or hire a personal trainer to share them, and you don't want everyone using your personal computer. Now don't get me wrong. I believe that you must receive Jesus personally and that one of the benefits of salvation is that we can have a personal and intimate relationship with the living God. But, Jesus is not our personal possessive savior, He is the 'Savior of the world.' "[1]

> "As Jesus walked beside the Sea of Galilee, he saw Simon and his brother Andrew casting a net into the lake, for they were fishermen. 'Come follow me,' Jesus said, 'and I will make you fishers of men.' At once they left their nets and followed him. When he had gone a little farther, he saw James son of Zebedee and his brother John in a boat, preparing their nets. Without delay he called them, and they left their father Zebedee in the boat with the hired men and followed him" (Mark 1:16-20).

DAY 2

THE ENCOUNTER OF A LIFETIME

6. You must make major adjustments when God calls you to join Him.

No doubt John and the other disciples strongly felt their obligations to family and financial concerns. After all, they were commercial fishermen. We know that Peter had a wife to support, and John and James were certainly an integral part of their father's fishing industry. Zebedee likely had to hire two or three persons to replace his sons after they dropped their nets and took off with Jesus! Major adjustments were required for everyone concerned in the lives of all Jesus' disciples.

Sometimes it costs others more than it does you for you to follow Jesus. Jesus set the example in leaving Joseph's carpentry shop to do His Heavenly Father's bidding. If God calls you to be a missionary, your parents may have

"As they were walking along the road, a man said to him, 'I will follow you wherever you go.' Jesus replied, 'Foxes have holes and birds of the air have nests, but the Son of Man has no place to lay his head.' He said to another man, 'Follow me.' But the man replied, 'Lord, first let me go and bury my father.' Jesus said to him, 'Let the dead bury their own dead, but you go and proclaim the kingdom of God.' Still another said, 'I will follow you, Lord; but first let me go back and say good-by to my family.' Jesus replied, 'No one who puts his hand to the plow and looks back is fit for service in the kingdom of God'" (Luke 9:57-62).

more difficulty in parting from you than you have in going. I was so excited about following God's call that I didn't really understand the sacrifice parents made until I had grandchildren. Missionaries feel the separation when a loved one far away is sick or dies. The cost is included in the major adjustment.

Read Luke 9:57-62 in the margin. Talk to God about the major adjustments required of others if you make the major adjustment He asks of you.

Today many distractions exist to doing the will of God. You may undergo a major adjustment in your career, your financial situation, the concerns of your parents, or any number of areas. No one who obeys the Great Commission has been able to avoid the necessary rearrangement of priorities when God issues an invitation to join Him on mission. God may ask you to quit a well-paying job, to sell your house and car, to do added study, to have a garage sale to rid yourself of unneeded possessions, and generally to alter your whole lifestyle. Jesus could have argued with the Father about leaving the glory of heaven for a ministry as an itinerant preacher and as a sacrifice for sinful people. The disciples could have offered many reasons not to leave all to follow Jesus, but they didn't. They got up and went—no questions asked. Jesus' supernatural magnetism called for unswerving loyalty!

Separate the decision-making phase from the problem-solving phase. You may want to have all the problems solved before you make the decision. The Lord wants you to make the right decision; then He will help you solve the problems!

In the margin write from memory as much of this week's memory verse as you can.

7. As you obey God and He accomplishes His purpose through you, you experience God's glory.

John and the other disciples had many great experiences ahead of them as they went on mission with Jesus. Not all were pleasant. They ran into much opposition along the way. But what an experience and what an education they received from God's Son!

It is the same in your world. As God's Holy Spirit anoints and fills you, you will operate in God's power and authority to bring the good news to people. Those who have never known the concept of forgiveness will be astonished that such is available to them. Recently, I was present when a Hindu girl attended a Bible study for the first time in her life. She kept repeating that she couldn't believe forgiveness was offered to cover all her sin. That concept was so foreign to her in her own religion that it was almost too good to be true! People all over the world are waiting for that same good news.

Are you ready for the next step in God's revelation of Himself and His purpose for your life? ☐Yes ☐No ☐Not yet

Will you stop and ask Him to lead you through whatever experience He desires that will help you join Him on mission? Write an expression of your willingness to be on mission with Him.

_____

_____

You saw John's initial experiences with Jesus and the way he responded to the Lord. You may have had an experience with God and wonder to what it will lead. God has a design for your life. That experience is one step in His grand design.

Read Jeremiah 29:11 in the margin. Try imagining what God has planned for your life. Then read Ephesians 3:20-21 in the margin and experience a sense of wonder at what God has planned for you.

John's life is a good example of what God can do with ordinary people who join Him on mission.

1. God chose you to be on mission with Him to reconcile a lost world to Himself.

We know that God chose John long before Christ called him to join Him on mission. Jesus prayed all night before He asked the disciples to follow Him. The Father communicated to the Son exactly who should make up that privileged group of twelve. John was blessed to be chosen for that relationship. In God's special purpose for him, he was to be in Jesus' inner circle, along with his brother, James, and Peter.

Beyond that, John became Christ's intimate friend, who reclined closest to Him at the Last Supper (see John 13:25; 21:20). The crucified Christ commissioned John to take care of His mother (see John 19:26). John was even closer to Jesus than He was to His own family members! Jesus had four half-brothers and at least two half-sisters, who were Mary's children; yet He entrusted His mother to John's care. The bond between Jesus and John was something special! You too can have a special bond with Christ.

Read Mark 3:31-34 in the margin. Fill in the blank below.

Those Jesus considered family: _____

Christ didn't allow John to grow close to Him just for John's benefit. The Lord's focus was on reconciling a lost world to Himself. Because John was close, he could hear Jesus' heartbeat for the world. John was chosen to live a long life (at least 90 years) so that he could influence the world with Christ's message of reconciliation. You have been chosen for the same incredible purpose! God will use you in the unique way He has planned for your life as you go on mission with Him.

" 'I know the plans I have for you,' declares the Lord, 'plans to prosper you and not to harm you, plans to give you hope and a future' " (Jer. 29:11).

"Now to him who is able to do immeasurably more than all we ask or imagine, according to his power that is at work within us, to him be glory in the church and in Christ Jesus throughout all generations, for ever and ever! Amen" (Eph. 3:20-21).

"Jesus' mother and brothers arrived. Standing outside, they sent someone in to call him. A crowd was sitting around him, and they told him, 'Your mother and brothers are outside looking for you.' 'Who are my mother and brothers?' he asked. Then he looked at those seated in a circle around him and said, 'Here are my mother and my brothers! Whoever does God's will is my brother and sister and mother' " (Mark 3:31-34).

Because John was close, he could hear Jesus' heartbeat for the world.

2. God calls you to Himself to be on mission with Him.

God's call is not to a position or a program but to intimate fellowship with Him. John experienced that as no other disciple did. This is clear when he called himself "the disciple whom Jesus loved" (John 13:23).

Write a phrase you would use to describe your relationship with Jesus.

_____

_____

John experienced the joy of observing His Lord at close range under all kinds of circumstances. At certain times John, James, and Peter were present when other disciples were excluded. No doubt the Lord had a special plan in mind for the part they would play in His kingdom.

Read Mark 5:34-43 in your Bible. Answer the following *T* (true) or *F* (false).
____ 1. Jesus let only Peter, James, and John follow Him.
____ 2. People laughed at Jesus when He said the child was not dead.
____ 3. Jesus allowed only the parents and three disciples to remain.
____ 4. The girl took a long time to awaken when Jesus spoke to her.
____ 5. Jesus gave strict orders that she should not be allowed to eat.

No doubt John and the other two disciples were astonished at Jesus' faith in this situation. They heard His encouraging words to the stricken father, in contrast to His authoritative attitude toward the unbelieving mourners. They observed that His presence changed the home's atmosphere from noisy commotion to quiet privacy, as He shut out all but those who had faith in Him. His gentleness with the young girl must have impressed them, as well as His humility in not wanting anyone to know. John, James, and Peter were privileged to observe this divine miracle. Think what they reported to the other disciples! (The first three answers above are true.)

> God confirms His choice of you when you recognize His call and follow Him.

You have the incredible opportunity of being Jesus' intimate disciple today. He calls you to help Him complete His task. God confirms His choice of you when you recognize His call and follow Him. You choose the level of intimacy you want to have with Him!

3. God initiates a covenant of promise and obedience with you.

Have you ever been offered a job situation that was too good to turn down? On that memorable day when Jesus called John to follow Him, He promised him something money could not buy—to make him a "fisher of men."

With a word Jesus changed his whole career. Jesus didn't have a contract for John to sign, guaranteeing him a certain wage for the work he would do in God's kingdom. But He gave John a promise. Great courage and faith were necessary for John to leave everything behind. Catching people would be hard work, but it was much more important than catching fish!

Perhaps the Lord has called you to leave the work in which you have become skilled to be on mission with Him. He may ask you to leave a comfortable lifestyle or your parents' home for a much less certain existence that doesn't guarantee even a minimum wage! John didn't stop and count the cost or cling to his creature comforts. He was drawn by the magnetic personality of the Lord and by the urgency of His mission to a lost world of men and women dying in their sin. The Lord called him to a lifetime commitment of obedience and faith, promising him an eternal reward for his faithfulness. John made that covenant with Christ and, having put his hand to the plough in the kingdom of God, never looked back!

Perhaps Jesus has called you to use your skills and relationships where you are to fulfill His mission in the world. Perhaps He tells you that you are to experience His glory by adopting a simpler lifestyle and giving the difference so that others might hear.

Perhaps He tells you that you are to experience His glory by adopting a simpler lifestyle.

Check what you would be willing to leave to join Christ on mission.
- ☐ Your career
- ☐ A comfortable home
- ☐ A good salary
- ☐ Your family
- ☐ Your close friends
- ☐ Other _____

DAY 3

PREPARED TO EXPERIENCE GOD'S GLORY

Jesus knew that the disciples needed His character formed in them before they were prepared to carry out His commission. For three years He set them an example of love, humility, servanthood, obedience, faithfulness, and suffering. He discipled and mentored John and the others to build these characteristics into their lives. He commanded them to wait in Jerusalem until the Spirit came on them in power. After that experience they were never the same again!

4. God prepares you for His mission.

Evangelist D. L. Moody was preaching to great crowds when two elderly women repeatedly said to him, "We are praying for you." Finally, he asked them what they were praying in his behalf. They answered, "We are praying for you that you may receive the power." Moody was miffed that they thought he wasn't filled with the Spirit, but something in his spirit prompted him to listen. He talked with them further, and that began his search for the filling of the Spirit. A few days later, as he walked down the street in New York City, the Spirit of God fell on him and revealed Himself to Moody. He recorded, "I had such an experience of His love that I had to ask Him to stay His hand."[2] After experiencing God's glory, Moody was used to bring hundreds of thousands to the Lord instead of a few hundred. At that point his whole ministry was completely changed.

It was the same after Pentecost. The Holy Spirit came on all 120 who were gathered, and they were all speaking as He gave them utterance. When Peter gave the invitation, 3,000 people came to Christ!

Reading Moody's story was the turning point in my life. I recognized how much I needed to be filled with the Spirit. Anything that has happened in my life is because the Spirit did it—not because I did it. In those early days after that experience I told the church I pastored, "If I don't show up one Sunday, it's because I'm not filled with the Spirit. If I'm not filled with the Spirit, I don't have anything to tell you. So if I don't show up, pray for me." I always showed up, but I had some close calls. I sometimes had to do some fervent praying before I approached the pulpit. God wants to fill you with His Spirit because it is the Spirit of God who is the power and who does the work!

It is the Spirit of God who is the power and who does the work!

What is the strongest evidence that you are filled with the Holy Spirit?

_____

5. God sends you to the place where He can best work through you to accomplish His mission.

God planned for John to have a big role in His mission. He would be imprisoned and beaten for his faith. Herod would behead James, John's brother. John would be asked to go to the outcast Samaritans to examine those who had believed. He would be exiled to the Isle of Patmos, where he would have a revelation of Christ, which he would record as the last book of the Bible.

What kind of preparation would Jesus give John so that he could do what God planned for his life? More than John could have ever imagined.

Have you ever been frustrated because someone asked you to do a job and you had no idea how it fit into the bigger scheme of things? God tells you what you need to know when you need to know it. Jesus carefully monitored the progress of John and His other disciples. He gave them more responsibility as they were faithful in the small tasks.

In your Bible look up the Scripture passages listed in the margin. Match the references with the ways Jesus prepared John for his ministry after Pentecost and for his Isle of Patmos exile.

a. Luke 9:16
b. Luke 9:1-6
c. Luke 9:54-55
d. Luke 9:49-50
e. Matthew 20:20-24
f. Luke 22:46
g. Luke 9:28-36

____ 1. Early in Jesus' ministry John was sent with the other disciples from village to village to preach the gospel and heal people.
____ 2. John took part in the feeding of the five thousand.
____ 3. John, with James and Peter, was privileged to be on the Mount of Transfiguration and see Jesus glorified.
____ 4. John needed correction from Christ when he tried to stop someone driving out demons in Jesus' name.
____ 5. John came in for rebuke when he and his brother wanted to call down fire on a Samaritan village.
____ 6. John and James drew indignation from other disciples when their mother requested special places in Christ's kingdom for her two sons.
____ 7. John was reprimanded by Jesus in Gethsemane for sleeping when he should have been praying.

Step-by-step John gradually moved from acquaintance to friend of Jesus. The correct answers in the previous exercise are *1. b, 2. a, 3. g, 4. d, 5. c, 6. e, 7. f.*

God looks for dependable people to be His friends so that when He sends them out, He can depend on them to do His work. In the margin see Jesus' words on this subject. In the normal course of events a servant doesn't understand what the master has in mind. A servant is usually told to go plow the back 40 acres or mop the floor or prepare lunch. He expects no thanks. He has done his duty. Jesus says, "I'm not just commanding you to go do a job. I call you friends because I have told you the Master's business. Everything I learned from My Father I have made known to you." What is the Master's business?

Read John 4:34-38; 15:14-16; 17:4 in your Bible. Then write what you think the Master's business is.

_____

_____

Jesus revealed what His work is. The Master's business, through His disciples, is producing fruit that will last so that He can reap an everlasting harvest through them. The Lord desires to produce fruit through you as He sends you on a lifetime quest for His kingdom for the glory of God!

6. God guides you on His mission.

Once when I preached at Southwestern Seminary, I said that like a flashlight, God gives you only so much light and the light will not shine a foot farther until you take a step. Months later, I met a man who had responded to the invitation. He was on his way to be a missionary in Japan. He said, "When I stepped out, I didn't know where I was going, but I took the next step. When I did, God showed me the next step." When you walk in the light God gives you, He gives you more light and guides you so that people can glorify Him.

John became a faithful friend and dependable disciple as the Lord guided him throughout his lifetime. He partnered with Peter to become an effective team player as God led them into various circumstances. John was with Peter and James in the garden of Gethsemane as the Lord asked them to pray during His agony (see Mark 14:33). Through John's influence Peter was permitted into the high priest's courtyard as Christ was led to trial (see John 18:16). Mary Magdalene found the two together when she ran to tell them of Jesus' resurrection, which means that John continued to be Peter's friend even after his infamous denial of the Lord. The two of them ran to the tomb together to verify Mary's story (see John 20:2-9).

After Christ's ascension the Lord guided John and Peter to testify before the Jewish rulers of the day. Standing before the Sanhedrin, they did not flinch. Commanded not to speak or teach in Jesus' name, Peter and John, empowered by the Holy Spirit, replied: " 'Judge for yourselves whether it is right in God's sight to obey you rather than God. For we cannot help speaking about what we have seen and heard' " (Acts 4:19-20). As an old man, exiled to Patmos for his faith in Christ, John endured loneliness and suffering without complaint (see Rev. 1:9).

You can't depend on someone unless he or she consistently obeys.

Can God really depend on you to obey as He guides you? If you say, "I obey most of the time," does that mean 65 percent of the time, or 70 percent, or 80 percent? How much can you trust someone who is dependable some of the time? What if you sent him on a mission during the 15 percent of the time he was undependable? An unfaithful person is like a lame foot in times of trouble, according to Proverbs 25:19. You can't depend on somebody unless he or she consistently obeys. God doesn't expect perfection, but He does expect faithfulness.

What percent of the time can God count on you to be obedient when He guides you to do something? _____ percent

Recall times in your life when God could count on your faithfulness.

_____

_____

_____

7. God uses you to bring glory to His name through His mission.

As you see John's development, does it inspire you to hope that you can be used effectively in God's kingdom? Watching this young Son of Thunder is fascinating as He is transformed into the Apostle of Love. As Jesus looked from the cross at this disciple whom He loved, He knew that John had the potential to become a pillar in the Jerusalem church, the bishop of the church at Ephesus, and the writer of five books of the New Testament. As John continued to follow the Lord obediently, his character was transformed. He was able to shoulder the responsibility God had prepared for him. No doubt his daily concern for Christ's mother prepared him for the care he would exercise for the churches over which he was given oversight. In his later years his main theme was love, which he exemplified in great measure.

As John continued to follow the Lord obediently, his character was transformed.

God uses ordinary people to take on God-sized tasks. Whether He leads you to witness in a prison, to share Christ in another country, to be exiled, to change your lifestyle where you live, or to teach a Sunday School class, He will equip and empower you, as He did John, and will use you mightily!

Ask God to guide you and use you in His kingdom and for His glory. Write your commitment here.

_____

_____

_____

※※ ～ DAY 4 ～ ※※

WHEN JESUS APPEARS

Today we move past John's lifetime to focus on John's influence on the church. As you study John's influence, think about your influence on your present church and on any other churches God leads you to. God revealed Revelation last because it is directed to the churches of these last days. As time has passed, the love of many has grown cold. They are no longer on mission with God. They need a fresh word from God and a challenge to join Him on mission.

In Revelation Jesus walks among the churches and speaks to their pastors. First-century heresies take a toll on the church of Christ. The seven churches of Asia Minor, especially the one at Ephesus, where John had been bishop, were dear to him. Their weakened condition grieved him. The One who holds " 'the keys of death and Hades' " (Rev. 1:18) spoke to His corporate body through John and showed them the remedy for their condition! I believe God told John what to say to them to address the many kinds of situations His churches face on mission with Him. His return to earth may occur at any time. He comes through the Holy Spirit every day and speaks through His messengers about the church's condition. God is concerned about His people because His mission through them requires a relationship with Him.

Jesus visits His churches personally. Jesus walks among the lampstands, which symbolize the churches, and holds in His hand the stars that represent His messengers. He gives a message to John for the messengers of the churches.

Read Revelation 1:10-18 in your Bible. Imagine with me how you would react as you saw the glorified Christ.

Relive John's experience, in exile on Patmos, as he worshiped the Lord one Sunday. First he heard a loud voice like a trumpet. He turned around quickly and saw Christ walking among seven golden lampstands (representing the seven churches). The first thing that caught his attention was one "like a son of man" dressed in a white robe with a golden sash around his chest. John noticed that His head and hair were white as snow and His eyes were like blazing fire. I think that he could not look continually into those blazing eyes and dropped his eyes to the ground, because the next thing he mentioned is Christ's feet that were like bronze glowing in a furnace. Suddenly he heard Christ's voice like the sound of rushing waters. At that he looked up and saw Christ's hands, which held the seven stars representing the churches. His eyes drifted up once again, and he saw the sharp double-edged sword coming out of Christ's mouth. That's when he fell to the ground as if he were dead. How will you feel when you meet Christ face-to-face? Every account in the Bible shows people overcome by His presence.

Read the passages in the margin. Stop and recognize that Christ stands before you, whether or not you can see Him. Stop and worship Him in all His holiness.

> God revealed Revelation last because it is directed to the churches of these last days.

> "With the tip of the staff that was in his hand, the angel of the Lord touched the meat and the unleavened bread. Fire flared from the rock, consuming the meat and the bread. And the angel of the Lord disappeared. When Gideon realized that it was the angel of the Lord, he exclaimed, 'Ah, Sovereign Lord! I have seen the angel of the Lord face to face!'" (Judg. 6:21-23).

> "Like the appearance of a rainbow in the clouds on a rainy day, so was the radiance around him" (Ezek. 1:28)

> "When Simon Peter saw this, he fell at Jesus' knee and said, 'Go away from me, Lord; I am a sinful man!'" (Luke 5:8).

Christ commended the churches for some things but condemned them for others and warned them of impending judgment if they did not repent. What would Christ say to today's churches? What does He say to your church?

1. God says, "To be on mission with Me, return to your first love."

Read Revelation 2:1-7 in your Bible. Compare the strengths and weaknesses of the church at Ephesus to those of your church.

Note that the many strong qualities of this church are completely counterbalanced by the major weakness—loss of their first love for the Lord. Only 35 years earlier Paul had written to commend them for their faith and love (see Eph. 1:15-16). How far they had fallen in just one generation! Today the corporate body of Christ suffers from the same disease. More than 70 percent of the churches in the United States have plateaued for years. If Satan can tempt your church to leave its first love for God, he has won a victory.

"Hear, O Israel: The Lord our God, the Lord is one. Love the Lord your God with all your heart and with all your soul and with all your strength. These commandments that I give you today are to be upon your hearts" (Deut. 6:4-6).

In the margin read Deuteronomy 6:4-6, which Christ repeated as the first and great commandment. You demonstrate your love by your actions. On a scale of 1–10 (1 = highest) evaluate yourself and your church by writing the numbers beside the phrases that best fit your church and your life.

	My Church	Me
1. Thrilled by experiencing God's glory in worship	____	____
2. Fervent in prayer	____	____
3. Telling others of your Lover	____	____
4. Thoughts don't wander during worship	____	____
5. Actions are as intensive as talk about Him	____	____
6. Focused on God's mission more than your own	____	____
7. Seeking God's glory more than your own	____	____

If you fail at love, you fail absolutely. The remedy for this church's situation was twofold: remember and repent. Christ reminds the members of the height of their first experience of love for Him. (Read Eph. 3:15-21 in your Bible to see how far they had fallen.) No other remedy existed for them but to repent and do the things they did at first—in simple terms, love and obey Him.

How much is your church like the church at Ephesus? Repentance was the key to the revival of their relationship with Him. Repentance means you and your church turn back and obey what He commands. Real and lasting spiritual awakening will occur only through prayer and obedience.

Stop now and pray until—
- you are aware of God's presence;
- you are awed by God's presence and holiness;
- you are alarmed by His convicting call;
- you are awakened to your first love.

As you pray, you may hear a clarion call that reveals God's impending judgment on your sin or on your church's sin and His view of it, as the church at Ephesus did. Christ's promise to those who were overcomers—those who obeyed Him—was that He would give them the right to eat from the tree of life in God's paradise. With that eternal prospect in view, you have great incentive to overcome your lethargy in the Christian life and return in repentance to the white-hot heat of your first, intimate love for Christ.

Check the commitments you will make to return to your first love.
☐ Ask God to set your heart on fire for Himself or the lost.
☐ Commit yourself to daily Bible study and keep on fire for Him.
☐ Pray. Enlist others in the corporate body to pray with you and for you.

Jesus gives you the remedy for your situation, just as He did the church at Ephesus: remember and repent, asking Him to rekindle your love for Him! Enlist others to pray with you and for you. Then be on mission with the Lord in your church to share the message of revival and spiritual awakening with others

2. God says, "To be on mission with Me, stay faithful even to the point of death."

Read Revelation 2:8-11 in your Bible. Fill in the following blanks.

1. The Lord knew their _____ and _____

   yet proclaimed they were _____.

2. Their main problem was _____ from the synagogue of Satan.

3. Their greatest fear was they would have to _____ persecution.

4. The devil was going to put some of them in _____—to _____them.

5. If they were _____unto death, they would receive a crown of _____.

The church at Smyrna faced suffering on every side. Members experienced afflictions and poverty, as well as slander and persecution. But Christ considered them rich in such circumstances, because their faithfulness in severe trials would earn them a crown of life. He also promised those who were overcomers that they would not be hurt by the second death, which would separate them from God forever.

Many believers and churches in Third World countries face such persecution today. One young Muslim believer in North Africa was savagely beaten by fundamentalist Muslims when he began writing a book to refute the Qur'an. In the hospital he cried out, "They're trying to kill me!" However, a doctor there assured him he no longer needed to fear the three men he had named who beat him because they had earlier been pronounced dead on arrival at the emergency room. The believer is now writing books to prove that Jesus is the Son of God.

Christ knows the situations His faithful ones face. He has endured great suffering for them and has set an example of overcoming the evil one. He is standing with them in every trial, even as He stood by John as he suffered persecution and exile. American Christians in the past were so sheltered that they didn't think of the possibility of persecution in their lifetime. Prejudice, persecution, terrorist attacks, and the shootings of believers in churches and schools in America have made Christians in the United States more attuned to that prospect. Persecution will someday be the norm for the corporate body of Christ all over the world. Be prepared to be an overcomer, no matter what the circumstances.

Pause and pray. Ask God to strengthen you and your church in the areas of weakness He sees.

3. God says, "To be on mission with Me, you must be pure in doctrine and life."

Read Revelation 2:12-17 in your Bible.

Have you ever felt uncomfortable around someone who seemed to see right through you to the heart of what you were thinking or doing? The Pergamum church must have felt the same way when it realized that the Lord knew its faults. Members were to experience "the sharp, double-edged sword" (Rev. 2:12) of His mouth, which spoke directly to their condition. Even though members of this body remained true to His name and did not renounce their faith when one of their number was martyred, major problems required their attention. Heresies enticed the church people to live ungodly lives. Again, the Lord called them to repentance, promising the overcomers rewards of hidden manna and a white stone with a new, individual name written on it.

Current heresies have sapped the strength of many churches. Many have watered down the gospel and allowed New Age thinking to crowd out Christ's claims. Others tolerate blatant sexual practices condemned by God's Word.

Check the heresies that threaten to prevent your church from being on mission.
☐ universalism ("In the end all people will be saved.")
☐ relativism ("There is no absolute truth.")
☐ humanism ("We can do it alone.")
☐ secularism ("Leave God out of this.")
☐ sensualism ("If it feels good, do it.")

Only truth will keep you doctrinally pure in this day when the edges of everything are blurred. As a well-taught student of the Word, you can be a catalyst to keep the church of Jesus Christ holy until He comes again for His bride!

4. God says, "To be on mission with Me, stop tolerating sexual immorality."

Read Revelation 2:18-29 in your Bible. Answer the following questions.

1. How many things did Christ know about them? (v. 19) _____

2. What did Christ hold against them? (v. 20) _____

3. Into what was this woman leading the church?_____

4. What was she unwilling to do?_____

5. What was the penalty for those who followed her ways? _____

6. What two rewards will those who overcome receive? _____

_____

The church at Thyatira had many good qualities, but it also had an outstanding weakness. Immorality was rampant because members refused to deal with a situation requiring discipline. However, the One "who searches hearts and minds" (Rev. 2:23) and would repay each according to his or her deeds was well aware of their condition and required an accounting. Intense suffering was ahead if they would not repent. Some were not led astray, however, and the Lord promised to give them authority over the nations and the morning star.

Today many churches are unwilling to take disciplinary actions when people refuse to repent of immorality and other serious sins that quench God's fire. No wonder many churches are cold and lifeless!

What is your church's disciplinary policy for serious sin? (If you don't know, try to find out.)

_____

_____

Name a spiritual friend you will ask to hold you accountable for sexual purity.

_____

5. God says, "To be on mission with Me, you must wake up."

Read Revelation 3:1-6 in your Bible. Answer T (true) or F (false).
_____ 1. The Sardis church members had a reputation for being dead.
_____ 2. The Lord had found their deeds complete in the sight of God.
_____ 3. They were to obey what they had heard and repent.
_____ 4. Christ was coming to them as a thief if they did not wake up.
_____ 5. Many people in Sardis had not soiled their clothes.
_____ 6. The overcomers would be dressed in white.
_____ 7. Christ would acknowledge the overcomers before His Father.

A tree that looked perfectly healthy once fell on the roof of my house. Its root system had been damaged earlier. Eventually, the hidden root system deteriorated to the point that it couldn't withstand winds that toppled the tree. That tree was like the Sardis church. The Lord saw that it was dead though appearing alive. He saw that what remained needed strengthening. He admonished members to remember, obey, and repent. To the few spiritually alive ones, He promised the privilege of walking with Him in white garments. The overcomers in the Sardis church would never have their names blotted out from the book of life.

Your church may be like the church at Sardis—full of activity and programs but lacking spiritual power. Many churches in the corporate body of Christ try to do His work in their own strength.

Christ loved the Sardis church and wanted to see it restored to its former vitality. That could occur only as members sought spiritual awakening through prayer. The following four steps are keys to revival.

1. The Holy Spirit *convicts* you of your sins. This occurs by truly listening to God as He assesses your relationship with Him. It means more than reading the Bible and listening to sermons. It means hearing God speak to you and call you to leave the parameters you set on Him.

2. You experience *contrition* for your sin, resulting in repentance and turning to God.

3. You *confess* your sin to God and, as He leads, to others. Usually, He convicts you of broken relationships and sinful actions on the way to the deeper sins of a broken relationship with Him and disobedience.

4. You are *cleansed* of your sins by the blood of Christ.

Does your church regularly pray for revival and spiritual awakening?
☐ Yes ☐ No

Will you be a catalyst for your church's spiritual awakening? ☐ Yes ☐ No

Will you remind your church of the need to pay attention to the four elements of revival listed above? ☐ Yes ☐ No

6. God says, "To be on mission with Me, you must enter the open door."

Read Revelation 3:7-13 in your Bible. Underline three good qualities of this church, circle three blessings Christ would bestow on this church, and put parentheses around three names that would be written on the overcomers in this church.

This church of brotherly love seems to be the only one that Christ highly commends. Members appeared to have loved and obeyed Him to a greater degree than those in any of the other six churches. Their one weakness seemed to be in the area of strength; they had only a little of it. Even under those conditions they had kept His Word, had not denied His name, and had obeyed His command to endure patiently. The rewards for this would be an open door placed before them, acknowledgment by those in the synagogue of Satan that they were beloved by God, and the promise that they would be kept from the hour of trial that would test the whole world. They were admonished to hold on to what they had so that their crown would not be taken away. The overcomers would be made pillars in the temple of God. They would have the name of God, the new Jerusalem, and Christ written on them. This church was on mission with God, influencing the pagan world around it. It had not stopped depending on the Spirit of God, so He was opening a door of opportunity for them.

What doors of opportunity is God opening for our church? Pray daily that you and your church will be faithful to those opportunities that God is placing before you.

7. God says, "To be on mission with Me, you must let Me in."

Read Revelation 3:14-22 in your Bible. In a sentence describe what was wrong with this church.

_____

The lukewarm Laodicean church was hypocritical. Members said they were rich and needed nothing, but Christ saw them as wretched, pitiful, poor, blind, and naked. They boasted of their own accomplishments but could not see their desperate spiritual condition. Christ had what they needed if they would only humble themselves, pray, seek His face, and turn from their wicked ways. The Lord's unconditional love was evident in His willingness to rebuke and discipline them. Their immediate need was to be earnest and repent. Obviously, they ignored their relationship with Him to the point that He felt like an outsider, having to knock to gain admittance to their hearts.

Does this church sound like many you know? How many churches have you observed that are honestly on fire for God, to the point that they impact their world for Christ? Today your church and mine—in fact, all of Christ's churches—need to be set ablaze by the fire of the Spirit! Pray that God's Holy Spirit will ignite your heart and cause the light of your life to burn brightly so that all may see it and glorify your Father in heaven!

On a scale of 1-10 (10 being highest) how on fire are you and your church? _____ you _____ your church

DAY 5

GLORY TO GOD

Have you ever skipped to the last page of a good book just to see how things would turn out? As you look at the end of time as Revelation describes, the final scene around the throne is fascinating! Who is there? How did they get there? Does the end have anything to do with the beginning? How exciting to realize that God's vision of history's final scene concludes the assignment He began with Abraham to bless all the peoples of the world!

"These were all commended for their faith, yet none of them received what had been promised. God had planned something better for us so that only together with us would they be made perfect" (Heb. 11:39-40).

"They sang a new song:
    'You are worthy to take
        the scroll
    and to open its seals,
    because you were slain,
    and with your blood
        you purchased men
        for God
    from every tribe and
        language and people
        and nation.
You have made them to be
    a kingdom and priests
    to serve our God,
    and they will reign on the
    earth' " (Rev. 5:9-10).

"I looked and there before me was a great multitude that no one could count, from every nation, tribe, people and language, standing before the throne and in front of the Lamb. They were wearing white robes and were holding palm branches in their hands. And they cried out in a loud voice:
    'Salvation belongs to
        our God,
    who sits on the throne,
    and to the Lamb' "
(Rev. 7:9-10).

Read Revelation 3:20; 4:1-10 in your Bible. Get heaven's perspective on God's eternal mission. As you read, worship God.

1. Eternity shows the consummation of God's mission through His obedient people.

Even though Abraham and all the heroes of the faith you have studied were unable to see the outcome of their obedience, God used their faith-filled lives to advance to a very specific end—the scene before you in Revelation. God invites you to join Him by faith (see Heb. 11:39-40 in the margin). When you walk in faith, you determine to willingly obey what God has revealed without seeing how everything will be done or accomplished. To experience God's glory on mission with Him requires that you walk by faith, not by sight.

From the first century, in which John lived, the Lord has built His church in miraculous ways. As the apostles fanned out and witnessed and discipled all nations, God began sweeping many people into the kingdom. In a similar way, God works today in unusual ways in many places, calling people to Himself.

For example, in 1900 only 3 percent of all the African people were Christians. Today Africa is 46 percent Christian. Christians will soon be the majority. In 1900 in Latin America fewer than 40,000 evangelicals existed. Today almost 40 million are evangelical. In Asia in 1980 about 16 million Christians existed. Today we can count more than 100 million.

You and I are given the best opportunity in all of history to reach those God desires to be a part of His corporate body. Every year new people groups hear the gospel for the first time. Some come to Christ and start churches and sometimes church planting movements.

God directs you to places, people, and positions so that His name will be glorified in all the earth. He is moving all of history to a specific end. What He has done in the past and what He will do in the future bear directly on what He invites you to do today! Are you aware that you live in the greatest day of mission advance in history? Are you involved in Christ's mission so that the world's peoples may glorify God?

What plan do you have to be more involved in His mission today?

_____

2. God is fulfilling His mission through His people.

From the beginning of Genesis God has been behind the scenes propelling history toward Revelation's compelling conclusion. John was privileged to see the culmination of redemptive history. His thrilling report allows you to observe a wonderfully triumphant scene around the throne of God in heaven!

Read the Revelation 5:9-10; 7:9-10; and 14:6-7 in the margin on this page and page 189. Underline the sections that describe the crowd standing before the throne.

People from every nation, tribe, and language stand before the throne. The promise made to Abraham and his heirs is fulfilled. As history comes to an end, John tells us that the blessing has indeed reached all the peoples of the world!

From Abraham, through Moses and David, Jesus, Peter, Paul, and John, you have now observed the beginning, middle, and end of God's story. He made a promise. He made an oath. He made a way through the redemptive work of Jesus so that you can play an important part in the fulfillment of His mission. You will stand around the throne of God rubbing shoulders with individuals who have heard through you the good news that rescued them from the kingdom of darkness.

The mission to bless all the peoples of the world is God's plan to bring all peoples into the family of God. The final scene of history is not a throng of individuals standing before the throne recounting their blessings one by one. Rather, it is a scene of all the peoples of God—a family drawn from every language, tribe, and people—giving honor and glory to the rightful Lord over all.

Today God initiates work around this world as never before. Do you realize the number of people who are alive today with the possibility of hearing the gospel? It took from the time of creation until 1830 for the world's population to reach one billion. It took another 97 years to add the second billion—by 1927. It took another 34 years, to 1964, to add the third billion. It took only 14 years to reach the fourth billion. In October 1999 the world surpassed six billion, and it is still escalating. That possibly means that the majority of people who have ever lived are alive today. God gives enormous opportunities!

What is God doing in your church to get all of you to join Him on mission to the unreached of this world?

_____

_____

_____

"I saw another angel flying in midair, and he had the eternal gospel to proclaim to those who live on the earth—to every nation, tribe, language and people. He said in a loud voice, 'Fear God and give him glory, because the hour of his judgment has come. Worship him who made the heavens, the earth, the sea and the springs of water' " (Rev. 14:6-7).

3. Eternity is the fulfillment of God's eternal plan.

God blesses His people so that they in turn will bless all peoples. Because He loves His creation and wants its highest good, God desires that all people worship Him with all of their being throughout the endless ages. He welcomes the untold billions of His creation to be blessed guests at the marriage supper of the Lamb. There they will worship Him forever and will be blessed by His presence with them always!

The world will not be won to Christ with business as usual. As you go on mission with Him, be willing to do new things, break old paradigms, and work in every possible way with your brothers and sisters in the body of Christ to spread the gospel today to those who have never worshiped Him! Now is the time to decide whether you are willing to change the question from "What can I do?" to "What will it take to reach all the peoples of the world?"

4. All peoples will worship God and give Him all the glory.

Representatives from all tribes, tongues, and peoples will worship God and the Lamb. You have a glimpse of all God has planned for eternity.

State God's mission. God's mission is _____

_____

Read the following quotes by John Piper. Choose below what *you* believe are the right answers.

"Missions is not the ultimate goal of the church. Worship is. Missions exists because worship doesn't. Worship is ultimate, not missions, because God is ultimate, not man."

"The great sin of the world is not that the human race has failed to work for God so as to increase His glory, but that we have failed to delight in God so as to reflect His glory. For God's glory is most reflected in us when we are most delighted in Him."

"God is calling us above all else to be the kind of people whose theme and passion is the supremacy of God in all of life. No one will be able to rise to the magnificence of the missionary cause who does not feel the magnificence of Christ. There will be no big world vision without a big God."[3]

1. The ultimate goal of the church is—
   - ❑ missions;
   - ❑ God;
   - ❑ worship.
2. The great sin of the human race is—
   - ❑ not working to increase God's glory;
   - ❑ failing to delight in God's glory;
   - ❑ not living a worthy life.
3. God is calling you, above all else, to—
   - ❑ have a passion for the supremacy of life;
   - ❑ feed on the magnificence of Christ;
   - ❑ have a big vision.

You may have agreed with Piper in number 1 that worship is the ultimate goal of the church. However, I marked *God* because one can easily have a crusade about something short of Him. So your goal is not even all peoples worshiping Him around the throne. It is God Himself. I agree with Piper in the second question that failing to delight in God's glory is the human race's greatest sin. When He is your focus, your joy, your satisfaction, then you want to increase His glory. In number 3 God calls you to feed on Christ's magnificence. He is your vision, and His being glorified by all peoples is so much bigger when you see and worship Him. So He is the fuel of missions and the center of your life.

Every day you face hundreds of decisions of one kind or another. You are pulled; you are distracted. Sometimes even in your best moments you don't get to what is ultimate. Even focusing on experiencing the glory of God is one step short of focusing on God. So neither missions nor worship is ultimate—God is.

You can get enamored with a telescope and forget to see the object at which it is pointed. You can get caught up in praise and forget the Object of praise. Too often what occurs in worship services is the praise of praise or the joy of praise, but somehow it misses focusing on God, His supremacy, His passion for His name, and His glory. Focus on Him even more than on His passion for His people and even more than all the peoples of the world around the throne worshiping Him. True worship involves submitting yourself to God, abdicating your own self, giving devotion to God, adoring Him, exulting in Him, and glorifying Him.

God desires that His people glorify Him in all things. You glorify God by worshiping Him. You glorify God as you let the glory of God shine to all corners of the globe. You glorify God by giving Him the credit for all He has done. You honor Christ as sovereign Lord as you confess Him, praise Him, and proclaim Him to all peoples of the world! Blessed be His name forever and ever!

> *Sometimes even in your best moments you don't get to what is ultimate.*

> Abraham: Experiencing God's Glory Through His Promises
> Romans 4:20-21

Read in your Bible the verses listed below and worship and glorify God.

Revelation 1:5	Revelation 14:7
Revelation 4:11	Revelation 15:4
Revelation 5:9-13	Revelation 19:1
Revelation 7:10-12	Revelation 19:6-7
Revelation 11:15	Revelation 21:23
Revelation 11:17	Revelation 21:26

> Moses: Experiencing God's Glory Through His Purpose for His People
> Exodus 14:4

> David: Experiencing God's Glory Through His Preeminent Kingdom
> 1 Chronicles 16:10-31

Read from your Bible the verses listed in the margin about how each of the Seven understood the mission of God—that He be glorified. Underline the phrases that indicate that God worked in them to show His glory.

> Jesus: Experiencing God's Glory Through His Person
> John 17:4

> Peter: Experiencing God's Glory Through His Power
> 1 Peter 4:10-11

It's unanimous! All of the Seven glorify God and His name. Abraham "grew strong in his faith, giving glory to God." Moses showed how God got the glory over Pharaoh "for his namesake, that he might make known his mighty power." David urged all nations to glorify God, His name, and His praise. Jesus said that He had glorified the Father as intended and then said He endured the cross to glorify His name. Peter says that God's power is manifested in His gifts to the glory of God. Paul says God's glory was manifested in Christ and is reflected in us. John pictures all peoples praising, glorifying, and worshiping God. The Bible is the story of God's glory.

As this book was going to press I had to speak at the funeral of Genessa Wells, a 24-year-old missionary on a two-year assignment. She was within two weeks of finishing her term of service when she was killed in a bus accident in Egypt. Below is part of the last email she sent.

> Paul: Experiencing God's Glory Through His Passion
> 2 Corinthians 4:6
> 2 Corinthians 3:18
> 1 Corinthians 10:31

> John Experiencing God's Glory Through His Presence
> Revelation 5:9-14

This summer has definitely been the busiest summer of my life. I came to France on the third of June, knowing that I was going to do a project called Northern Lights but knowing very little about it until I actually arrived. Looking back, it was a little tougher physically, spiritually, and mentally than I had expected. I also grew more, learned more, and my eyes were opened to more than I had expected. I wouldn't change a thing if I could. ... It seems that everything we do all comes down to one thing. His glory. I pray that all of our lives reflect that: His glory.

The last two years I have spent time in five different countries. France is the first one I have been in where a believer can share their faith freely. It seems like a floodgate was opened in my heart. After almost two years, I found myself in a country full of opportunities. No longer did I have to be so careful to share in a private, safe way, I was free to tell them of the biggest need in their life. They also (the lost) felt free to listen. Suddenly I felt like Paul going into the city gates to preach about the way, the truth, and the life. And I had a passion for it that I never knew God had given me. He's given it to me for His glory.

A few minutes before the accident, she witnessed to another passenger. At only 24 years of age Genessa discovered the glory of being on mission with God—living God's purpose for His glory. Now she is glorifying God with the multitudes around the throne. May God grant that you and I will do as well in the time He has given us. It is all about Him!

As you look back at previous weeks to check your answers, identify at least one Scripture and statement that you want to make sure is a part of your life from now until you glorify God with all peoples in heaven.

What Scripture in the study is the most meaningful to you? Why?

_____

What statement is most memorable to you?

_____

_____

Read Revelation 19:1-10 in your Bible. Sing a song of praise to God!

---

[1] Jeff Lewis, *God's Heart for the Nations* (Riverside, CA: The Global Center, California Baptist University, 2000), 24.

[2] Arthur Percy Fitt, *Moody Still Lives: Word Pictures of D.L. Moody* (New York: Fleming H. Revell Co., 1936), 27–29.

[3] John Piper, *Let the Nations Be Glad* (Grand Rapids, MI: Baker Book House, 1993), 49, 51, 54.

GROUP LEADER GUIDE

On Mission with God: Living God's Purpose for His Glory combines daily individual study and a weekly small-group process to help Christians understand the heart of God and His mission. This leader guide provides step-by-step guidance for leading group sessions that follow each week's individual study.

THE PROCESS OF *ON MISSION WITH GOD*

On Mission with God employs an interactive learning process. Each day for five days a week, members are expected to study a segment of the material and complete activities that relate to what they read. Each day's work requires from 30 to 40 minutes of private study time.

At the end of the week's study, members gather for group sessions. The sessions help members reflect on the concepts and experiences in *On Mission with God* and apply the ideas to their lives.

Although persons may benefit from completing the studies totally on their own without a group experience, they will miss the critical element Jesus' disciples experienced: relationships with one another in Christ's presence. As members share ways they are growing in their ability to understand the heart of God and His mission, others give feedback and are encouraged in their own challenges and victories. Therefore, individuals are strongly urged to connect with other believers to study this material.

On Mission with God consists of nine group sessions—an orientation session and eight sessions supporting the eight weeks of material in the member book. Each week builds on the previous one and is a prerequisite for the one that follows.

Some members will desire to participate in an *On Mission with God* study because they have had a positive experience with *Experiencing God: Knowing Doing the Will of God*, a 12-week study by Henry T. Blackaby and Claude V. King. Churches and individuals throughout the world have used this material to help them learn how to know and do God's will. Helping members understand the slight difference in format between these two studies is important. In *Experiencing God* Henry Blackaby and Claude King apply to Moses the basic truths of *Experiencing God*. In *On Mission with God* these basic truths are applied to seven biblical characters to explore ways these seven were on mission with God and to inspire participants to be on mission with Him, as well.

The study of *Experiencing God* is not a prerequisite for this course. Members will benefit from *On Mission with God* whether or not they have studied *Experiencing God*. Taking this study first, before *Experiencing God*, is perfectly acceptable. Ideally, *On Mission with God* will take members deeper into more specific aspects of knowing and following God's will and understanding the heart of God than they could examine during their study of *Experiencing God*.

STEPS FOR OFFERING *ON MISSION WITH GOD* IN YOUR CHURCH

1. *Pray.* Seek God's direction in determining whether a study of *On Mission with God* is appropriate for your church.
2. *Seek approval.* If you are a church-staff member, discuss your proposal with your pastor, fellow staff members, deacon body, pertinent committees, or whoever guides the approval process in your church. If you are a church member, consult your pastor or an appropriate church-staff member before scheduling a study of this resource. Provide the pastor and/or staff member with a copy of the member book and direct attention to this leader guide. Help church leaders understand the process, goals, content, and procedures.

3. Select leaders and provide training. Use the section "How to Train Leaders" on page 196 in this leader guide to train persons to lead *On Mission with God* groups. Refer to the section "Who can lead an *On Mission with God* group?" on this page as you recruit persons to lead.

4. Set a time, date, and place. The optimal time for *On Mission with God* groups to meet is outside the typical church schedule. If you are scheduling these sessions on the church calendar, try to set a different time from any normally scheduled activity. Consider a weeknight (other than Wednesday-night activities), a weekday for those available to participate, a Saturday, or a Sunday afternoon between morning and evening worship. However, if such a plan is not possible, you can adapt the leader material for any setting—discipleship training, Wednesday-night prayer meeting, women's or men's groups, or Sunday-morning Bible study.

One option for a meeting site is to schedule group meetings for the same place at the church each week. Check the church schedule to make sure a distracting activity is not scheduled for a room nearby. (See "How to Lead a Small Group.")

You may choose to conduct sessions in members' homes. If you move from one home to another each week, ensure that hosts do not compete to serve the best refreshments. Offer simple refreshments before or after the session. Plan a short break without extending the session. Begin and end each session on time.

5. Recruit members. Schedule at least a four-week period to register members and to promote the study. Promote by placing announcements in church publications and on bulletin boards; by placing displays around the church; by sharing testimonies in worship services, Bible-study classes, and discipleship groups; and by showing the promotional segment on videotape 1.

Make certain each group you enlist contains no more than eight persons. If groups are larger than eight, each member may not have an opportunity to participate each week.

One way to organize groups is to strive for homogeneity among members. For example, a group can be formed of all retirement-age persons, all young married couples, or all single adults. Another way to organize a group is to blend a variety of ages and life circumstances in which members can learn

from one another's age and stage of life. Supply trained leaders for each group.

6. Order materials. At least six weeks prior to the starting date, order one member book for each participant. If a couple participates, order individual books for both the husband and wife. Be certain to order a book for the leader. *On Mission with God* resources include:
• *On Mission with God Member Book* (ISBN 0-6330-1855-4)
• *On Mission with God Leader Kit* (ISBN 0-6330-1856-2)

7. Set fees. Ask members to purchase their own books unless the church has decided to subsidize the cost. Ask members to pay at least part of the cost to invest in *On Mission with God*.

8. Arrange child care. Decide whether you will provide child care for group members' children. Child care will allow some persons to participate who could not otherwise do so. Ideally, the church can offer this as a complimentary service to members if meetings are held at a time during the week when child care is not normally provided for church activities. However, the church could also arrange child care for a fee.

9. Get started. Read the leader guide and complete the member material yourself before you attempt to lead the study. Work at least one week ahead of the group you lead. For example, before you conduct the orientation session, be sure you have studied week 1, completed the interactive activities, and watched the corresponding video segments so that you can give members any special instructions necessary for the following week's study.

HOW TO LEAD A SMALL GROUP

1. Who can lead an On Mission with God *group?* Any mature Christian, either a layperson or a church-staff member, can lead the group. A person may resist leading a group on this topic because he or she may think, *I'm still struggling in the area of knowing God's will for my life. I strive to be an on mission Christian, but I'm not there yet.* In reality, the ideal leader is a fellow struggler—someone who relates to the issues involved and who is perhaps just a little farther down the road than the rest of his or her group members in terms of surrendering every aspect of his or her life to God's control. An ideal group leader is someone who has struggled to know and do God's will and who can transparently share from his or her own experiences. Because the group leader leads by modeling, recruiting leaders who are role models in terms of striving to know and do God's will is important. Assure leaders you recruit that this leader guide provides ample, detailed instructions on how to lead the group. It is recommended, though not required, that a leader have completed *Experiencing God: Knowing and Doing the Will of God* before the person leads *On Mission with God*.

2. What are some traits of an effective group leader? This person has the following qualities.

- Is a growing Christian, a person of prayer, and someone who has faith in what God can do
- Has a commitment to keep confidential information private
- Is an active member of the sponsoring church
- Relates well to people
- Has a knowledge of Scripture
- Senses God's call to be involved in a ministry of helping others learn how to join God on mission
- Is comfortable in the presence of people who share painful life experiences. In the process of these group discussions, members may reflect on hurtful times they have responded improperly to God's call or on other wrong choices they have made in relating to God or others. A person who feels comfortable only when those around him or her are cheerful and upbeat may need to reconsider whether he or she is appropriate to lead an *On Mission with God* group.

3. What are some skills that a group leader needs? A successful group leader will use the following group-leadership techniques.

- Maintain eye contact as members share. When appropriate, nod your head or use occasional verbal phrases to indicate that you are listening to what someone is saying.
- Use good listening skills. To encourage sharing, make sure you or another member offers some type of response when any group member shares.
- Try to read body language and nonverbal cues. Attempt to draw out people who are, for example, listening intently, withdrawing, or looking as though they are full of pain. Depend on God for sensitivity.
- Affirm strong emotions, such as tears. Phrases like "I sense hurt in what you just shared" or "I'm sure

that must have been disappointing" help members identify their emotions and validate them.

- Avoid allowing one member to dominate discussions. If someone has talked too long, gently try to steer the conversation to someone else. Help the person summarize. Watch for the slightest break in a monologue to turn the conversation to someone else. State, "I'm wondering whether anyone else has a thought to share on this subject."
- Steer the group away from giving advice. Help members share their own experiences ("Something that has worked for me is …" or "Here's what I've learned …" instead of "What you should do is …").

4. What is an effective room arrangement? Use the following ideas to make the room arrangement and physical environment aid the group process.

- Arrange chairs in a circle so that members can see each other face-to-face.
- Place in the circle only enough chairs to seat members who attend the session. If you know of absences already, withdraw that number of chairs from the circle. If someone fails to show up by the time the group starts, withdraw that person's chair.
- Remove any unnecessary items in the room. Groups work best when chairs are free of tables and members are seated in a circle without any distractions in front of them.
- Position training equipment, such as a television monitor, so that all members can easily see it.

5. What are some guidelines for healthy group life?

- Announce to the group that you will begin and end on time. Begin the group even if all members have not arrived. Conclude at the designated hour. Be dependable. If a member arrives late, continue the group process matter-of-factly and without undue attention to the tardiness.
- Ask members to avoid bringing drinks, candy, mints, or gum to group sessions. These items can detract from an atmosphere conducive to sharing.
- Provide a box of tissue at each group session. Position it on the floor in the center of the room. Instruct members to feel free to take a tissue if they need one. Providing tissues helps demonstrate to members that this is a safe place to express emotions.
- Ask members to agree to confidentiality—what is said in the group remains in the group. Urge members to refrain from mentioning group matters

even in well-meaning, outside-the-group prayer requests in which they supply no specific names. Although no names may be mentioned, the circumstances stated may be just enough to enable a nonmember to identify the actual situation. At that point confidentiality has been breached, just as though the name of the person involved had been stated.

• If members must miss a session, ask them to keep up with the group by completing assignments in the member book for the material missed.

HOW AN *ON MISSION WITH GOD* GROUP SESSION WORKS

1. Each group session is from one to two hours in length. Time increments for each segment of the session are provided in the individual session plans in this leader guide.
2. Members complete all weekly assignments before the group sessions.
3. *On Mission with God* may be used in two different plans: the Standard Plan and the Split-Session Plan. Choose the plan that best meets members' needs.
4. Sessions are divided into the following segments: Introductory Time, Group-Discussion Time, Preview Next Week's Assignments, and Closure. Suggested time increments are furnished for the various segments. A variety of group experiences encourages sharing, promotes fellowship, and breaks monotony.
5. Leaders are highly encouraged to use the video that accompanies the material. Group session plans instruct leaders on how to use the video.

The Standard Plan

1. Each group session is either 1 or 2 hours in length. Time increments are provided in this leader guide for the segments of each session. When two times are listed (for example, 30–55 mins.), the first number (30) indicates the recommended time for the 1-hour session; the second number (55) is for the 2-hour session.
2. Members complete their assignments in the member book before the group session.
3. At each session members deal with the preceding week's assignments by discussing them in the group setting. Each session prepares members for the following week by previewing the next week's material.

4. The leader uses the leader guide as directed. The first half of the session deals with material in part 1; the second half involves part 2.

The Split-Session Plan

1. This plan allows any or all group sessions to be split into two meetings. The group-session time for each meeting is reduced to one hour. The number of weeks required to complete the course is doubled.
2. The purpose of the Split-Session Plan is to—
• allow groups that are unable to complete all assignments each week to spread them over two weeks;
• allow groups that want to meet during the regular church schedule to split the group session into two 60-minute segments;
• allow groups that want to spend more time in content review or in group activities to have two weeks to do so;
• make the study more self-paced so that any committed group can fit the course into its schedule.
3. All groups begin using the Standard Plan as the norm. If most members express the desire to slow down after a couple of weeks, discuss adopting the Split-Session Plan to spread the assignments over two weeks. Return to the Standard Plan as soon as members catch up. If members want to continue using the Split-Session Plan, ask for their commitment to the additional weeks necessary to complete the course.
4. In the Split-Session Plan members complete assignments in days 1–3 for week 1 and in days 4–5 for week 2. Simply use part 1 of the session plan for the first week and part 2 for the second week.

HOW TO TRAIN LEADERS

1. Churches electing to study *On Mission with God* can benefit from conducting leader training several weeks before the study. After leaders are enlisted, ask them to commit to a two-hour training session to equip them to lead *On Mission with God* groups.
2. Ask leaders to read the introductory material and complete week 1 in their member books before attending the training.
3. If more than eight leaders attend the training session, divide the group and ask another leader to lead separate training for one group while you lead the other.
4. Prepare the meeting room.

- Provide a circle of chairs for the number of participants.
- Prepare name tags if necessary.
5. Sample training schedule (2 hours)
a. Introduction (20 mins.). Ask participants to introduce themselves to one another. Ask each participant to tell one struggle and one victory he or she has experienced in knowing and doing God's will.
b. Describe the plan for the *On Mission with God* study in your church (20 mins.). Explain the rationale for the church's scheduling the emphasis, the benefits to the individual church member, and the benefits to the church as a corporate body. Overview the plans that are being made for church preparation, promotion, enlistment, child care, fees, and scheduling.
c. Review the main points in "How to Lead a Small Group" (p. 194). Invite questions (30 mins.).
d. Review the format of the member book and instructions for completing daily assignments (30 mins.). Explain that the interactive format allows members to read the text and then answer questions that relate to the material they have read. Discuss questions or comments. Review the organization of the leader guide. Direct leaders to the "Before the Session" and "After the Session" segments that are to be used to prepare for and review after each session.
e. Explain the importance of offering follow-up studies after members complete *On Mission with God*. For example, if a church has not offered *Experiencing God: Knowing and Doing the Will of God*, it could be used to help members reinforce what they learned in *On Mission with God*. Other possibilities include *MasterLife*, a sequential, developmental discipling process, and *The Mind of Christ*, a discipleship study that teaches believers how to think the thoughts of Christ.
f. Lead the group leaders in conversational prayer for the upcoming studies (10 mins.). Pray for growth in the lives of individual members and in the life of the church through *On Mission with God*.

A KEY DECISION

On Mission with God is written with the assumption that members have already received Jesus Christ as their Savior. However, participants may possibly realize as they study that they have never invited Christ into their lives. Be alert to this possibility. Be available to answer questions for members who accept Christ during the study. (See "How to Find New Life in Christ.") Arrange for them to talk to a pastor or another church leader. Consider giving them a copy of *Survival Kit: Five Keys to Effective Spiritual Growth* (0-8054-9770-6), available by writing to LifeWay Church Resources Customer Service; One LifeWay Plaza; Nashville, TN 37234-0113; by calling toll free (800) 458-2772; by emailing *customerservice@lifeway.com*; by ordering online at *www.lifeway.com*; or by faxing (615) 251-5933. Do not discourage these persons from continuing the study. This course is designed to help Christians at any stage of spiritual growth.

OBTAINING A LIST OF MISSIONS AGENCIES

Hundreds of missions agencies exist in the United States and around the world. Some focus worldwide, others on selected areas. Some send volunteers as well as short-term and career missionaries, while others focus only on special needs. To obtain a full list of all agencies, order *Mission Handbook: U.S. and Canadian Christian Ministries Overseas* by the Evangelism and Missions Information Service Department at the Billy Graham Center at Wheaton College in Wheaton, IL 60187-5593; call (630) 752-7158; email *emis@wheaton.edu*; or visit *www.billygrahamcenter.org*.

A FINAL NOTE FOR LEADERS

Because of the subject matter of *On Mission with God*, leaders may observe some class members who feel led to make a major decision, such as surrendering their lives to missions service or making another lifestyle alteration to be on mission with God. Be available to counsel them or get someone like a church-staff member or a Christian counselor to counsel them if you don't feel comfortable in this role. Leaders can refer members considering missions service to a recommended missions agency (see "Obtaining a List of Missions Agencies").

A new Christian may also express a desire to serve Christ as a missionary. However, missions-sending agencies often will not appoint someone unless he or she has been a Christian for a set amount of time. Missions agencies can explain to them what guidelines apply in their situations.

If a member suddenly decides to withdraw from the group in the middle of the study, that person may feel called to missions and is running from that call in a crisis of belief. Be sensitive to this possibility and try to help the member verbalize what is going on. Try to keep the member involved in the study so that the person receives group support and proper grounding.

ORIENTATION SESSION

SESSION GOALS

By the end of this session, members will be able to demonstrate their commitment to participate in *On Mission with God* by—
- telling the name of each member's favorite Bible character;
- identifying the five perspectives from which they will study each Bible character;
- explaining the seven realities of *Experiencing God* and the spiritual-markers diagrams;
- being prepared to complete next week's assignments.

BEFORE THE SESSION

☐ Have available enough copies of *On Mission with God* for all members.
☐ Review the introductory material and week 1, "Introducing Your Seven Mentors for the Journey." Complete the learning activities for week 1 to stay ahead of the group.
☐ Determine whether you will use the group-session format with the video or without it. You are highly encouraged to use the video. Arrange to have a VCR and a monitor available for your weekly sessions.
☐ Pray for group members. Ask the Lord to prepare you to lead the group.
☐ Read "During the Session," which follows.
☐ Arrange for simple refreshments to be served at the beginning of the session (optional).

☐ Arrange in a circle only enough chairs for each member and yourself.
☐ Prepare name tags for those you expect to attend.
☐ Plan to stay within the time given for each activity.

DURING THE SESSION (50-60 MINS.)

Lead an Introductory Activity (10–15 mins.)
1. Welcome participants and direct them to the refreshments. Invite each person to make a name tag. As members arrive, introduce each one to the others in the room if they don't know one another.
2. Begin promptly. Assure the group that you will begin and end each session on time. If members want to fellowship after the sessions, they may do so, but they can count on you to close the sessions on time.
3. As an icebreaker, ask each person to state the name of his or her favorite Bible character. Ask each person to explain in no more than two sentences why he or she chose this character as a favorite. Explain that the study of *On Mission with God* will focus on seven Bible characters who were on mission with God. Tell members that they will begin to identify with the seven featured characters as they study ways God used each to accomplish His purposes. Tell members that by studying these characters, participants will be able to explain God's pattern of doing extraordinary things through ordinary people to glorify His name among all peoples, and they will see how He wants to do the same through them.

Show the Promotional Videotape for *On Mission with God* (10 mins.)
Ask members to identify, as they view the video, what they think being on mission with God means. After the video allow members to share answers. Add this time to the next activity if you don't use the video.

Review the Five Perspectives and the *Experiencing God* and Spiritual-Markers Diagrams (15–20 mins.)
Briefly review with members the seven realities of *Experiencing God*, as the diagram (figure 1, p. 10) in the member book illustrates. Tell members that regardless of whether they have previously participated in an *Experiencing God* study, they will become

familiar with these seven tenets through the *On Mission with God* study. Also review the spiritual-markers diagram (figure 2, p. 10). Refer members to the five perspectives from which they will study each character (p. 7). Explain that members will begin to see their own lives from these five perspectives.

Explain the Format of *On Mission with God* (5 mins.)

Refer members to the introduction. State that members will complete five days of weekly work before they attend each session. At the group session they will discuss insights gained in individual study during the week. Encourage members to devote a period of time each day to that day's assignment rather than hurriedly studying all five days' work at once. Explain that their study will be more meaning-ful if they do it sequentially and allow time to process each day's insights before moving on to another day's work.

Preview Next Week's Assignments (5 mins.)

1. Direct members to week 1, "Introducing Your Seven Mentors for the Journey."
2. Briefly preview the content of week 1. Ask members to complete week 1 before the next group session. Tell them that the week's work will overview ways God used each of the seven biblical characters to glorify His name among all peoples. The seven weeks of work that follow week 1 will examine these characters in depth.
3. Direct members to the group covenant (p. 3). Review the covenant's concepts, explained in "What Are Some Guidelines for Healthy Group Life?" (p. 195). Members will be asked to sign the covenant at the next session.
4. Conduct the orientation session as a single session. For groups following the split-session plan, assign days 1–3 of the material for the first week of session 1 and days 4–5 for the second week of session 1.

Closure (5 mins.)

1. Announce the time and place for the next session.
2. Suggest that each person enlist a prayer partner (someone other than a fellow group member) before the next session. Explain to members that they will greatly benefit from having another Christian individual who will commit to pray for them about the way God wants to use this study in their lives.
3. Close in prayer. Suggest that members ask God for something they want to accomplish in the study.
4. Request members' prayers for you as you facilitate the group during the weeks that follow.

After the Session

☐ Before the next group session pray specifically for each member.

☐ Call each group member and encourage him or her in the study of week 1. Answer any questions group members may have.

☐ If any persons expressed doubt about participating in the study, you may want to enlist others in their places. Ask that they complete week 1, "Introducing Your Seven Mentors for the Journey," before the next session.

☐ Use the following questions to evaluate your leadership.

• Was I thoroughly prepared? Did I follow the leader guidelines for this session?

• Did I provide positive leadership? Was I the kind of leader 2 Timothy 2:24-25 describes?

• Did I create a group feeling during the opening minutes? Did it deepen?

• Did I help group members communicate with one another?

• Did members understand the course's goals, methods, and requirements?

• Was I enthusiastic about what *On Mission with God* can do in members' lives and church?

☐ Read "Before the Session" for group session 1 to determine the amount of preparation you will need for the next group session. At the top of the group session 1 material in this leader guide, record when you will do your preparation.

☐ Carefully study week 2 and complete all exercises. You will preview week 2 for members during session 1.

GROUP SESSION 1

SESSION GOALS

By the end of this session, members will be able to demonstrate their progress in achieving the *On Mission with God* goals by—

- explaining the difference between being on mission with God and being a missionary;
- revealing one opportunity God placed in their path during the past week to join Him in His work;
- describing one way they believe God is preparing them to be on mission with Him;
- praying about other members' goals while they participate in *On Mission with God*.

BEFORE THE SESSION

☐ Review week 1. Read and complete the learning activities for week 2 to stay ahead of the group.
☐ Pray daily for each group member. Ask the Lord to give you wisdom to prepare for and lead the group session.
☐ Master this week's material in the leader guide.
☐ Review the goals for this session.
☐ If you are meeting in a member's home, check with the host or hostess to be sure he or she is expecting the group this week.
☐ Arrange the meeting place so that members can sit in a circle.
☐ If you have the video, arrange for a VCR and monitor to show the video.
☐ Have name tags ready to use while members are still learning one another's names.
☐ Remember to encourage those who have problems completing assignments. Praise them for what they do; ask others to share any insights that might be helpful.

STANDARD PLAN

DURING THE SESSION (1-2 HRS.)

Prepare to take a stand-up break in the middle of the session if necessary. If you are using the longer time period (2-hour session), plan to take a 10-minute break when the time seems opportune and natural.

Part 1
Introductory Time (15–20 mins.)
1. Greet members as they arrive. Begin on time. Be alert to any signs of progress or problems members may be facing. Open the session with prayer. Ask for special prayer requests (5 mins.).
2. Draw their attention back to the group covenant (page 3) that you discussed last week. Ask everyone to take a moment to sign the covenant and then pray silently, committing themselves to this study of *On Mission with God* (5 mins.).
3. Show the session 1, part 1 videotape to set the scene and to prepare for sharing (10 mins.). If you do not have the video, take more time in the Group-Discussion Time.

Group-Discussion Time (35–70 mins.)
Choose from the following steps during your discussion time. Realize that far more questions are provided for you than you will likely have a chance to use with your group. Allowing members to share freely is far more important than legalistically adhering to a plan you develop for the group session.
1. Ask a volunteer to answer this question: Since the Bible is a book about God, why does 60 percent of the Bible consist of accounts about people? (*Because God reveals Himself through His relationships with people so that all can understand*) Be alert to individuals who seem eager to share. Allow time for them to do so. Emphasize that, as a group, you will help one another develop a heightened awareness of situations in which God is at work.
2. Briefly discuss this question: Do you agree or disagree that the seven mentors on whom this study focuses reveal God's mission? Why or why not?
3. Ask members to explain the difference between being on mission with God and being a missionary. (*Being on mission includes being involved with God as He reconciles all things to Himself through Christ. A missionary is a person who, in response to God's call and gifting, leaves his or her comfort zone and crosses cultural, geographic, or other barriers to proclaim the gospel and live out a Christian witness in obedience to the Great Commission.*) Help members understand that all Christians are to be on mission with God whether or not God calls them to be missionaries.
4. Ask volunteers to answer these questions: In the case studies of the seven mentors, who took the

initiative? (*God*) How did God speak to them? Why did they have to fully experience God?

5. Remind members that day 2 asked them to be alert to opportunities to see where God was at work in their lives. Ask each member to share briefly about opportunities God placed in his or her path this week to join Him in His work.

6. Ask members how they reacted to the concept that their salvation did not occur just for them but for the purpose of redeeming a lost world. Ask members if this represented a new concept for them and how they feel when they realize the personal responsibility that comes with salvation.

7. Refer to the dialogue (p. 19) in which the seven biblical characters discuss the major adjustments they were asked to make. Ask a couple of members to share with which of the seven biblical characters to be studied they most identify right now.

8. Invite a volunteer to answer this question: How does your personal experience match the seven spiritual markers these seven mentors experienced? (If you are splitting the session, end discussion here.)

Part 2

9. Call on a volunteer to choose any one of the Seven and tell how much he or she thinks the Bible character realized that he was influencing his generation and generations to come.

10. Ask someone to answer this question: In what ways do you influence other Christians in the body of Christ?

11. Ask someone to share with the group the mission statement he or she wrote (p. 25) in day 4.

12. Ask a volunteer to describe something he or she has done to bring God the glory instead of drawing glory or recognition to himself or herself.

13. Ask one person to share his or her response to this statement: Describe one way you believe God is preparing you or has prepared you to be on mission with Him.

14. Ask for several group members to answer these questions: What is the Bible about? How did the Seven glorify God? What is God's threefold purpose?

15. Call on a volunteer to answer the following: In what ways are you committed to the rest of the world (other peoples) in this age of globalization, world markets, and immigration?

16. Ask each member: What do you think God wants to do in your life during this course?

17. Show the session 1, part 2 videotape (15 mins.). Ask members to brainstorm applications of the video segment to their own lives and to their church. If you do not have the video, take more time in the Group-Discussion Time.

18. Close this portion in a time of prayer. Ask each member to pray for the person on his or her left. Ask God to help that member accomplish the goal he or she just voiced for the course.

Preview Next Week's Assignments (5–10 mins.)
1. Briefly preview the content of week 2, "Abraham on Mission with God: A Blessing for All Peoples." Tell members they will be able to understand and explain how God is connecting their lives, like Abraham's, to His mission to bless all peoples.
2. Remind members to pray for one another and with their prayer partners during the week. Explain that praying for one another is an important part of *On Mission with God*.

Closure (5–10 mins.)
1. Announce the time and place for the next session.
2. Stand and join hands in a prayer of dismissal. Voice a closing prayer asking God to help members understand what His mission is for them and look for His activity in their lives in the week ahead.

AFTER THE SESSION

☐ Evaluate the session by listing what you believe was effective and ways you can improve.

☐ Make a prayer list for each person in your group so that you can record needs to be prayed for and answers to your prayers. Pray daily for each group member (see Phil. 1:6-8).

☐ Contact any person who seems to need encouragement. Be an encourager who helps group members grow.

☐ Read "Before the Session" for group session 2 to determine the amount of preparation you will need for the next group session. At the top of the group session 2 material in this leader guide, record when you will do your preparation.

☐ Carefully study week 3 and complete all the exercises. You will preview week 3 for members during session 2.

SPLIT-SESSION PLAN

First Week
Follow session 1 of the Standard Plan except for the following adjustments.
1. Remind members that your group is using the Split-Session Plan. This means they have completed only days 1–3 for the first week of this session. Ask them to complete days 4–5 for next week.
2. If you have the video, show it during the first week of this session, at the time allotted in the session plan (p. 200).
3. Close the session in prayer, asking members to thank God for something they learned during their study so far.

Second Week
Follow the Standard Plan for session 1 with the following changes. Use shorter times for each activity to allow for these steps.
1. As members arrive, greet them cordially. Ask for prayer requests. Offer an opening prayer, focusing specifically on the matters mentioned.
2. During the introductory time ask volunteers to summarize important points from last week.
3. Move on to the discussion questions. Begin with question 9 (previous questions were covered during last week's group time).
4. Preview next week's work. Assign members days 1–3 in week 2, "Abraham on Mission with God: A Blessing for All Peoples."

GROUP SESSION 2

SESSION GOALS

By the end of this session, members will be able to demonstrate their progress in achieving the *On Mission with God* goals by—
• identifying ways God encounters them;
• describing ways they identify with Abraham's victories and challenges;
• pledging that they will specifically pray this week for their church and its role in God's mission.

BEFORE THE SESSION

☐ Review week 2. Read and complete the learning activities for week 3 to stay ahead of the group.
☐ Call all members of the group to ask them how they are doing on their assignments and to encourage them.
☐ Master this week's material in the leader guide.
☐ Check with the host or hostess to be sure he or she is expecting the group this week.
☐ If you have the video, arrange for a VCR and a monitor to show the video during the session.
☐ Arrange the meeting room so that members can sit in a circle.

STANDARD PLAN

DURING THE SESSION (1-2 HRS.)

Prepare to take a stand-up break in the middle of the session if necessary. If you are using the longer time period (2-hour time session), plan to take a 10-minute break when the time seems opportune and natural.

Part 1
Introductory Time (15–20 mins.)
1. Begin the session on time even if all members are not yet present. The purpose of this early period is to allow members to share their progress on any problems they are having in their work. Begin with prayer for this session's activities (5–10 mins.).
2. Show the session 2, part 1 videotape to set the scene and to prepare for sharing (10 mins.). If you do not have the video, take more time in the Group-Discussion Time.

Group-Discussion Time (35–70 mins.)
Choose from these steps.
1. Ask members to tell how they identified with the opening question of their week 2 study: "Can you recall a time when you knew you were making a decision that would affect your entire life?" (p. 37). Briefly share your own experience, and members will follow suit.
2. Comment that Abraham did not have Scripture to hear from God but still heard Him clearly. Ask each member to mention one way God encounters him or her—either the ways checked during the day

2 exercise on this subject (p. 36) or other ways. Explain that during the study members will learn to be even more attuned to recognize times in which God encounters them.

3. Call on a volunteer who seems willing to respond to this question: What three things did God ask Abraham to leave behind when He asked him to go to a distant land? Ask whether any member has ever felt God asking a similar sacrifice of him or her and how the member responded. Ask the member to describe the outcome.

4. Ask volunteers to answer: Describe a time when you, as Abraham did at one time, responded in fear, rather than faith, to something to which God called you. What happened as a result?

5. Call on a member to state what the object lesson was that God gave Abraham when he complained that he didn't have a son.

6. Ask a volunteer to answer: Describe a time in the past when God blessed an adjustment you made to follow Him. This may be the answer members gave in the learning activity on this subject during day 2 (p. 37) or another answer.

7. Ask members to recall the crucial incident that turned Abraham's fear to faith that God would fulfill His promises. Call on a volunteer willing to share a defining moment in his or her life when the person truly experienced that the Lord provides.

8. Ask volunteers to share how they experienced God this week and what they believe He is saying.

9. Ask members to work in pairs to check their recall of this week's memory verse.

(If you are splitting the session, end discussion here.)

Part 2

10. Ask the group what promises God made to Abraham and his descendants.

11. Discuss the concept you first read about in week 1—that blessing is never just for yourself but is to be passed along to others. Ask members how they respond to this concept. Call on a volunteer to share a time when this was true in his or her life. Share your own experience in this area.

12. Ask two volunteers to share one way they believe God has blessed their church to make it physically or spiritually fruitful.

13. Ask volunteers to state reasons they act short-sightedly and ignore the fact that God sees the big picture, as He did with Abraham.

14. Discuss the concept you studied in day 4—that God is not only working in your life but also preparing His people in your generation for His mission. Discuss evidence of this that members see in your church as He involves people there to be on mission with Him. Ask members to identify ways they could envision your church being even more involved in bringing glory to God among all peoples. Ask what type of involvement they could have in the actions they describe.

15. Call on each member to briefly share the way he or she most identified this week with Abraham's struggles and victories.

16. Ask a volunteer to share any indication that God wants to use him or her in His larger purpose for the world. Affirm any member who shares.

17. Ask a volunteer to answer this question: Why does God bless us individually and as a people?

18. Direct members' attentions to the section on Sarah (pp. 52–53). Ask a volunteer to share a time when he or she had to respond to his or her mate's experience with God.

19. Show the session 2, part 2 videotape (15 mins.). Ask members to brainstorm applications of the eternal perspective on Abraham's life to their own lives and to their church. If you do not have the video, take more time in the Group-Discussion Time.

Preview Next Week's Assignments (5–10 mins.)

1. Briefly preview the content of week 3, "Moses on Mission with God: A People Responsible for All Peoples." Tell members they will be able to understand how, when God personally encounters them, He wants to use them to make His name known to the nations.

2. Ask members to pledge to pray specifically this week for their church and its role in God's mission.

Closure (5–10 mins.)

1. Announce the time and place for the next session.

2. Close with a circle of prayer. Ask each member to think about ways they have already been involved in helping to extend the kingdom of God to the ends of the earth. Then ask members to pray brief prayers aloud that God will show them ways they can join Him in blessing the nations.

AFTER THE SESSION

☐ Evaluate the session by listing what you believe was effective. Consider ways to improve in future sessions.
☐ Pray daily for each group member. Record prayers prayed and prayers answered.
☐ Contact any person who seems to be struggling with the assignments.
☐ Read "Before the Session" for group session 3 to determine the amount of preparation you will need for the next group session. At the top of the group session 3 material in this leader guide, record when you will do your preparation.
☐ Carefully study week 4 and complete all the exercises. You will preview week 4 for members during session 3.

Split-Session Plan

First Week
Follow session 2 of the Standard Plan except for the following adjustments.
1. If you have the video, show session 2, part 1 during the first week of this session, at the time allotted in the session plan (p. 201).
2. In closing, ask members to pray sentence prayers that God would help them make whatever adjustments are necessary to follow Him.

Second Week
Follow the Standard Plan for session 2 with the following changes. Use shorter times for each activity to allow for these steps.
1. As members arrive, be sensitive to struggles any are having in doing their weekly work. Ask if any member can share an answer to or update on a prayer request mentioned previously. Offer the opening prayer, mentioning these items and asking God to bless the meeting's activities.
2. During the introductory time ask volunteers to summarize important points from last week.
3. Move on to the discussion questions. Begin with question 10 (previous questions were covered during last week's group time).
4. Preview next week's work. Assign members days 1–3 in week 3, "Moses on Mission with God: A People Responsible for All Peoples."

GROUP SESSION 3

SESSION GOALS

By the end of this session, members will be able to demonstrate their progress in achieving the *On Mission with God* goals by—
• identifying the last time they clearly heard God speaking;
• praying with another group member about a crisis of faith that the member currently faces as God speaks to him or her;
• committing to pray about ways God can use them as ordinary people to carry out His kingdom purposes;
• describing the most prominent way God revealed Himself during this week's work.

BEFORE THE SESSION

☐ Review week 3 and read and complete the learning activities for week 4 to stay ahead of the group.
☐ Pray daily for each group member.
☐ Master this week's material in the leader guide.
☐ Review the goals for this session.
☐ Check with the host or hostess to be sure he or she is expecting the group this week.
☐ If you have the video, arrange for a VCR and a monitor to show the video during the session.
☐ Arrange the meeting room so that members can sit in a circle.

Standard Plan

DURING THE SESSION (1–2 HRS.)

Prepare to take a stand-up break in the middle of the session if necessary. If you are using the longer time period (2-hour time session), plan to take a 10-minute break when the time seems opportune and natural.

Part 1
Introductory Time (15–20 mins.)
1. Fellowship with early arrivers. Ask for questions members may have about their weekly work. Begin on time.

2. Ask members to share ways they have seen God at work around them this week. Begin by sharing your experience. If you are open and honest, you will set the stage and make others' sharing easier.

3. Pray an opening prayer thanking God for evidence of His work.

4. Show the session 3, part 1 videotape to set the scene and to prepare for sharing (10 mins.). If you do not have the video, take more time in the Group-Discussion Time.

Group-Discussion Time (35–70 mins.)
Allowing members to share freely during group sessions is far more important than legalistically adhering to a plan for the group session that you develop before the session begins. Group members sometimes arrive at the sessions eager to share something that happened in their lives during the previous week that relates to the week's content. Be sensitive to this need and be flexible. Allow opportunities for everyone to respond during the session. Choose from these steps.

1. Ask a volunteer to answer this question: Can you identify with the Henry Blackaby illustration in the opening paragraphs of week 3? Have you ever been in an obscure, out-of-the-way place where you believed you had no chance of being used by God? If so, what happened?

2. Call on volunteers to answer this question: Have you ever been like Moses and tried to do God's work by yourself? What do you believe you learned from that experience? Emphasize that in this week's lesson, as well as throughout the entire study, they should see how only activities that are in concert with God are blessed and used by Him.

3. Ask someone to tell how he or she answered this question from day 2: "When was the last time you clearly heard God speaking?" (p. 59).

4. Discuss the four ways of God (pp. 64–65). Ask members to comment on one of the ways they have experienced God working.

5. Ask, Why did God deliver Israel from Egypt? (*promise and purpose*) Ask for comments on the account of the missionary who thanked God for Marx and Lenin.

6. Ask members in pairs to quote to each other the memory verse for this week.

7. Ask volunteers to share a time when they recognized that God was trying to get their attention, as

He did with Moses at the burning bush, and involve them in His mission.

8. Ask all members to briefly share what they described in day 2 as a crisis of faith they now face as God speaks to them (p. 60). Ask members to pause and pray in pairs for the concerns expressed about individual crises of faith.

(If you are splitting the session, end discussion here.)

Part 2
9. Ask a volunteer to answer this question: How do you think the great I AM sees our day?

10. Ask a volunteer to answer: What was the importance of the exodus for other nations/peoples?

11. Discuss the ways of God with His people. Ask members to give an example of one of these ways in their personal lives or in the life of their church.

12. Ask group members how they reacted when they read this statement in day 4: "Your life is connected to God not just so that you will experience His glory but also so that you can participate in His purposeful mission" (p. 69). Note that this is a recurring theme throughout the study. Ask members to share how they respond when they read this theme.

13. Call for someone to respond to this statement from day 4: "Describe a circumstance in which God has stirred up your church's cozy nest or is now stirring your nest" (p. 70).

14. Ask volunteers to share a time God pushed them off a cliff, figuratively, causing them to fly by faith.

15. Ask members this question: What is God's eternal mission revealed through Moses?

16. Call on a member to share how he or she answered the day 5 questions about how his or her church rates in terms of being the type of people God desires today (pp. 72–73).

17. Ask volunteers to share their answers to the closing questions in day 5 (p. 75).

18. Show the session 3, part 2 videotape. Ask members to brainstorm applications of the video segment to their lives and to their church. If you do not have the video, take more time in the Group-Discussion Time.

Preview Next Week's Assignments (5–10 mins.)
1. Briefly preview the content of week 4, "David on Mission with God: Establishing a Kingdom Without End." Tell members that they will be able to understand and describe how God revealed through David

that His seed would rule all nations and His kingdom would be for all peoples.

2. Ask members to pray this week, as they study, that God will reveal how He can use them, as ordinary people, in the same way David, who began as a mere shepherd boy, was used in God's kingdom.

Closure (5–10 mins.)

1. Announce the time and place for the next session.
2. Close with a circle of prayer. Ask members to cite what they believe is the most important revelation God has given them during this week's study. Close the prayer time by thanking God for the revelations just mentioned and asking Him to continue revealing Himself to participants.

AFTER THE SESSION

1. Use the following questions to evaluate how well you led the session.
☐ Do members care for one another? Are they trusting one another and being more open?
☐ Are there blockages in communication?
☐ Is the group becoming cliquish? Do I need to encourage members to reach out?
☐ Do some members show undesirable attitudes toward other members? Should I take them visiting together and/or pair them more often?
☐ Are members helping disciple one another? Do they see me as a growing disciple who is also learning from them?
2. Contact all members of the group this week to encourage or challenge them as needed as they complete their assignments. Remember that you are their servant.
3. Read "Before the Session" for group session 4 to determine the amount of preparation you will need for the next group session. At the top of the group session 4 material in this leader guide, record when you will do your preparation.
4. Carefully study week 5 and complete all the interactive exercises. You will preview week 5 for members during session 4.

Split-Session Plan

First Week
Follow part 1 of session 3 as it is outlined in the Standard Plan except for the following adjustments.

1. If you have the video, show session 3, part 1 during the first week of this session, at the time allotted in the session plan (p. 205).
2. As a closing prayer, ask members to say sentence prayers that God would get their attention about His mission for each person's life in whatever way He desires. Ask them to pray that God would move in such a direct, visible way that they would make no mistake about what He wants them to do.

Second Week
Follow the Standard Plan for part 2 of session 3 with the following changes. Use shorter times for each activity to allow for these steps.

1. Ask members to express specific praise about their experiences in *On Mission with God* so far. Call on a couple of volunteers to lead the opening prayer time, thanking God for the praises mentioned and asking Him to bless the session's activities.
2. During the introductory time ask volunteers to summarize important points from last week.
3. Move on to the discussion questions. Begin with question 9 (previous questions were covered during last week's group time).
4. Preview next week's work. Assign members days 1–3 in week 4, "David on Mission with God: Establishing a Kingdom Without End."

GROUP SESSION 4

SESSION GOALS

By the end of this session, members will be able to demonstrate their progress in achieving the *On Mission with God* goals by—
• sharing a way they have seen God at work in seemingly mundane activities in their lives;
• explaining a major adjustment they made in their lives to join God on His mission;
• sharing a way God can use them to help bring about spiritual awakening in their church;
• praying for and receiving the prayers of fellow members, asking that God help them be conscious daily of the kingdom role for which each person prayed.

BEFORE THE SESSION

☐ Review this week's material and complete the learning activities for week 5 so that you can stay ahead of the group.

☐ Pray daily for each group member.

☐ Master this week's material in the leader guide.

☐ Review the goals for this session.

☐ Check with the host or hostess to be sure he or she is expecting the group this week.

☐ Arrange the meeting room so that members can sit in a circle.

☐ If you have the video, arrange for a VCR and a monitor to show the video during the session.

Standard Plan

DURING THE SESSION (1–2 HRS.)

Prepare to take a stand-up break in the middle of the session if necessary. If you are using the longer time period (2-hour time session), plan to take a 10-minute break when the time seems opportune and natural.

Part 1

Introductory Time (15–20 mins.)

1. Arrive early. Greet each member as he or she arrives. Ask for reports on prayer requests voiced previously.

2. Ask each member to share a way he or she has seen God at work in seemingly mundane activities in his or her life. Voice a prayer giving thanks for praises reported. Ask God to show members during this session how important we are to Him despite our ordinariness.

3. Show the session 4, part 1 videotape to set the scene and to prepare for sharing (10 mins.). If you do not have the video, take more time in the Group-Discussion Time.

Group-Discussion Time (35–70 mins.)

Choose from these steps.

1. Call on a volunteer to identify the reason David gave for his defeating Goliath.

2. Ask volunteers to share a way they have been aware that God has pursued them with His love, just as He did David. Briefly share first, and members will follow suit.

3. Ask a willing member to share a way he or she has experienced the Holy Spirit's reassurance—either through Scripture, prayer, circumstances, confirmation by the body of Christ, or the counsel of a trusted Christian—to join God on His mission. Reassure members that if they are unable at this point to identify a specific way this has occurred in their lives, the study of *On Mission with God* will heighten their awareness of times when this special reassurance of the Holy Spirit occurs.

4. Ask these questions: When you realize that God has chosen you, called you to Himself, and given you promises of what He will do through you, does that mean things will go easily for you after that? Why or why not?

5. Ask members in pairs to check each other's accuracy in quoting this week's memory verse.

6. Ask members to share major adjustments they have made in order to join God on mission. As they saw in day 1, this could mean anything from rearranging their lives to having a longer quiet time to contacting a missions agency.

7. Ask each member to describe one way God calls him or her.

8. Call on volunteers to describe what experiences have helped prepare them for God's mission. It might be the type they checked in day 3 (p. 84) or another example.

9. Ask a volunteer to answer this question from day 3: "What are some abilities you have seen God call forth from you that you didn't realize you had?" (p. 85).

10. Ask each member to briefly describe a time when God moved him or her out of a comfort zone to better serve Him. Share your experience first.

11. Call on all members to state one way they believe God can use them to bring about spiritual awakening in their church.

12. Ask volunteers to name one promise God has made to them in Scripture. As members share their promises, ask them to describe ways they have seen God fulfill this promise if He has already.

(If you are splitting the session, end discussion here.)

Part 2

13. Ask a volunteer to recall a time when your church persevered through adversity. (See the question on p. 90.)

14. Ask the group this question: How should God's people (the church) discern God's will?

15. Ask: How is God using your church to fulfill His mission before the eyes of a watching world?

16. Ask: What is the kingdom of God? Discuss the four answers from day 5 (pp. 92–97).

17. Ask members to share their responses to one of the seven statements about the kingdom (p. 95).

18. Ask members to discuss what they think would be required for them to become men or women after God's own heart, as David was described. Remind members that this description applied to David despite the fact that he failed God many times.

19. Call on all members to state one way they believe God can use them to bring about spiritual awakening in their church.

20. Show the session 4, part 2 videotape. Ask members to brainstorm applications of the video segment to their own lives and to their church. If you do not have the video, take more time in the Group-Discussion Time.

Preview Next Week's Assignments (5–10 mins.)

1. Briefly preview the content of week 5, "Jesus on Mission with God: A Savior for All Peoples." Tell members they will be able to understand and explain how Jesus reconciles the lost to God and to defend the position that He is the only way to salvation.

2. Ask members to pray this week, as they study, that God will reveal how they can be instruments to bring others to know Jesus' saving power.

Closure (5–10 mins.)

1. Announce the time and place for the next session.

2. Close with a circle of prayer. Ask each member to pray that the person on his or her right will daily be conscious of God's kingdom purposes for him or her.

AFTER THE SESSION

1. Contact members who are having difficulty completing their work to see if you can help.

2. Pray daily for each group member. Record their prayer requests. Pray that God will reveal to them the roles He has in mind for them in keeping with His plan for the salvation of the nations.

3. Read "Before the Session" for group session 5 to determine the amount of preparation you will need for the next group session. At the top of the group session 5 material in this leader guide, record when you will do your preparation.

4. Carefully study week 6 and complete all the exercises. You will preview week 6 for members during session 5.

Split-Session Plan

First Week

Follow part 1 of session 4 as it is outlined in the Standard Plan except for the following adjustments.

1. If you have the video, show session 4, part 1 during the first week of this session, at the time allotted in the session plan (on this page).

2. Close in prayer. Pray for each member by name, asking that God will do what is necessary to make each person a man or a woman after His own heart.

Second Week

Follow the Standard Plan for part 2 of session 4 with the following changes. Use shorter times for each activity to allow for these steps.

1. As members arrive, spend time discussing any questions they have about their work so far. Call on volunteers to share any victories they experienced in their spiritual lives during the past week. Pray a brief prayer and invite others to pray also.

2. During the introductory time ask volunteers to summarize important points from last week.

3. Move on to the discussion questions. Begin with question 13 (previous questions were covered during last week's group time).

4. Preview next week's work. Assign members days 1–3 in week 5, "Jesus on Mission with God: A Savior for All Peoples."

GROUP SESSION 5

SESSION GOALS

By the end of this session, members will be able to demonstrate their progress in achieving the *On Mission with God* goals by—

• reporting the names of persons through whom God has communicated His love to them;

• sharing their struggles in joining God on His mission to save all people from their sins;

- discussing how their church can become a missions-strategy center;
- giving to and receiving support in areas that keep them from fully obeying the Great Commission.

BEFORE THE SESSION

- Review week 5 and complete week 6 to stay ahead of the group.
- Pray daily for each group member.
- Master this week's material in the leader guide.
- Review the goals for this session.
- Check with the host or hostess to be sure he or she is expecting the group this week.
- Arrange the meeting room so that members can sit in a circle.
- If you have the video, arrange for a VCR and a monitor to show the video during the session.

Standard Plan

DURING THE SESSION (1-2 HRS.)

Prepare to take a stand-up break in the middle of the session if necessary. If you are using the longer time period (2-hour session), plan to take a 10-minute break when the time seems opportune and natural.

Part 1
Introductory Time (15–20 mins.)
1. Be available to greet members as they arrive. As an opening exercise, ask each member to describe the way he or she first experienced the fact that God was at work around him or her.
2. Ask each member to name one person through whom God has communicated His love. Stop and pray. Thank God for the individuals named and for the experiences shared.
3. Show the session 5, part 1 videotape to set the scene and to prepare for sharing (10 mins.). If you do not have the video, take more time in the Group-Discussion Time.

Group-Discussion Time (35–70 mins.)
Choose from these steps.
1. Ask a volunteer to answer these questions: What have you discovered is standing in your way of complete obedience to God? What would it take

for you to get beyond this barrier to experience complete obedience to Him?
2. Say to the group, Perhaps you have never thought about Jesus on earth experiencing the Father as others do (the seven realities). Ask, Where was God at work around Jesus when He was born?
3. Call on a volunteer to share the answer he or she wrote to the question in day 1 about ways Jesus has used the Bible, prayer, and circumstances in his or her life to speak about joining His mission to reconcile the peoples of the world to Himself (p. 102-103).
4. Ask members, How in the life of Jesus did the Holy Spirit use the four ways God speaks to us? (*He doesn't mention the people of God because in Jesus' day they had not heard from God for four hundred years, and they always gave the wrong advice.*)
5. Ask members to share their struggles in joining God on His mission to save all people from their sins. After each person has shared, ask members to stop and pray silently for the person on their right about concerns voiced.
6. Call on several members to answer how it makes them feel to realize that God had a plan for them, just as He did for Jesus, from before the creation of the world. Remind members that their study of *On Mission with God* will continue to emphasize the fact that God foreknew the mission of our lives and will encourage us to learn more about that mission as we learn more about His activity.
7. Call for answers to this question: How did the Father use Satan to prepare Jesus for future temptations? (See day 3, p. 107-108)
8. Ask members to work in pairs to recite this week's memory verse.
9. Ask members to report to the group how they answered the questions in day 3 about temptations (p. 107-108). Ask each member to share with the group how he or she would answer if Satan posed each temptation to him or her.
(If you are splitting the session, end discussion here.)

Part 2
10. Ask this question: Is your church an Acts 1:8 church that serves Jerusalem, Judea, Samaria, and the uttermost parts of the earth? In what areas does it need to be strengthened the most?
11. Call on a volunteer to describe ways he or she is a new creation because of Christ, as Paul testified

in 2 Corinthians 5:17. Then ask, How motivated are you to testify of this fact to the world?

12. Ask, What factors today are causing the world to become more of a global village than ever? Ask a volunteer to describe one way he or she has already responded to this situation. (*Example: I am learning Spanish because my company deals with many people from Latin America.*)

13. Ask members to discuss their responses to the question posed at the end of day 4: "What do you think God is doing in your life and in your church to send you to the place where He can best work through you to accomplish His mission?" (p. 114)

14. Ask: In what ways do you identify with Jesus in His earthly experiences? What incidents do you read about in the Bible that cause you to think, *Jesus must truly know just how I feel?*

15. Ask members how they responded to the final activity in this week's study (p. 119).

16. Call on a volunteer to share ways he or she identified with Mary in the section that follows week 5 (pp. 120–22). Explain that even if members are not parents, they can sometimes find themselves feeling puzzled and misunderstood, as Mary must have felt in fulfilling her role in God's kingdom.

17. Show the session 5, part 2 videotape. Ask members to brainstorm applications from the video segment to their own lives and to their church. If you do not have the video, take more time in the Group-Discussion Time.

Preview Next Week's Assignments (5–10 mins.)
1. Briefly preview the content of week 6, "Peter on Mission with God: A Church for All Peoples." Tell members that they will be able to explain how the Holy Spirit awakened and empowered the church to be a witnessing community of faith for all peoples.
2. Ask members to pray this week, as they study, that God will reveal His role for each member to be a catalyst for spiritual awakening, as Peter was.

Closure (5–10 mins.)
1. Announce the time and place for the next session.
2. Ask each member to confess one thing that keeps him or her from obeying all that Christ commanded. In a circle of prayer ask each member to pray about what he or she confessed, asking God to help him or her carry out the Great Commission to its fullest.

AFTER THE SESSION

1. Pray for those who are struggling to keep up with the assignments. Pray that they will wisely use their time during the coming week to catch up.
2. Contact the persons who are having difficulty completing weekly work. Ask whether you can help.
3. Pray daily for each member. Record their prayer requests. Pray that God will reveal to them what roles He has in mind for them in keeping with His plan for the salvation of the nations.
4. Read "Before the Session" for group session 6 to determine the amount of preparation you will need for the next group session. At the top of the group session 6 material in this leader guide, record when you will do your preparation.
5. Carefully study week 7. You will preview week 7 for members during session 6.

Split-Session Plan

First Week
Follow part 1 of session 5 as it is outlined in the Standard Plan except for the following adjustments.
1. If you have the video, show session 5, part 1 during the first week of this session, at the time allotted in the session plan (p. 209).
2. In closing, ask members to state one way they have experienced God surprising them with a next step on the journey—a step they could never have imagined taking. Pray for members, asking God to keep them open to ways He would use them rather than ways they might choose for themselves.

Second Week
Follow the Standard Plan for part 2 of session 5 with the following changes. Use shorter times for each activity to allow for these steps.
1. Greet each member and begin promptly. Ask each member to tell one way he or she is seeking to model his or her life after Jesus, the focus of this week's study. Ask each to pray a sentence prayer asking God to help him or her continue to model this trait.
2. During the introductory time ask volunteers to summarize important points from last week.
3. Move on to the discussion questions. Begin with question 10 (previous questions were covered during last week's group time).

4. Preview next week's work. Assign members days 1–3 in week 6, "Peter on Mission with God: A Church for All Peoples."

GROUP SESSION 6

SESSION GOALS

By the end of this session, members will be able to demonstrate their progress in achieving the *On Mission with God* goals by—

- naming persons instrumental in their coming to Christ and stating ways their concepts of God's will have grown;
- describing a time when they acted on something God told them to do and were surprised by the outcome;
- stating how they would respond to Jesus' call to "follow Me";
- sharing with the group a Scripture reference God has given them as a life verse, a verse for the year, or a verse for a particular situation.

BEFORE THE SESSION

- Review week 6 and complete week 7 to stay ahead of the group.
- Pray daily for each group member.
- Master this week's material in the leader guide.
- On newsprint, poster board, or a chalkboard write the three things Peter learned about visions (p. 131).
- Check with the host or hostess to be sure he or she is expecting the group this week.
- Arrange the meeting room so that members can sit in a circle.
- If you have the video, arrange for a VCR and a monitor to show the video during the session.

Standard Plan

DURING THE SESSION (1–2 HRS.)

Prepare to take a stand-up break in the middle of the session if necessary. If you are using the longer time

period (2-hour session), plan to take a 10-minute break when the time seems opportune and natural.

Part 1
Introductory Time (15–20 mins.)
1. Welcome members as they arrive. As an opening activity, ask members to share the name of the person who brought them to Jesus. As they answer, also ask them to share one way their concept of God's will has grown since they came to Christ.
2. Offer a prayer thanking God for the instrumental persons named. Ask God to help each member likewise be instrumental in the lives of others.
3. Show the session 6, part 1 videotape to set the scene and to prepare for sharing (10 mins.). If you do not have the video, take more time in the Group-Discussion Time.

Group-Discussion Time (35–70 mins.)
Choose from these steps.
1. Call on a volunteer to tell about a time—as the disciples did with Jesus—when someone advised the person what to do without considering what God wanted. This might be a current situation the member faces or one in the past. Ask how the situation turned out and what action he or she eventually took.
2. Call on anyone who might be willing to discuss how God is in the process of getting into his or her boat, just as Jesus did with Peter. Ask how God indicates He is involving Himself in the person's work. Remind members that during the remainder of the study, members will continue to identify ways God is involving Himself in our lives.
3. Ask members to share about a time when they acted on something God told them to do and were surprised by the outcome, just as Peter was when he cast his nets at Jesus' command.
4. Ask members to discuss what answer they would give if Jesus were to say to them at this moment, "Follow Me, and I will use you to bring glory to God." Ask members to pray that God will help their fellow members seek to be used by God.
5. Pause for a moment and ask members to quote this week's memory verse. Ask members to work in pairs to check each other's accuracy.
6. Ask each member to share a Scripture reference God has given them as a life verse, a verse for the year, or a verse for a particular situation.

7. Draw attention to the newsprint, poster board, or chalkboard and discuss the three things Peter learned about visions (p. 131). Ask members to share which of the three statements they struggle with the most and any experiences they have had as God has revealed these facts to them.

8. Call on volunteers to describe one difficult experience God has used to develop their character for His mission.

9. Ask a volunteer to describe a time when God, through His Holy Spirit, transformed the person from fearful to fearless and from faithless to faithful, just as He did Peter.

10. Pose to group members this question from day 3: "Have you ever believed you have failed the Lord so badly that He would never send you on another mission?" (p. 134). Call on someone who seems willing to share.

(If you are splitting the session, end discussion here.)

Part 2

11. Ask members to discuss ways God can use them as catalysts to move their church toward spiritual awakening and being on mission with God.

12. In response to the discussion of the five principles in Acts 10 (day 5), call on volunteers to answer these questions.

a. Do you believe God initiates a desire in people's hearts to know Him, but they don't know how?

b. How is God interrupting you to get you out of your comfort zone so that you can tell someone about Christ?

c. What light has God given you about being on mission with Him?

d. Has anyone experienced God intervening when you went on mission with Him?

e. How has God accomplished His purpose in your life in a way that brought glory to Him?

13. Ask members: What is the only thing that will satisfy God's heart? (*That He be glorified among all peoples*) Call for answers.

14. Call for volunteers to answer this question: Can you think of a time when, like Peter, you initially allowed your prejudice or preconceived notions about someone to keep you from witnessing to a person or finding out what God wanted you to do?

15. Show the session 6, part 2 videotape. Ask members to brainstorm applications from the video segment to their own lives and to their church. If

you do not have the video, take more time in the Group-Discussion Time.

16. Close this time of discussion in prayer. Ask God to show members how He can use them in spite of failures and weaknesses.

Preview Next Week's Assignments (5–10 mins.)

1. Briefly preview the content of week 7, "Paul on Mission with God: A Gospel for All Peoples." Tell members that they will be able to understand and explain how God revealed through Paul the mystery of the ages, that He includes all peoples in His redemption and sends missionaries to all nations, tribes, tongues, and peoples.

2. Ask members to pray this week, as they study, that God will show them how they can follow Paul's example to live in such a way that their entire lives glorify Him.

Closure (5–10 mins.)

1. Announce the time and place for the next session.

2. Ask group members to share one spontaneous response they could make to someone who is culturally different from them. Ask how they could envision God at work in this encounter. Close by asking each person to pray aloud, asking God to keep him or her sensitive to ways ministering across cultural lines can be accomplished.

AFTER THE SESSION

1. Meet individually or in small groups with members who seem to be having problems com-pleting assignments. Pray with them about their problems. If necessary, enlist another member to work with them.

2. Pray for members. This is the best support you can give them as they seek to be on mission with God.

3. Continue to evaluate your leadership. Refer to the questions listed in earlier "After the Session" sections to focus on your leadership abilities.

4. Read "Before the Session" for group session 7 to determine the amount of preparation you will need for the next group session. At the top of the group session 7 material in this leader guide, record when you will do your preparation.

5. Carefully study week 8 and complete all the exercises. You will preview week 8 for members during session 7.

Split-Session Plan

First Week

Follow part 1 of session 6 as it is outlined in the Standard Plan except for the following adjustments.
1. If you have the video, show session 6, part 1 during the first week of this session, at the time allotted in the session plan (p. 211).
2. As you pray at the close of the session, call on a couple of volunteers to pray for the group, asking that God would send each member to the place where He can best work through him or her to accomplish His mission.

Second Week

Follow the Standard Plan for part 2 of session 6 with the following changes. Use shorter times for each activity to allow for these steps.
1. As members arrive, be alert to any questions members have or struggles they may be experiencing in completing their work. Ask for updates on prayer requests mentioned previously. Pray a brief prayer and invite others to pray also.
2. During the introductory time ask volunteers to summarize important points from last week.
3. Move on to the discussion questions. Begin with question 11 (previous questions were covered during last week's group time).
4. Preview next week's work. Assign members days 1–3 in week 7, "Paul on Mission with God: A Gospel for All Peoples."

GROUP SESSION 7

SESSION GOALS

By the end of this session, members will be able to demonstrate their progress in achieving the *On Mission with God* goals by—
* recounting times when they have experienced Christ in proportion to their obedience to Him;
* sharing ways they sensed that God was at work around them even when they were working against Him;

* giving examples of times when they immediately responded after God saved them;
* describing at least one person they know who could be considered an on-mission Christian.

BEFORE THE SESSION

* Review week 7 and complete the learning activities for week 8 to stay ahead of the group.
* Pray daily for each group member.
* Master this week's material in the leader guide.
* Check with the host or hostess to be sure he or she is expecting the group this week.
* Arrange the meeting room so that members can sit in a circle.
* If you have the video, arrange for a VCR and a monitor to show the video during the session.

Standard Plan

DURING THE SESSION (1–2 HRS.)

Prepare to take a stand-up break in the middle of the session if necessary. If you are using the longer time period (2-hour time session), plan to take a 10-minute break when the time seems opportune and natural.

Part 1
Introductory Time (15–20 mins.)
1. Begin the session on time even if all members are not present. Call on members to discuss their response to this statement made in day 1: "The more Paul obeyed, the more he experienced Christ" (p. 151). Ask, When has this been true in your life? Ask each member to briefly answer this question.
2. Pray for the outcome of today's session. Thank God for testimonies members shared about times when they experienced Christ through obedience.
3. Show the session 7, part 1 videotape to set the scene and to prepare for sharing (10 mins.). If you do not have the video, take more time in the Group-Discussion Time.

Group-Discussion Time (35–70 mins.)
Choose from these steps.
1. Ask a volunteer to share ways he or she has responded to God's revelations during the past month. Perhaps the volunteer may want to reflect

on how he or she answered a similar question posed in day 1 (p. 149).

2. Ask a couple of volunteers to describe major adjustments they have made since they became Christians and how they exercised faith to make those adjustments. Remind members that *On Mission with God* is designed to give increasing courage to people to act on faith even if doing

so requires major adjustments.

3. Ask members to share their answers to the following question: When have you sensed God at work around you even when you were working against Him—a similar situation to what Paul experienced?

4. Ask members to give examples of times when they immediately responded after God saved them. Perhaps they shared the experience with someone or shared Christ with someone.

5. Call on a member who might be willing to describe his or her most recent witnessing opportunity and the way God fulfilled His promise to be with us when we share the gospel.

6. Ask volunteers to share their responses to the list on page 156 of ways people go on mission and ways they think God might have in mind for them to touch unreached peoples.

7. Call for a discussion of this statement in day 3: "God will do His work with or without you" (p. 159). Ask members to describe how they feel when they realize that, as the lesson states, they are "privileged to be chosen, called, promised, prepared, sent, guided, and used to bring peoples to glorify Him for all eternity!" (p. 159).

8. Ask a volunteer to tell which kind of vessel he or she identifies with—gold, silver, wood, or clay. Ask the person to relate the illustration about the use of clay in the Phillips translation (p. 156).

9. Ask members in pairs to check each other's recall of their memory verse for the week.
(If you are splitting the session, end discussion here.)

Part 2

10. Review the 10 factors (points A–J, day 4, pp. 160–63) that characterize a biblical Church Planting Movement. Ask members to cite the action(s) they believe God could accomplish through them. (Refer to *Church Planting Movements* by David Garrison for modern-day CPMs.)

11. Ask each member to name one person with whom they are linked who could be considered

an on-mission Christian. Call for volunteers to describe an accountability relationship they have with another Christian or to name someone who is mentoring them.

12. Call on a member who is willing to share what he or she wrote as a personal statement of God's mission in his or her life (day 5, p. 165).

13. Ask members to discuss whether God is egotistical because He wants everyone to glorify Him. Ask if they had ever thought about glorifying God in this manner. Ask how they responded when they first read the statement "Because He is the one true God, no one or no thing should be glorified more than God is!" (p. 165).

14. Ask members to name the four reasons Paul listed in Romans 15 for God's mission to be for all peoples to glorify Him (pp. 166–67).

15. Ask, How do you know whether you are called to be a missionary? Invite answers.

16. Call for answers to this question: How do you respond to these statements in day 5: "God doesn't just work in spite of circumstances. He works through them" (p. 165)? Ask someone to describe a time when this has been a reality in the person's life.

19. Show the session 7, part 2 videotape. Ask members to brainstorm applications of the video segment to their own lives and to their church. If you do not have the video, take more time in the Group-Discussion Time.

Preview Next Week's Assignments (5–10 mins.)

1. Briefly preview the content of week 8, "John on Mission with God: All Peoples Worshiping God." Tell members that they will be able to describe how God will establish His kingdom and the way representatives of all peoples will worship and glorify Him forever in heaven.

2. Ask members to pray this week, as they study, that God will show them how they can follow John's example to help others realize that they are to continually worship God and to make others aware of His kingdom.

Closure (5–10 mins.)

1. Announce the time and place for the next session.

2. In closing, ask members to reflect on the activity at the conclusion of day 5 that helped members identify whether God might be calling them to serve as missionaries (pp. 167–68). Call for testimonies

from members who believe they have experienced a call. If any members testify that they believe they are being called, ask the other members to gather around those individuals for a time of prayer. If no one shares that he or she has been called, close by praying that all members will continue seeking God's will for their lives in whatever ways He chooses to use them.

AFTER THE SESSION

1. Call or meet with members who may be behind in their work. Offer individual help as needed.
2. Pray for members as they prepare for your final group session together.
3. Meet with members to discuss future opportunities for them to be on mission with God. Encourage all members to continue to grow in their obedience to God by implementing *On Mission with God* principles and practices in their lives and by participating in other biblically based studies that will help them grow spiritually.
4. Read "Before the Session" for group session 8 to determine the amount of preparation you will need for the next group session. At the top of the group session 8 material in this leader guide, record when you will do your preparation.

Split-Session Plan

First Week
Follow part 1 of session 7 as it is outlined in the Standard Plan except for the following adjustments.
1. If you have the video, show session 7, part 1 during the first week of this session, at the time allotted in the session plan (p. 213).
2. As you close the session with a prayer time, remind members of these statements from day 3: "God also used Paul to write almost half of the New Testament. Do you see how much glory God can get through one person's life?" (p. 158). Ask members to pray silently that God will be abundantly glorified by their lives, just as He was by Paul's. Offer a brief closing prayer.

Second Week
Follow the Standard Plan for part 2 of session 7 with the following changes. Use shorter times for each activity to allow for these steps.

1. In an opening activity ask each member to relate something he or she has grown to appreciate about the person seated on his or her right during the time the group has met together. Thank God for the expressions and for each member.
2. During the introductory time ask volunteers to summarize important points from last week.
3. Move on to the discussion questions. Begin with question 10 (previous questions were covered during last week's group time).
4. Preview next week's work. Assign members days 1–3 in week 8, "John on Mission with God: All Peoples Worshiping God."

GROUP SESSION 8

SESSION GOALS

By the end of this session, members will be able to demonstrate their progress in achieving the *On Mission with God* goals by—
- hearing other group members report progress they have observed in one another;
- identifying one obstacle that keeps them from immediately following Jesus, as the disciples did;
- stating one phrase that describes their relationship with Jesus;
- identifying Scriptures and statements that have been most meaningful to them during this study.

BEFORE THE SESSION

❑ Review week 8.
❑ Pray daily for each group member.
❑ Master this week's material in the leader guide.
❑ Check with the host or hostess to be sure he or she is expecting the group this week.
❑ Arrange the meeting place so that members can sit in a circle.
❑ If you have the video, arrange for a VCR and monitor to show the video during the group session. Note that both segments of the session 8 video are slightly longer than in previous weeks. Adjusted times are noted in the session plan.

Standard Plan

DURING THE SESSION

Prepare to take a stand-up break in the middle of the session if necessary. If you are using the longer time period (2-hour time session), plan to take a 10-minute break when the time seems opportune and natural.

Part 1
Introductory Time (21–26 mins.)
1. Greet members as they arrive. Begin on time. Ask members to report one change they have seen in the life of the person seated to their right since they began *On Mission with God*.
2. Ask members to pray for the person about whom they just spoke. Suggest that members ask God to help the person continue to live the commitments he or she made during this study.
3. Show the session 8, part 1 videotape to set the scene and to prepare for sharing (16 mins.). If you do not have the video, take more time in the Group-Discussion Time.

Group-Discussion Time (29–64 mins.)
Choose from these steps.
1. Ask volunteers to share ways God has revealed to them Himself, His purpose, and His ways.
2. Call for volunteers to share what they have learned during this study about Jesus' love for them. Note that John was called "the disciple Jesus loved" (John 20:2) but that each member could just as easily substitute his or her name in the place of John's because of the Master's deep love for all of us.
3. Ask each member to identify one obstacle that keeps him or her from immediately following Jesus, as the disciples did. Ask God to remove from each member's life the obstacle stated.
4. Ask members to describe major adjustments that would be required of other persons in their lives if members responded to God's call to follow Him, even to the ends of the earth.
5. Ask members to discuss Jeff Lewis's statement in day 1 that "Jesus is not our personal Savior" (p. 173). Ask them to discuss in what sense He is our personal Savior and in what sense He is not.
6. Ask members to work in pairs to check each other's memorization of this week's memory verse.

7. Ask someone to recount a time when God could depend on his or her faithfulness. The person might name something he or she described in the day 3 activity on page 179 or identify another incident.
8. Remind members of the day 3 material describing the way ordinary people—Christians in a restricted country—were used to do a God-sized task to minister to an unreached people group (pp. 179–80). Ask a volunteer to tell about a time when he or she was given a God-sized task to perform in spite of his or her ordinariness.
9. Ask members to share the phrase they used in the day 2 exercise on page 175 to describe their relationship with Jesus.
10. Ask members to close this period in prayer, asking God to help them truly live the type of relationship they just described.
(If you are splitting the session, end discussion here.)

Part 2
11. Ask members to identify which of John's messages to the seven churches is most needed by their church. Why?
12. Lead members in a discussion contrasting your church to the church of Ephesus. Ask members to state ways your church demonstrates its love for God; then ask for ways it fails to demonstrate its love. Ask each member to state ways he or she could personally act to bring about renewal in the church.
13. Call on someone who is willing to share the commitments he or she checked in the day 4 activity on page 182.
14. Ask members these questions: What is the role of worship in heaven? What is the role of worship in your church? What should you do to get ready to worship forever?
15. Ask members to share what they have learned during this study about being on mission with God and about living God's purpose for His glory.
16. Ask members to identify the Scriptures and statements they recorded at the end of day 5 (p. 192) that have been most meaningful to them during the study.
17. Ask, What changes are you making as God develops the seven spiritual markers in your life?
18. Show the session 8, part 2 videotape. (Note that this segment of the session 8 video is longer than in previous weeks.) Ask members to brainstorm applications of the video segment to their own lives and

to their church. If you do not have the video, take more time in the Group-Discussion Time.

Closure (10–20 mins.)
1. Conclude your study with a time of commitment and affirmation. Ask each member to tell the group how he or she believes God, during the course of the study, has led him or her to become more involved in His mission today.
2. As each person states his or her commitment, ask members to form a circle around the person. Ask each member to pray that God will help the individual fulfill the commitment stated. Encourage volunteers to become accountability partners for the person. Repeat this process until each person has stated a commitment and has been prayed around.
3. Express gratitude for the opportunity you have had to lead this *On Mission with God* group. Remind members that you will continue to be available to them for encouragement and support.

AFTER THE SESSION

1. Continue to pray that the Holy Spirit will work in each member's life.
2. Ask God to prepare you for further opportunities of service. Be aware of the possibility that He may direct you to lead another *On Mission with God* group or another biblical study in your church.
3. As much as is possible, remain in contact with group members, as the Holy Spirit leads. Continue to be available to meet with them or pray with them about ways the Lord is directing them.

Split-Session Plan

First Week
Follow part 1 of session 8 as it is outlined in the Standard Plan except for the following adjustments.
1. If you have the video, show session 8, part 1 during the first week of this session, at the time allotted in the meeting plan (p. 216).
2. In closing, ask a few volunteers to recall times in their lives when God could count on their faithfulness, just as He did in John's life. Voice a closing prayer thanking God for the experiences members just recounted. Ask Him to help each person be faithful in whatever ways He instructs them.

Second Week
Follow the Standard Plan for part 2 of session 8 with the following changes. Use shorter times for each activity to allow for these steps.
1. To kick off the session, express a special, individual word of thankfulness for each member. Mention an attribute of each member that you sincerely appreciate. Begin with prayer.
2. During the introductory time ask volunteers to summarize important points from last week.
3. Move on to the discussion questions. Begin with question 11 (previous questions were covered during last week's group time).

HOW TO HAVE NEW LIFE IN CHRIST

If you realize that you have never trusted Christ as your Savior or if you, as a leader, find that a group member has not trusted Christ, the following brief summary can help with that decision.

1. The Bible says that you are accountable for the sin in your life: "All have sinned and fall short of the glory of God" (Rom. 3:23).

2. A penalty exists for that sin: "The wages of sin is death" (Rom. 6:23).

3. You cannot earn, by good deeds, a way to wipe out that sin from your life: "It is by grace you have been saved, through faith—and that is not from yourselves; it is the gift of God—not by works, so that no one can boast" (Eph. 2:8-9).

4. God provided for your sin by sending His Son to die in your place. Instead of you, Jesus took the wages of sin on Himself by dying on the cross. Then God raised Him on the third day: "God demonstrates his own love for us in this: While we were still sinners, Christ died for us" (Rom. 5:8).

5. How do you claim this free gift of salvation that God has provided? "Everyone who calls on the name of the Lord will be saved" (Rom. 10:13). If this makes sense to you, then pray a prayer similar to this one:

> *"Dear God, thank You for going to the cross for me. I believe You did it because I am a sinner and You wanted to spend eternity with me. Thank You for forgiving me of my sins and giving me a new life. I want to change my ways and seek a relationship with You. Amen."*

Tell your pastor, a Christian friend, or your group leader about your decision.

CHRISTIAN GROWTH STUDY PLAN

Preparing Christians to Serve

In the **Christian Growth Study Plan (formerly the Church Study Course)** this book, *On Mission with God,* is a resource for course credit in the subject area Ministry of the Christian Growth category of diploma plans. To receive credit, read the book; complete the learning activities; show your work to your pastor, a staff member, or a church leader; and complete the following information. This page may be duplicated. Send the completed page to:

Christian Growth Study Plan
One LifeWay Plaza
Nashville, TN 37234-0117
Fax: (615) 251-5067
Email: *cgspnet@lifeway.com*

For information about the Christian Growth Study Plan, refer to the current *Christian Growth Study Plan Catalog.* Your church office may have a copy. If not, request a free copy from the Christian Growth Study Plan office, (615) 251-2525. Also available online at *www.lifeway.com/cgsp/catalog.*

On Mission with God
CG-0705

PARTICIPANT INFORMATION

Social Security Number (USA ONLY-optional)	Personal CGSP Number*	Date of Birth (MONTH, DAY, YEAR)

Name (First, Middle, Last)	Home Phone

Address (Street, Route, or P.O. Box)	City, State, or Province	Zip/Postal Code

CHURCH INFORMATION

Church Name

Address (Street, Route, or P.O. Box)	City, State, or Province	Zip/Postal Code

CHANGE REQUEST ONLY

☐ Former Name

☐ Former Address	City, State, or Province	Zip/Postal Code

☐ Former Church	City, State, or Province	Zip/Postal Code

Signature of Pastor, Conference Leader, or Other Church Leader	Date

*New participants are requested but not required to give SS# and date of birth. Existing participants, please give CGSP# when using SS# for the first time. Thereafter, only one ID# is required. **Mail to:** Christian Growth Study Plan, One LifeWay Plaza, Nashville, TN 37234-0117. Fax: (615)251-5067.

Rev. 3-01